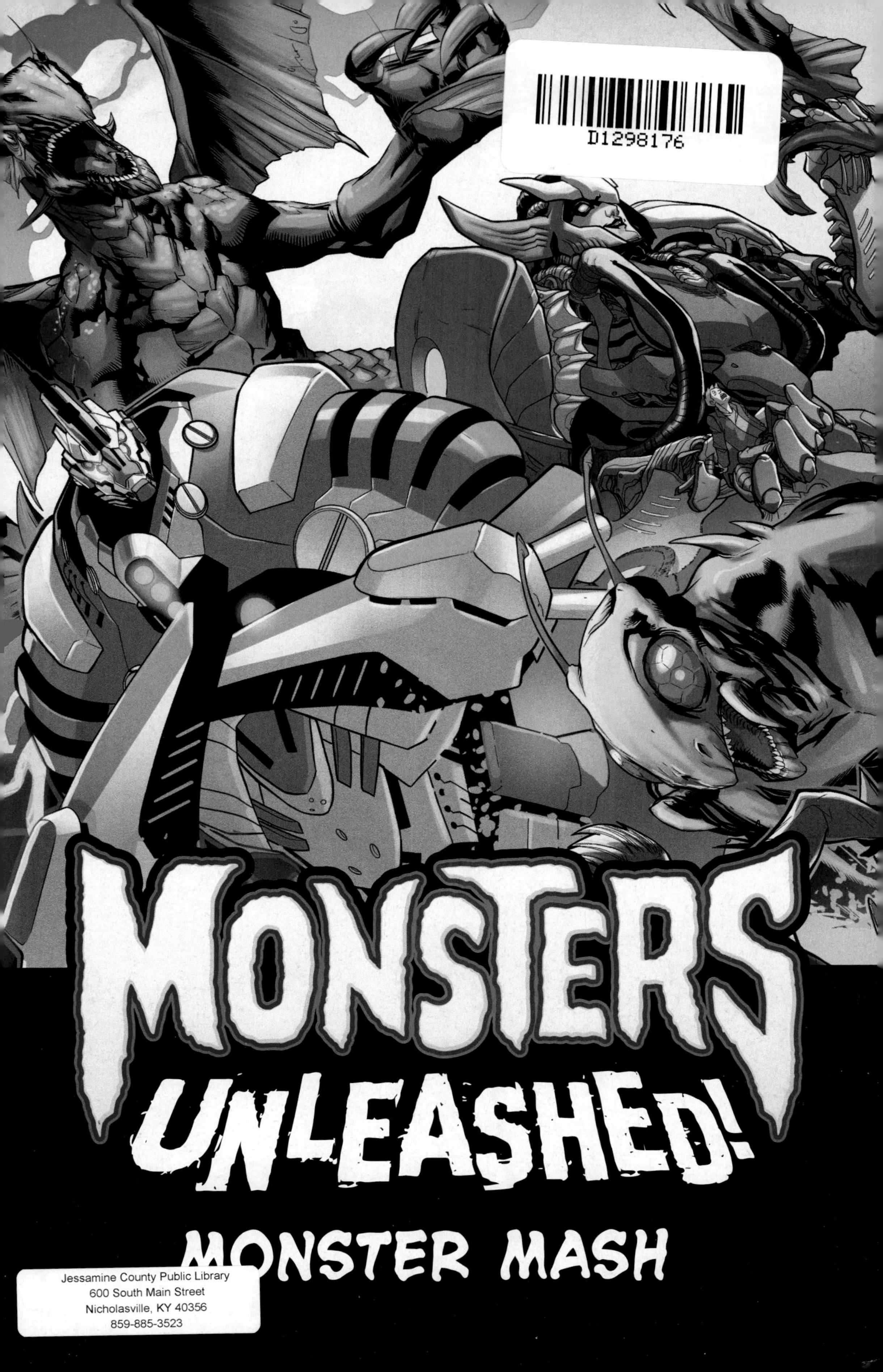

MONSTERS UNLEASHED!

MONSTER MASH

WHEN GIANT MONSTERS KNOWN AS **LEVIATHONS**
STARTED RAINING FROM THE SKY, THE HEROES OF EARTH
TURNED TO A BOY NAMED **KEI KAWADE** FOR HELP.

KNOWN TO THE WORLD AS **KID KAIJU**, KEI HAS THE INHUMAN ABILITY
TO SUMMON AND CREATE MONSTERS SIMPLY BY DRAWING THEM.

WITH THE HELP OF **FIVE NEW MONSTERS** — AEGIS,
HI-VO, SCRAGG, SLIZZIK AND MEKARA — KEI DEFEATED
THE LEVIATHONS' LEADER AND SAVED THE PLANET.

NOW, KEI AND HIS MONSTERS RESIDE ON THE LEGENDARY
ISLAND OF **MU**, JOINED BY MONSTER HUNTER TURNED PROTECTOR,
ELSA BLOODSTONE. TOGETHER THEY ARE READY TO HELP,
SHOULD THE REMAINING LEVIATHONS ON EARTH POSE A THREAT.

MONSTERS UNLEASHED VOL. 1: MONSTER MASH. Contains material originally published in magazine form as MONSTERS UNLEASHED #1-5. First printing 2017. ISBN# 978-0-7851-9636-5. Published by MARVEL WORLDWIDE, INC., a subsidiary of MARVEL ENTERTAINMENT, LLC. OFFICE OF PUBLICATION: 135 West 50th Street, New York, NY 10020. Copyright © 2017 MARVEL No similarity between any of the names, characters, persons, and/or institutions in this magazine with those of any living or dead person or institution is intended, and any such similarity which may exist is purely coincidental. **Printed in the U.S.A.** DAN BUCKLEY, President, Marvel Entertainment; JOE QUESADA, Chief Creative Officer; TOM BREVOORT, SVP of Publishing; DAVID BOGART, SVP of Business Affairs & Operations, Publishing & Partnership; C.B. CEBULSKI, VP of Brand Management & Development, Asia; DAVID GABRIEL, SVP of Sales & Marketing, Publishing; JEFF YOUNGQUIST, VP of Production & Special Projects; DAN CARR, Executive Director of Publishing Technology; ALEX MORALES, Director of Publishing Operations; SUSAN CRESPI, Production Manager; STAN LEE, Chairman Emeritus. For information regarding advertising in Marvel Comics or on Marvel.com, please contact Vit DeBellis, Integrated Sales Manager, at vdebellis@marvel.com. For Marvel subscription inquiries, please call 888-511-5480. **Manufactured between 10/6/2017 and 11/6/2017 by QUAD/GRAPHICS WASECA, WASECA, MN, USA.**

10 9 8 7 6 5 4 3 2 1

MONSTERS UNLEASHED!

MONSTER MASH

WRITER
CULLEN BUNN

ARTISTS
DAVID BALDEÓN (#1-4) &
RAMÓN BACHS (#4-5)

COLOR ARTISTS
MARCIO MENYZ (#1) &
CHRIS SOTOMAYOR (#2-5)

LETTERER
VC's TRAVIS LANHAM

COVER ARTISTS
ARTHUR ADAMS &
PETER STEIGERWALD (#1),
R.B. SILVA &
JASON KEITH (#2-4), AND
R.B. SILVA &
NOLAN WOODARD (#5)

ASSISTANT EDITOR
CHRISTINA HARRINGTON

EDITOR
MARK PANICCIA

COLLECTION EDITOR **MARK D. BEAZLEY**   ASSISTANT EDITOR **CAITLIN O'CONNELL**   ASSOCIATE MANAGING EDITOR **KATERI WOODY**   SENIOR EDITOR, SPECIAL PROJECTS **JENNIFER GRÜNWALD**   VP PRODUCTION & SPECIAL PROJECTS **JEFF YOUNGQUIST**

SVP PRINT, SALES & MARKETING **DAVID GABRIEL**   BOOK DESIGNER **ADAM DEL RE**   EDITOR IN CHIEF **AXEL ALONSO**   CHIEF CREATIVE OFFICER **JOE QUESADA**   PRESIDENT **DAN BUCKLEY**   EXECUTIVE PRODUCER **ALAN FINE**

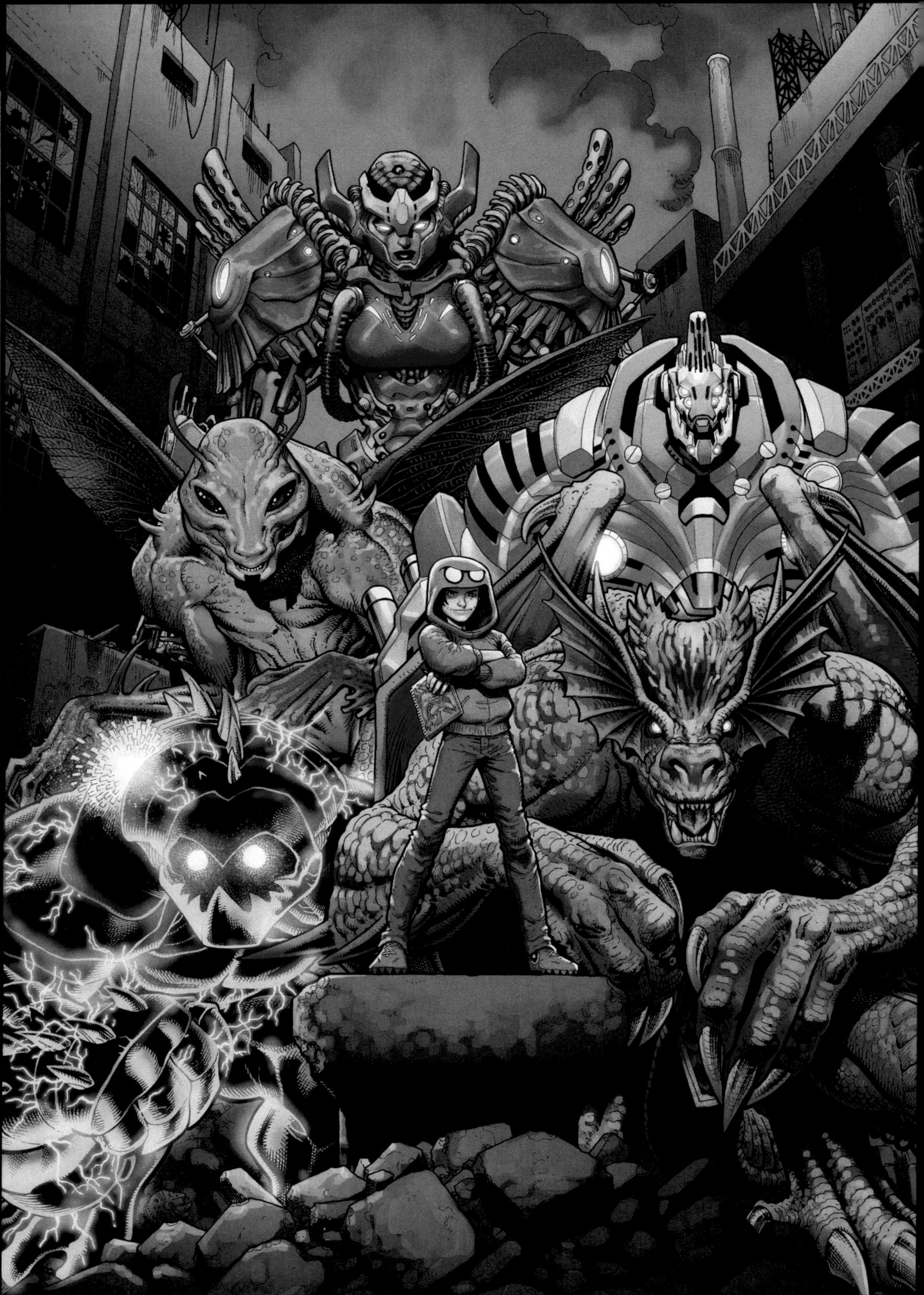

#1

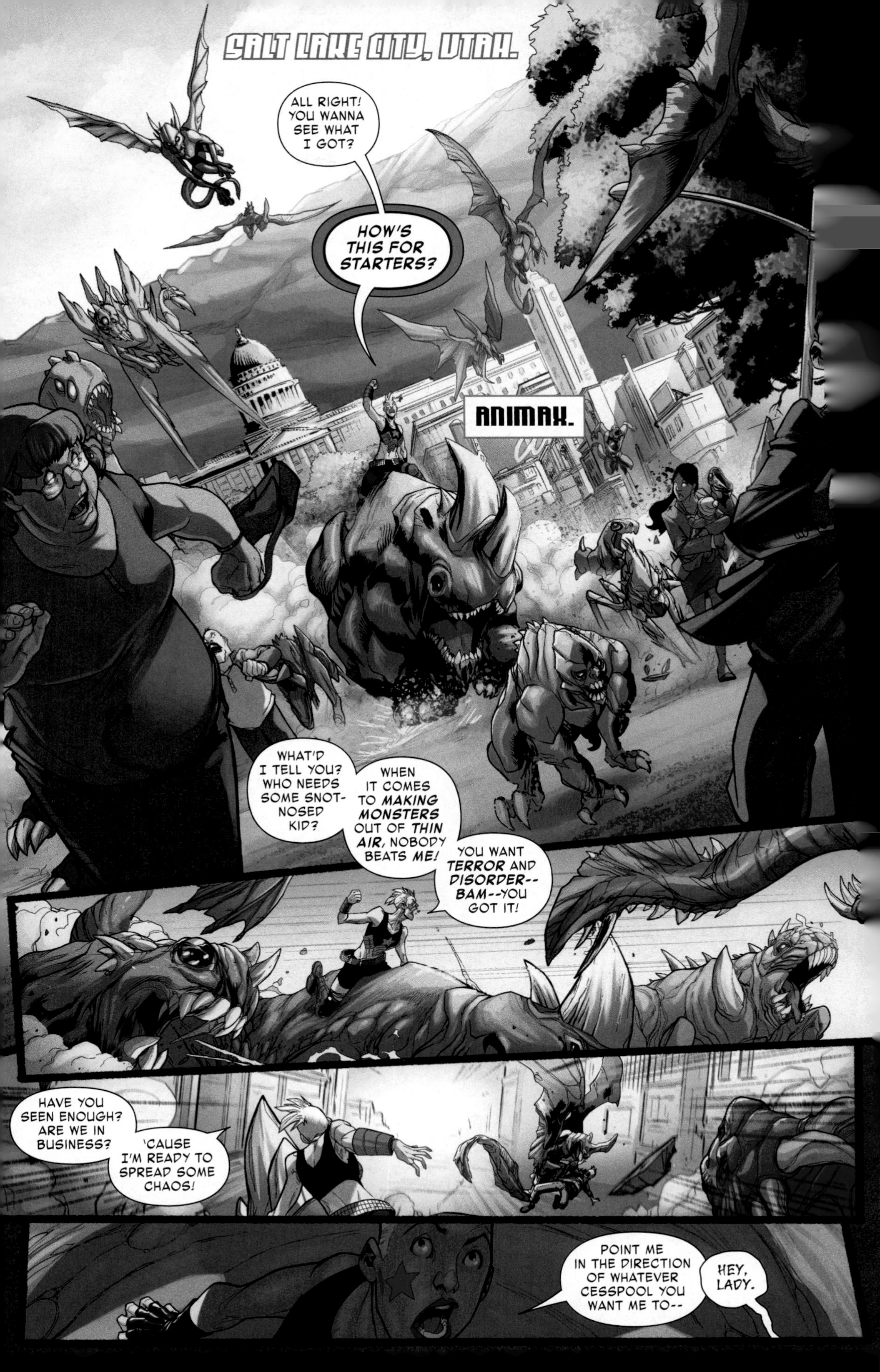

SALT LAKE CITY, UTAH.
ALL RIGHT! YOU WANNA SEE WHAT I GOT?
HOW'S THIS FOR STARTERS?
ANIMAX.
WHAT'D I TELL YOU? WHO NEEDS SOME SNOT-NOSED KID?
WHEN IT COMES TO MAKING MONSTERS OUT OF THIN AIR, NOBODY BEATS ME!
YOU WANT TERROR AND DISORDER--BAM--YOU GOT IT!
HAVE YOU SEEN ENOUGH? ARE WE IN BUSINESS?
'CAUSE I'M READY TO SPREAD SOME CHAOS!
POINT ME IN THE DIRECTION OF WHATEVER CESSPOOL YOU WANT ME TO--
HEY, LADY.

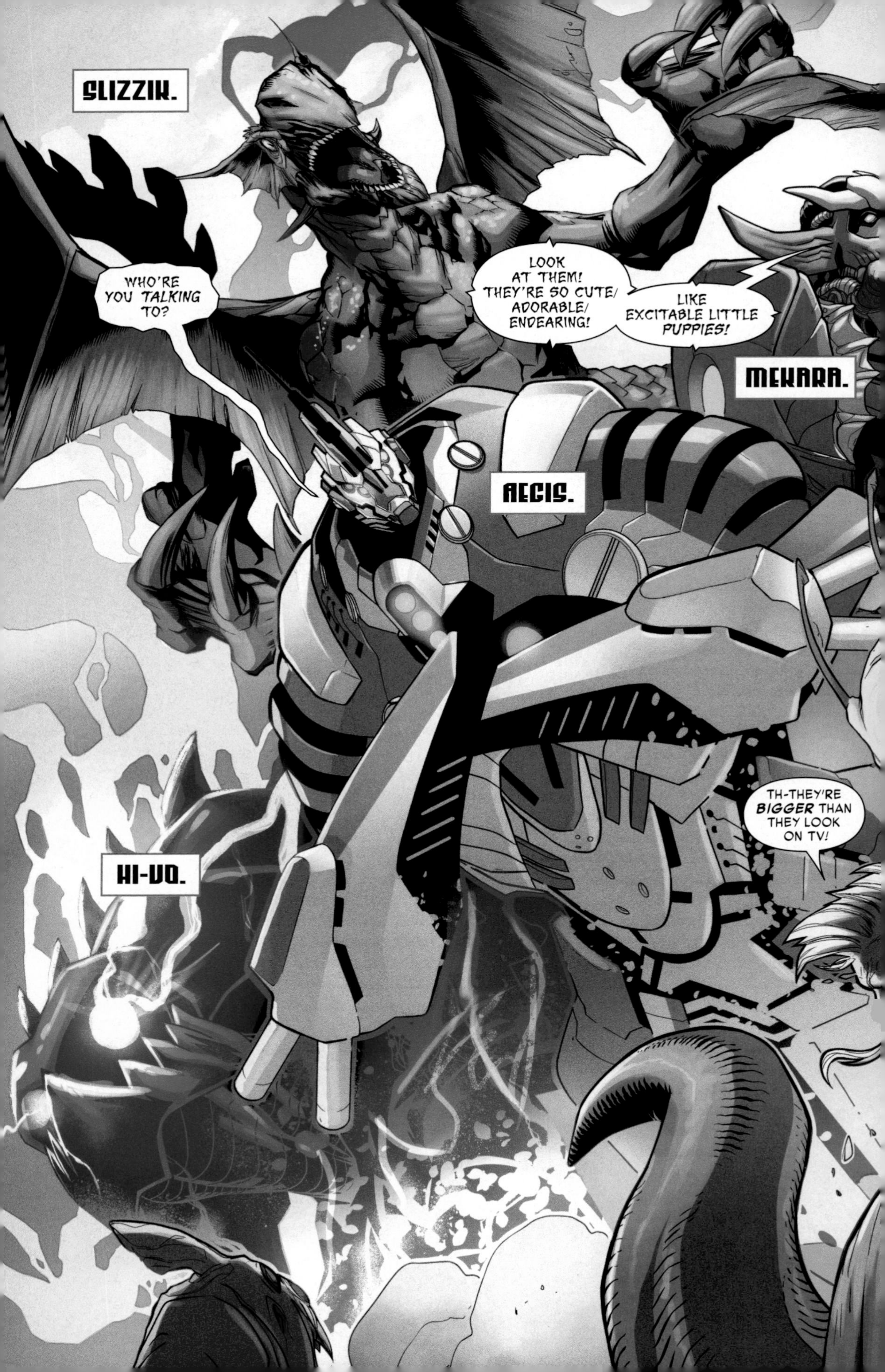
SLIZZIK.
WHO'RE YOU TALKING TO?
LOOK AT THEM! THEY'RE SO CUTE/ ADORABLE/ ENDEARING!
LIKE EXCITABLE LITTLE PUPPIES!
MEKARA.
AEGIS.
TH-THEY'RE BIGGER THAN THEY LOOK ON TV!
HI-VO.

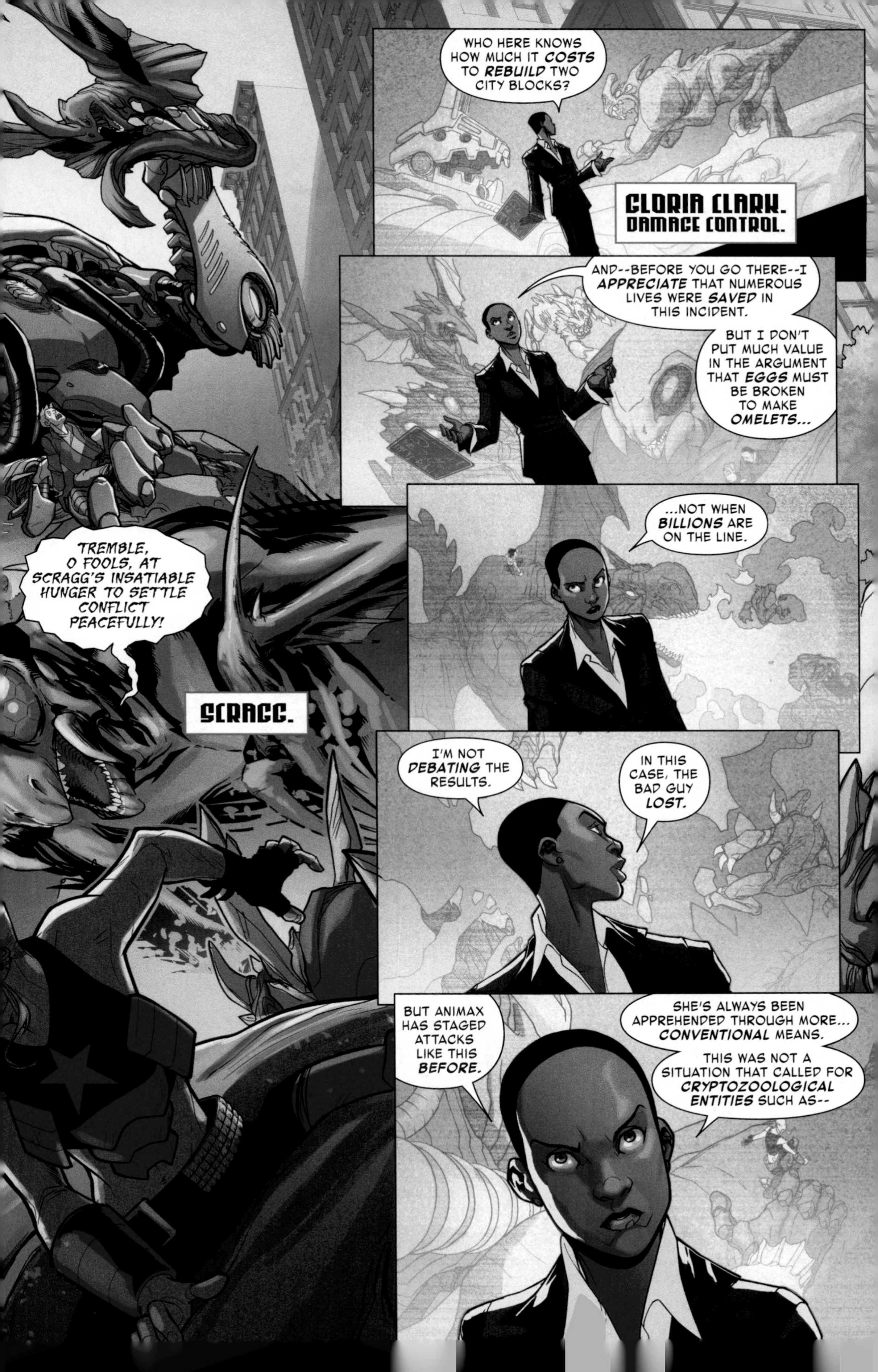
WHO HERE KNOWS HOW MUCH IT COSTS TO REBUILD TWO CITY BLOCKS?
GLORIA CLARK. DAMAGE CONTROL.
AND--BEFORE YOU GO THERE--I APPRECIATE THAT NUMEROUS LIVES WERE SAVED IN THIS INCIDENT.
BUT I DON'T PUT MUCH VALUE IN THE ARGUMENT THAT EGGS MUST BE BROKEN TO MAKE OMELETS...
TREMBLE, O FOOLS, AT SCRAGG'S INSATIABLE HUNGER TO SETTLE CONFLICT PEACEFULLY!
SCRAGG.
...NOT WHEN BILLIONS ARE ON THE LINE.
I'M NOT DEBATING THE RESULTS.
IN THIS CASE, THE BAD GUY LOST.
BUT ANIMAX HAS STAGED ATTACKS LIKE THIS BEFORE.
SHE'S ALWAYS BEEN APPREHENDED THROUGH MORE... CONVENTIONAL MEANS.
THIS WAS NOT A SITUATION THAT CALLED FOR CRYPTOZOOLOGICAL ENTITIES SUCH AS--

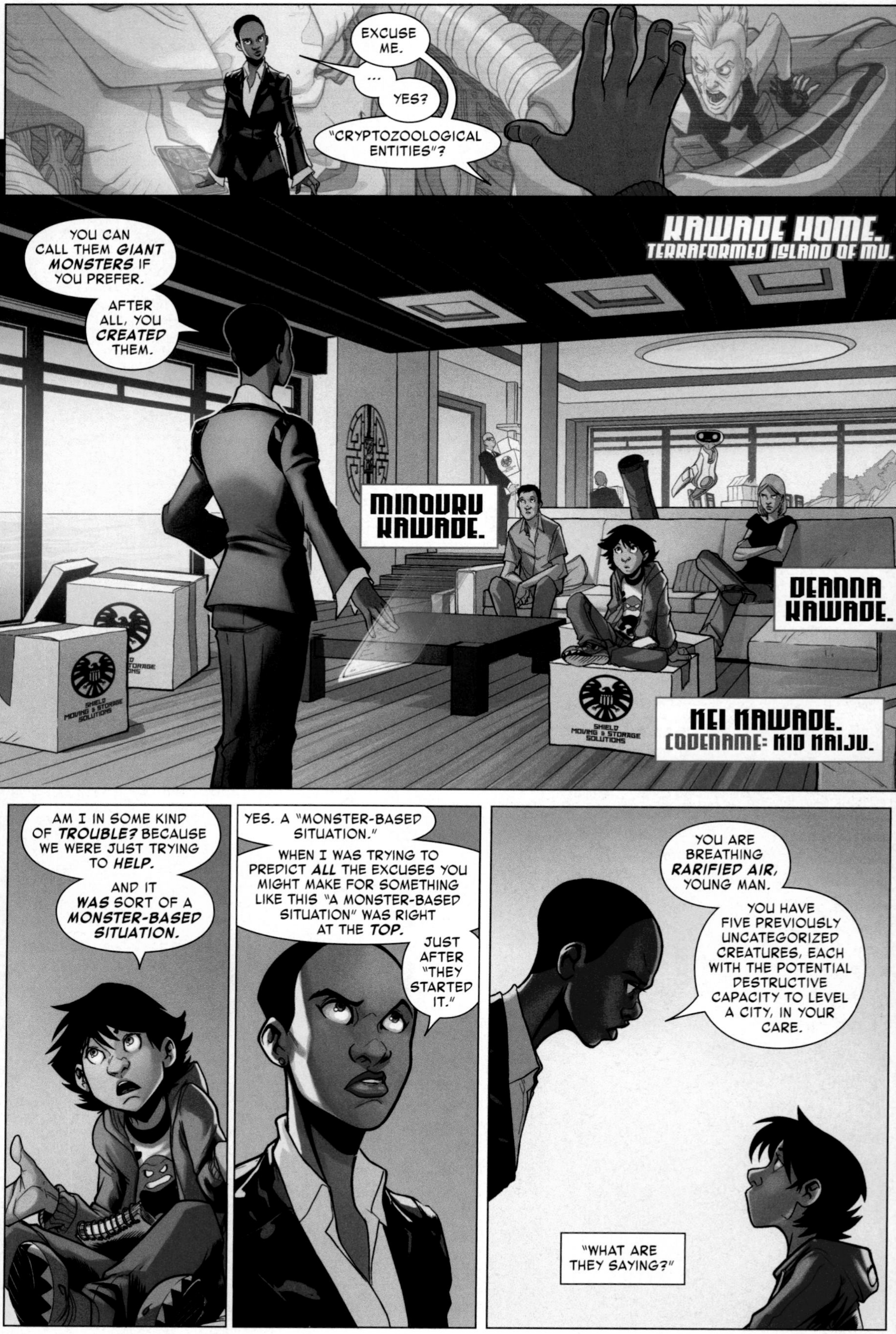
EXCUSE ME.
...
YES?
"CRYPTOZOOLOGICAL ENTITIES"?
KAWADE HOME. TERRAFORMED ISLAND OF MU.
YOU CAN CALL THEM GIANT MONSTERS IF YOU PREFER.
AFTER ALL, YOU CREATED THEM.
MINORU KAWADE.
DEANNA KAWADE.
KEI KAWADE. CODENAME: KID KAIJU.
SHIELD MOVING & STORAGE SOLUTIONS
AM I IN SOME KIND OF TROUBLE? BECAUSE WE WERE JUST TRYING TO HELP.
AND IT WAS SORT OF A MONSTER-BASED SITUATION.
YES. A "MONSTER-BASED SITUATION."
WHEN I WAS TRYING TO PREDICT ALL THE EXCUSES YOU MIGHT MAKE FOR SOMETHING LIKE THIS "A MONSTER-BASED SITUATION" WAS RIGHT AT THE TOP.
JUST AFTER "THEY STARTED IT."
YOU ARE BREATHING RARIFIED AIR, YOUNG MAN.
YOU HAVE FIVE PREVIOUSLY UNCATEGORIZED CREATURES, EACH WITH THE POTENTIAL DESTRUCTIVE CAPACITY TO LEVEL A CITY, IN YOUR CARE.
"WHAT ARE THEY SAYING?"

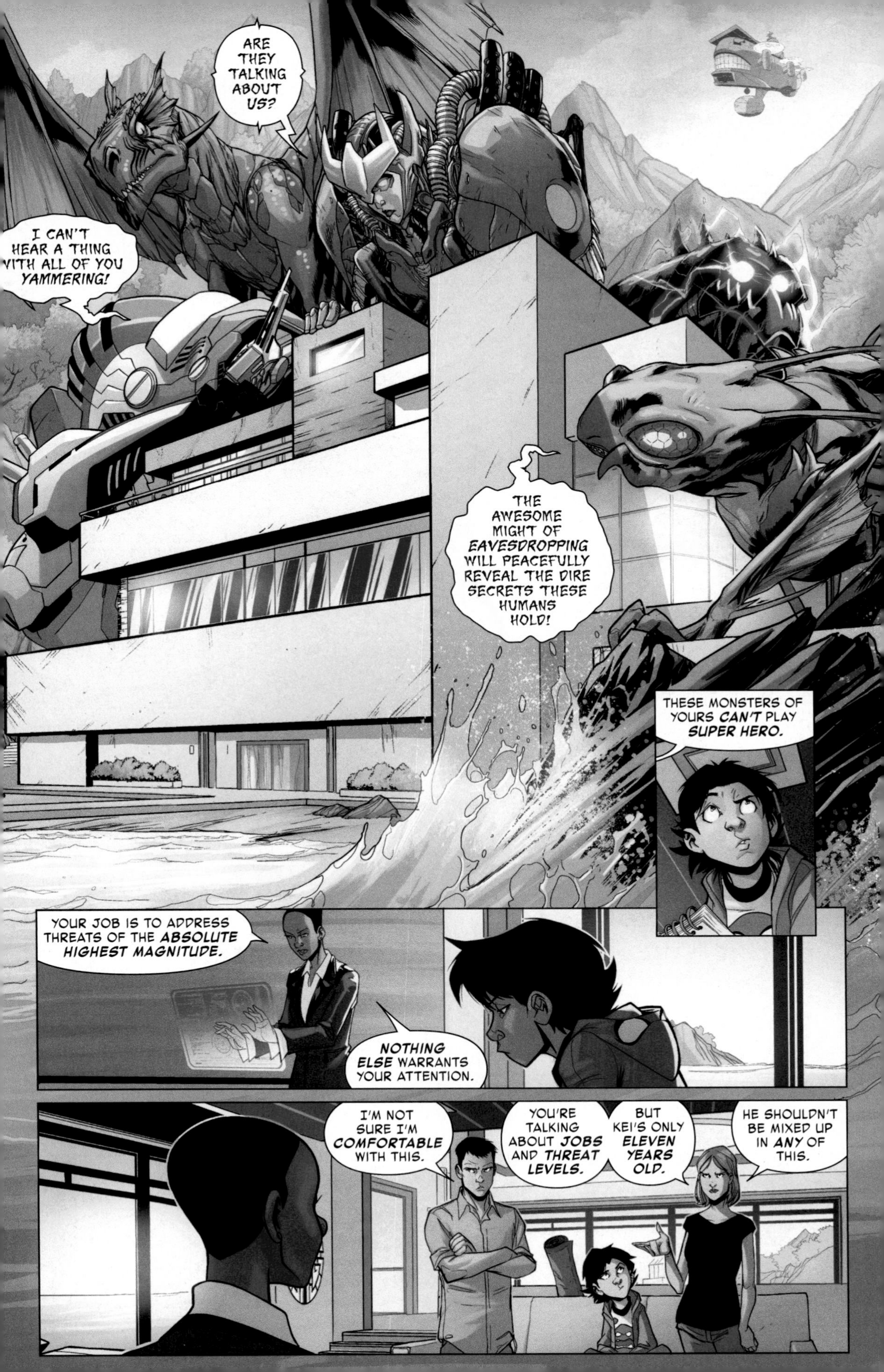
ARE THEY TALKING ABOUT US?
I CAN'T HEAR A THING WITH ALL OF YOU YAMMERING!
THE AWESOME MIGHT OF EAVESDROPPING WILL PEACEFULLY REVEAL THE DIRE SECRETS THESE HUMANS HOLD!
THESE MONSTERS OF YOURS CAN'T PLAY SUPER HERO.
YOUR JOB IS TO ADDRESS THREATS OF THE ABSOLUTE HIGHEST MAGNITUDE.
NOTHING ELSE WARRANTS YOUR ATTENTION.
I'M NOT SURE I'M COMFORTABLE WITH THIS.
YOU'RE TALKING ABOUT JOBS AND THREAT LEVELS.
BUT KEI'S ONLY ELEVEN YEARS OLD.
HE SHOULDN'T BE MIXED UP IN ANY OF THIS.

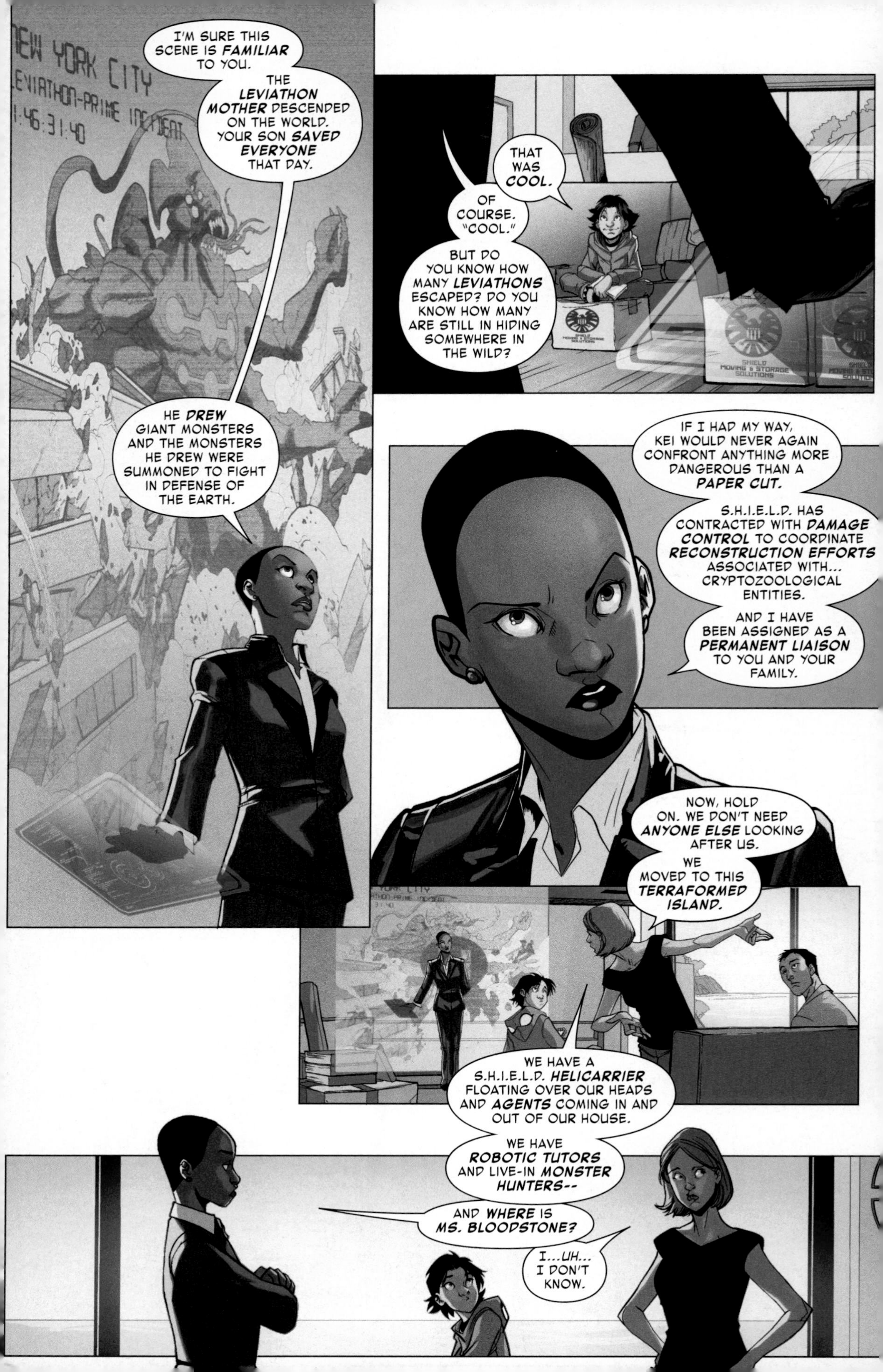

NEW YORK CITY
LEVIATHON-PRIME INCIDENT
1:46:31:40
I'M SURE THIS SCENE IS FAMILIAR TO YOU.
THE LEVIATHON MOTHER DESCENDED ON THE WORLD. YOUR SON SAVED EVERYONE THAT DAY.
HE DREW GIANT MONSTERS AND THE MONSTERS HE DREW WERE SUMMONED TO FIGHT IN DEFENSE OF THE EARTH.
THAT WAS COOL.
OF COURSE. "COOL."
BUT DO YOU KNOW HOW MANY LEVIATHONS ESCAPED? DO YOU KNOW HOW MANY ARE STILL IN HIDING SOMEWHERE IN THE WILD?
SHIELD MOVING & STORAGE SOLUTIONS
IF I HAD MY WAY, KEI WOULD NEVER AGAIN CONFRONT ANYTHING MORE DANGEROUS THAN A PAPER CUT.
S.H.I.E.L.D. HAS CONTRACTED WITH DAMAGE CONTROL TO COORDINATE RECONSTRUCTION EFFORTS ASSOCIATED WITH... CRYPTOZOOLOGICAL ENTITIES.
AND I HAVE BEEN ASSIGNED AS A PERMANENT LIAISON TO YOU AND YOUR FAMILY.
NOW, HOLD ON. WE DON'T NEED ANYONE ELSE LOOKING AFTER US.
WE MOVED TO THIS TERRAFORMED ISLAND.
WE HAVE A S.H.I.E.L.D. HELICARRIER FLOATING OVER OUR HEADS AND AGENTS COMING IN AND OUT OF OUR HOUSE.
WE HAVE ROBOTIC TUTORS AND LIVE-IN MONSTER HUNTERS--
AND WHERE IS MS. BLOODSTONE?
I...UH... I DON'T KNOW.

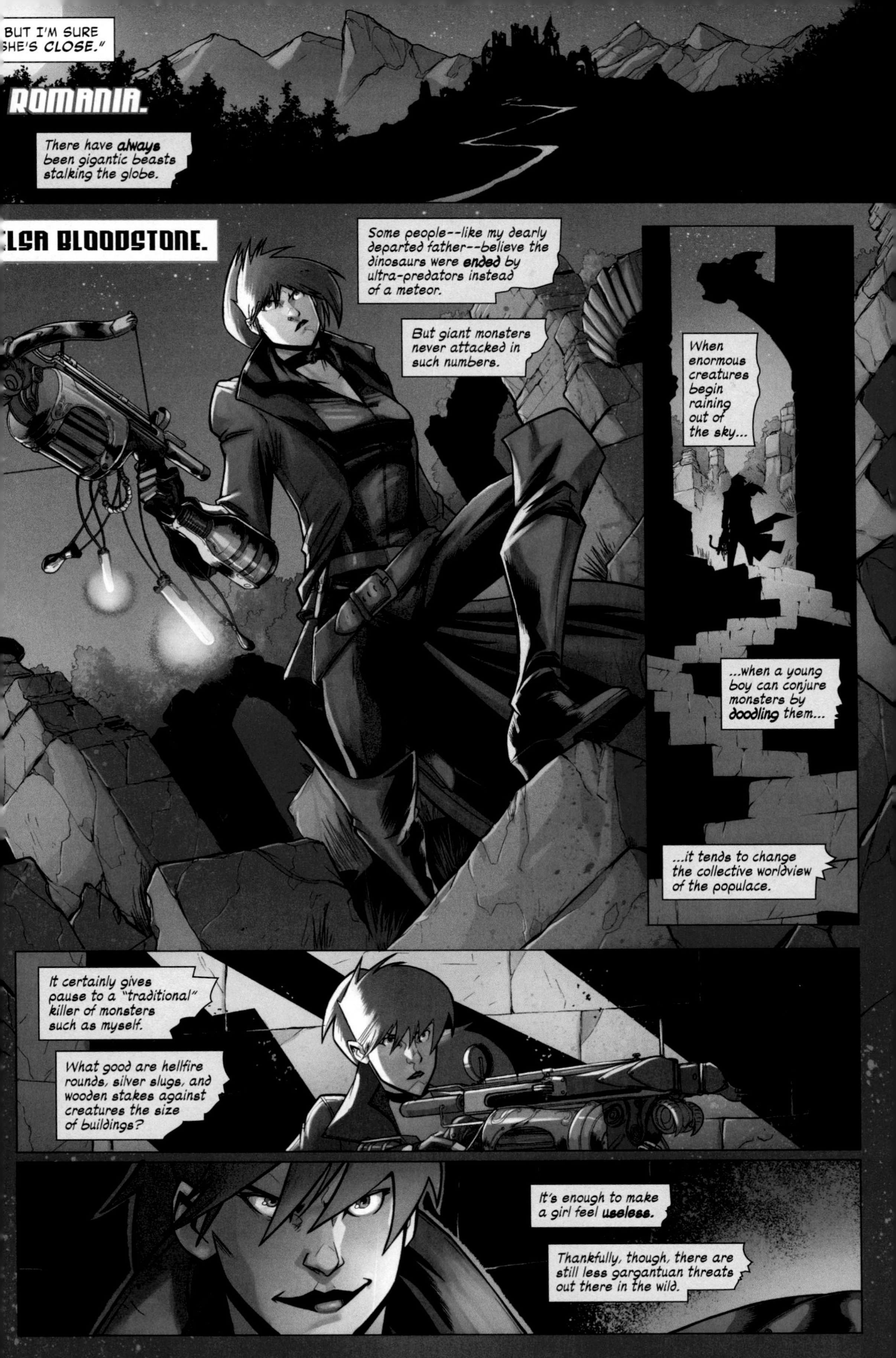

BUT I'M SURE SHE'S CLOSE."
ROMANIA.
There have always been gigantic beasts stalking the globe.
ELSA BLOODSTONE.
Some people--like my dearly departed father--believe the dinosaurs were ended by ultra-predators instead of a meteor.
But giant monsters never attacked in such numbers.
When enormous creatures begin raining out of the sky...
...when a young boy can conjure monsters by doodling them...
...it tends to change the collective worldview of the populace.
It certainly gives pause to a "traditional" killer of monsters such as myself.
What good are hellfire rounds, silver slugs, and wooden stakes against creatures the size of buildings?
It's enough to make a girl feel useless.
Thankfully, though, there are still less gargantuan threats out there in the wild.

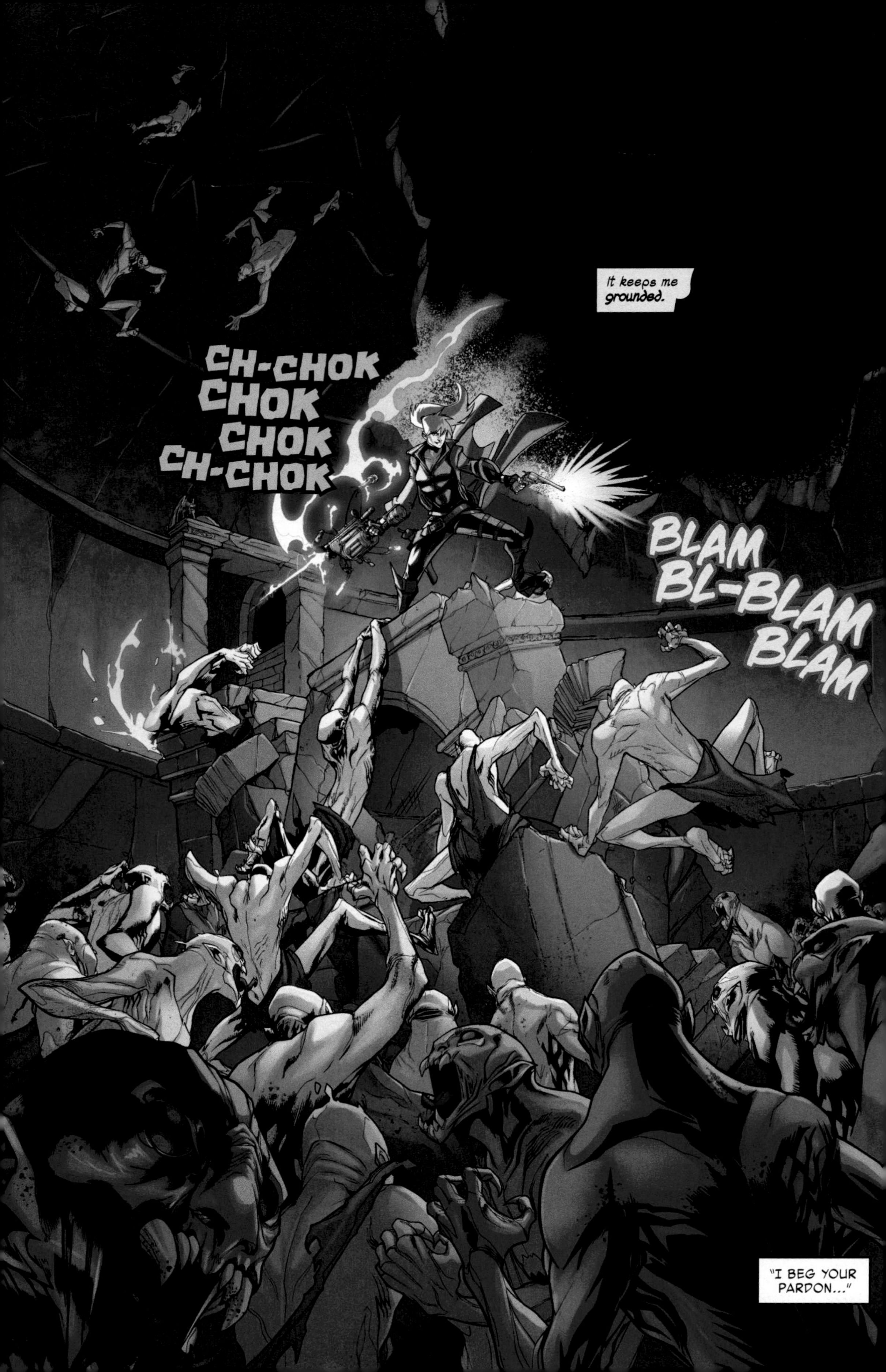
It keeps me grounded.
CH-CHOK CHOK CHOK CH-CHOK
BLAM BL-BLAM BLAM
"I BEG YOUR PARDON..."

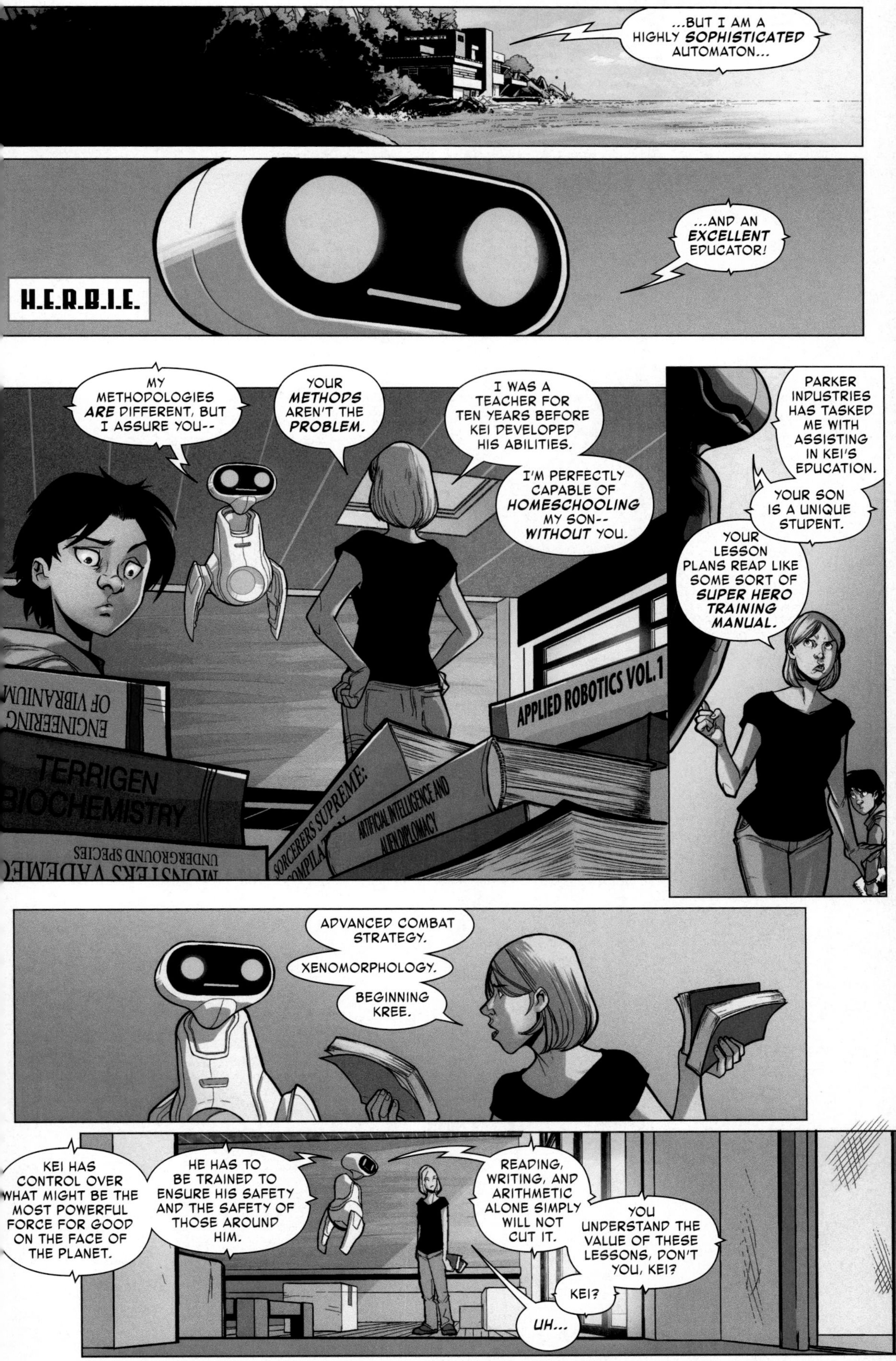
...BUT I AM A HIGHLY SOPHISTICATED AUTOMATON...
H.E.R.B.I.E.
...AND AN EXCELLENT EDUCATOR!
MY METHODOLOGIES ARE DIFFERENT, BUT I ASSURE YOU--
YOUR METHODS AREN'T THE PROBLEM.
I WAS A TEACHER FOR TEN YEARS BEFORE KEI DEVELOPED HIS ABILITIES.
I'M PERFECTLY CAPABLE OF HOMESCHOOLING MY SON-- WITHOUT YOU.
ENGINEERING OF VIBRANIUM
TERRIGEN BIOCHEMISTRY
MONSTERS VADEMEC UNDERGROUND SPECIES
SORCERERS SUPREME: COMPILA
ARTIFICIAL INTELLIGENCE AND ALIEN DIPLOMACY
APPLIED ROBOTICS VOL.1
PARKER INDUSTRIES HAS TASKED ME WITH ASSISTING IN KEI'S EDUCATION.
YOUR SON IS A UNIQUE STUDENT.
YOUR LESSON PLANS READ LIKE SOME SORT OF SUPER HERO TRAINING MANUAL.
ADVANCED COMBAT STRATEGY.
XENOMORPHOLOGY.
BEGINNING KREE.
KEI HAS CONTROL OVER WHAT MIGHT BE THE MOST POWERFUL FORCE FOR GOOD ON THE FACE OF THE PLANET.
HE HAS TO BE TRAINED TO ENSURE HIS SAFETY AND THE SAFETY OF THOSE AROUND HIM.
READING, WRITING, AND ARITHMETIC ALONE SIMPLY WILL NOT CUT IT.
YOU UNDERSTAND THE VALUE OF THESE LESSONS, DON'T YOU, KEI?
KEI?
UH...

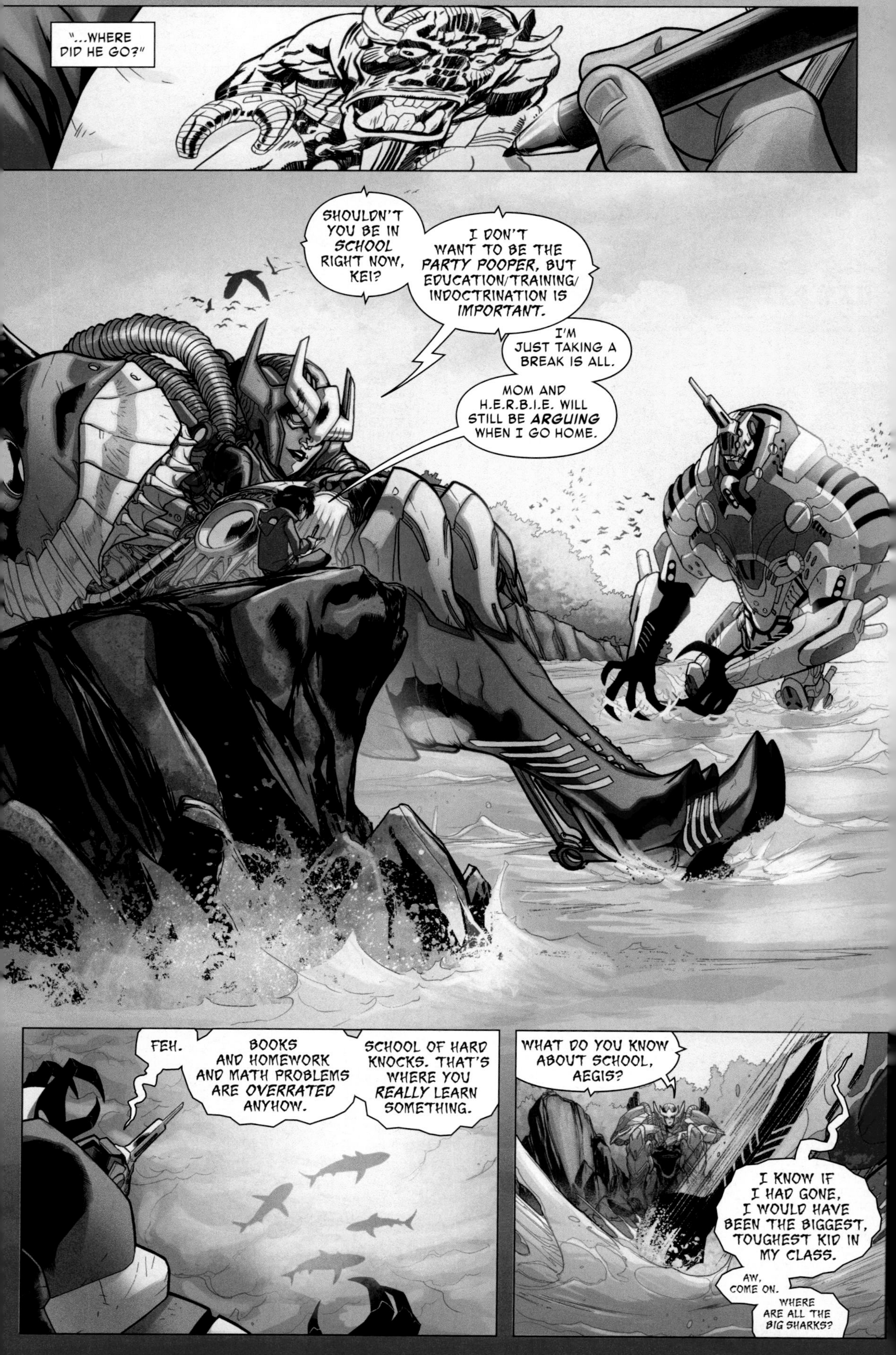
"...WHERE DID HE GO?"
SHOULDN'T YOU BE IN SCHOOL RIGHT NOW, KEI?
I DON'T WANT TO BE THE PARTY POOPER, BUT EDUCATION/TRAINING/ INDOCTRINATION IS IMPORTANT.
I'M JUST TAKING A BREAK IS ALL.
MOM AND H.E.R.B.I.E. WILL STILL BE ARGUING WHEN I GO HOME.
FEH.
BOOKS AND HOMEWORK AND MATH PROBLEMS ARE OVERRATED ANYHOW.
SCHOOL OF HARD KNOCKS. THAT'S WHERE YOU REALLY LEARN SOMETHING.
WHAT DO YOU KNOW ABOUT SCHOOL, AEGIS?
I KNOW IF I HAD GONE, I WOULD HAVE BEEN THE BIGGEST, TOUGHEST KID IN MY CLASS.
AW, COME ON.
WHERE ARE ALL THE BIG SHARKS?

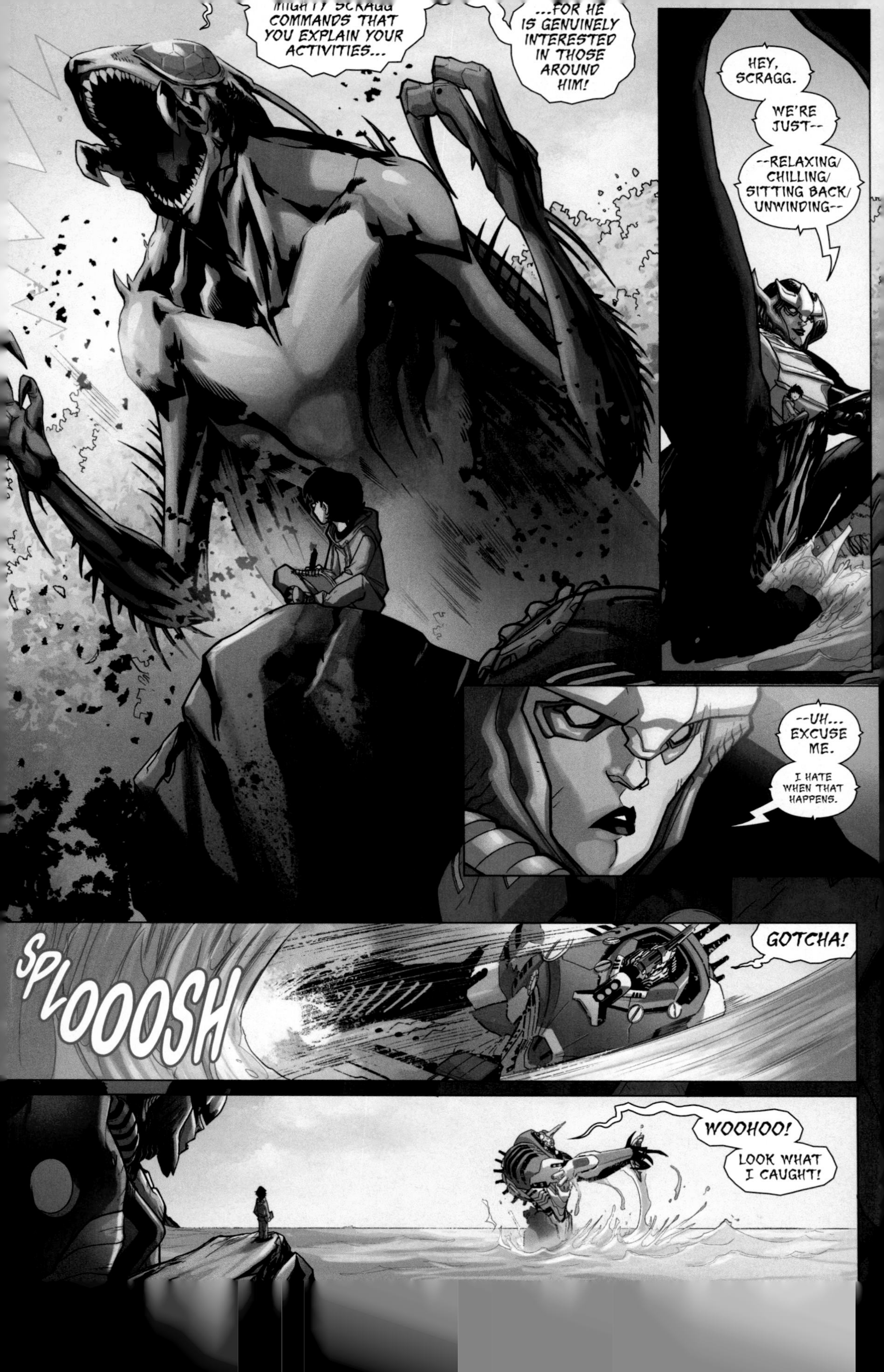
MIGHTY SCRAGG COMMANDS THAT YOU EXPLAIN YOUR ACTIVITIES...
...FOR HE IS GENUINELY INTERESTED IN THOSE AROUND HIM!
HEY, SCRAGG.
WE'RE JUST--
--RELAXING/ CHILLING/ SITTING BACK/ UNWINDING--
--UH... EXCUSE ME.
I HATE WHEN THAT HAPPENS.
SPLOOOSH
GOTCHA!
WOOHOO!
LOOK WHAT I CAUGHT!

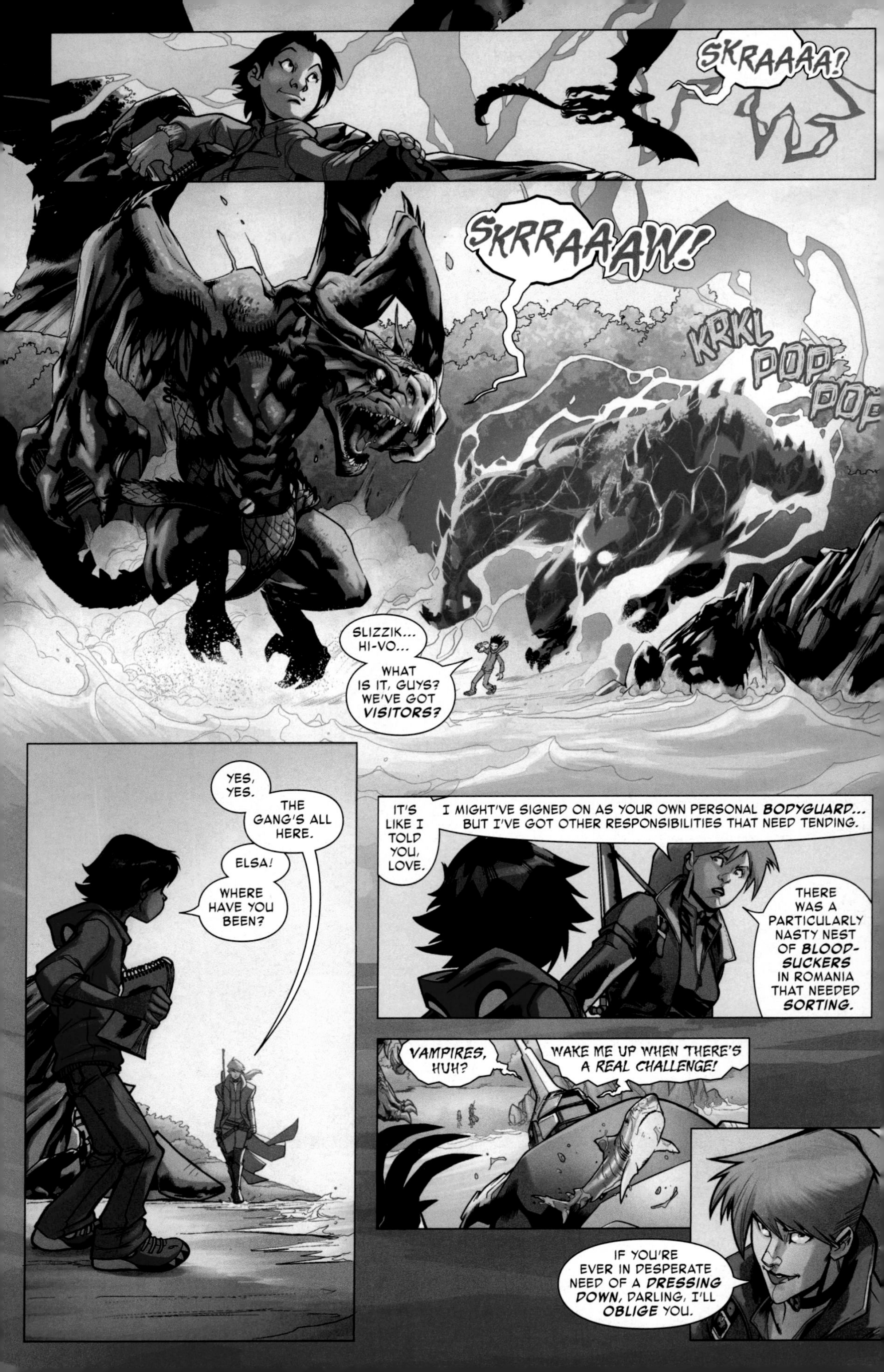
SKRAAAA!
SKRRAAAAW!
KRKL
POP
POP
SLIZZIK... HI-VO...
WHAT IS IT, GUYS? WE'VE GOT VISITORS?
YES, YES.
THE GANG'S ALL HERE.
ELSA!
WHERE HAVE YOU BEEN?
IT'S LIKE I TOLD YOU, LOVE.
I MIGHT'VE SIGNED ON AS YOUR OWN PERSONAL BODYGUARD... BUT I'VE GOT OTHER RESPONSIBILITIES THAT NEED TENDING.
THERE WAS A PARTICULARLY NASTY NEST OF BLOOD-SUCKERS IN ROMANIA THAT NEEDED SORTING.
VAMPIRES, HUH?
WAKE ME UP WHEN THERE'S A REAL CHALLENGE!
IF YOU'RE EVER IN DESPERATE NEED OF A DRESSING DOWN, DARLING, I'LL OBLIGE YOU.

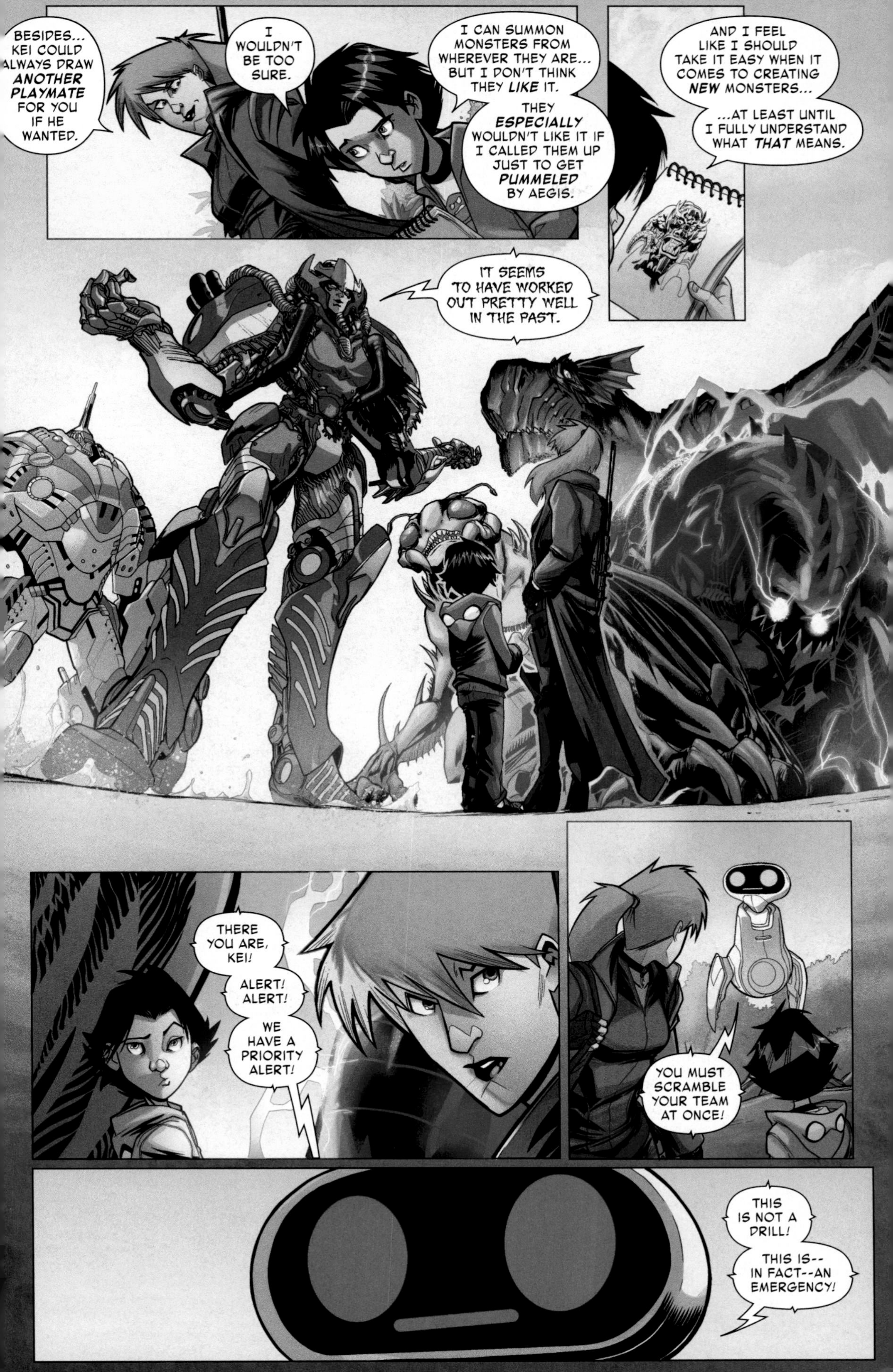
BESIDES... KEI COULD ALWAYS DRAW ANOTHER PLAYMATE FOR YOU IF HE WANTED.
I WOULDN'T BE TOO SURE.
I CAN SUMMON MONSTERS FROM WHEREVER THEY ARE... BUT I DON'T THINK THEY LIKE IT.
THEY ESPECIALLY WOULDN'T LIKE IT IF I CALLED THEM UP JUST TO GET PUMMELED BY AEGIS.
AND I FEEL LIKE I SHOULD TAKE IT EASY WHEN IT COMES TO CREATING NEW MONSTERS...
...AT LEAST UNTIL I FULLY UNDERSTAND WHAT THAT MEANS.
IT SEEMS TO HAVE WORKED OUT PRETTY WELL IN THE PAST.
THERE YOU ARE, KEI!
ALERT! ALERT!
WE HAVE A PRIORITY ALERT!
YOU MUST SCRAMBLE YOUR TEAM AT ONCE!
THIS IS NOT A DRILL!
THIS IS-- IN FACT--AN EMERGENCY!

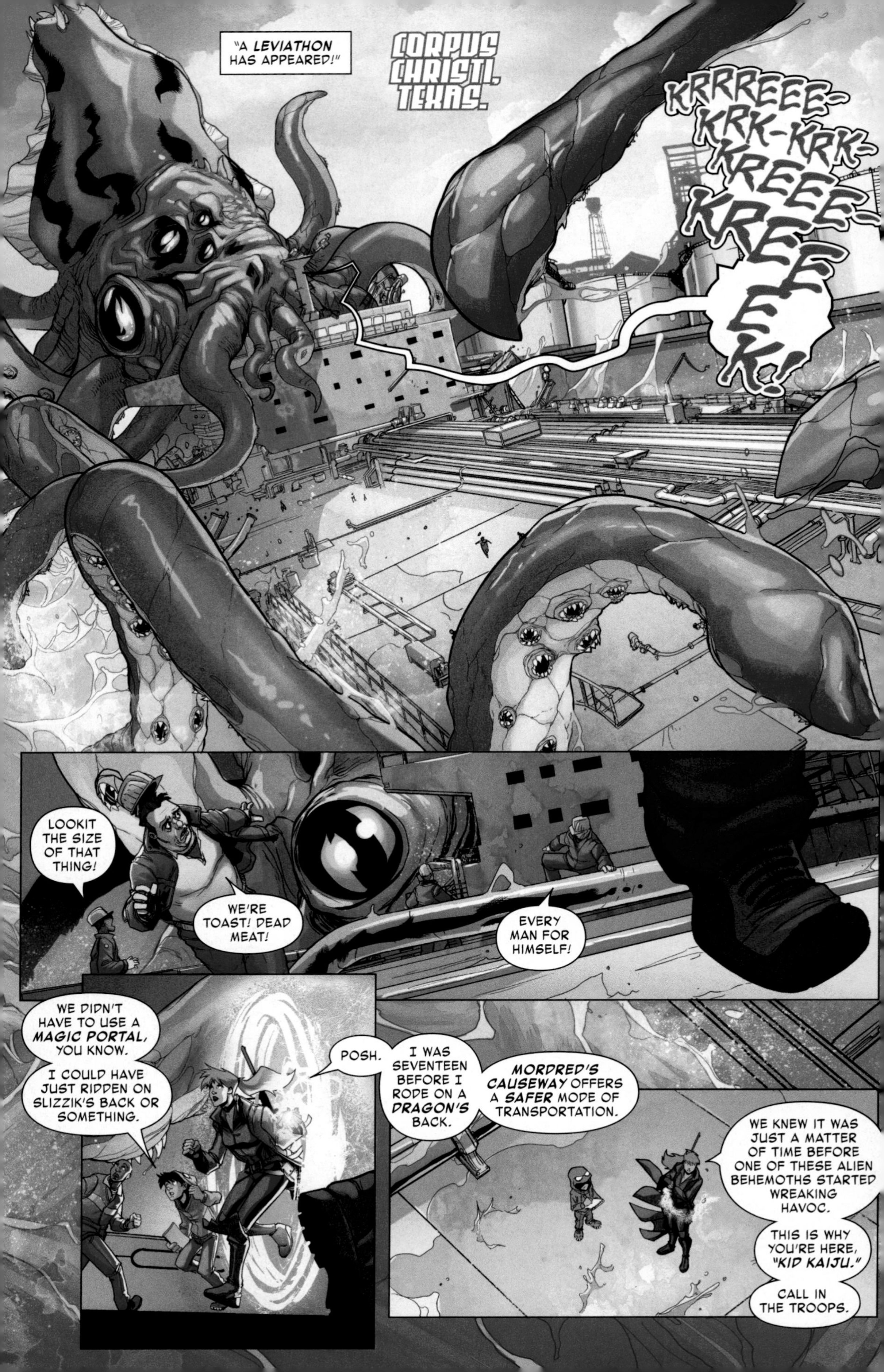

"A LEVIATHON HAS APPEARED!"
CORPUS CHRISTI, TEXAS.
KRRREEE-KRK-KRK-KREEEE-KREEEEK!
LOOKIT THE SIZE OF THAT THING!
WE'RE TOAST! DEAD MEAT!
EVERY MAN FOR HIMSELF!
WE DIDN'T HAVE TO USE A MAGIC PORTAL, YOU KNOW.
I COULD HAVE JUST RIDDEN ON SLIZZIK'S BACK OR SOMETHING.
POSH.
I WAS SEVENTEEN BEFORE I RODE ON A DRAGON'S BACK.
MORDRED'S CAUSEWAY OFFERS A SAFER MODE OF TRANSPORTATION.
WE KNEW IT WAS JUST A MATTER OF TIME BEFORE ONE OF THESE ALIEN BEHEMOTHS STARTED WREAKING HAVOC.
THIS IS WHY YOU'RE HERE, "KID KAIJU."
CALL IN THE TROOPS.

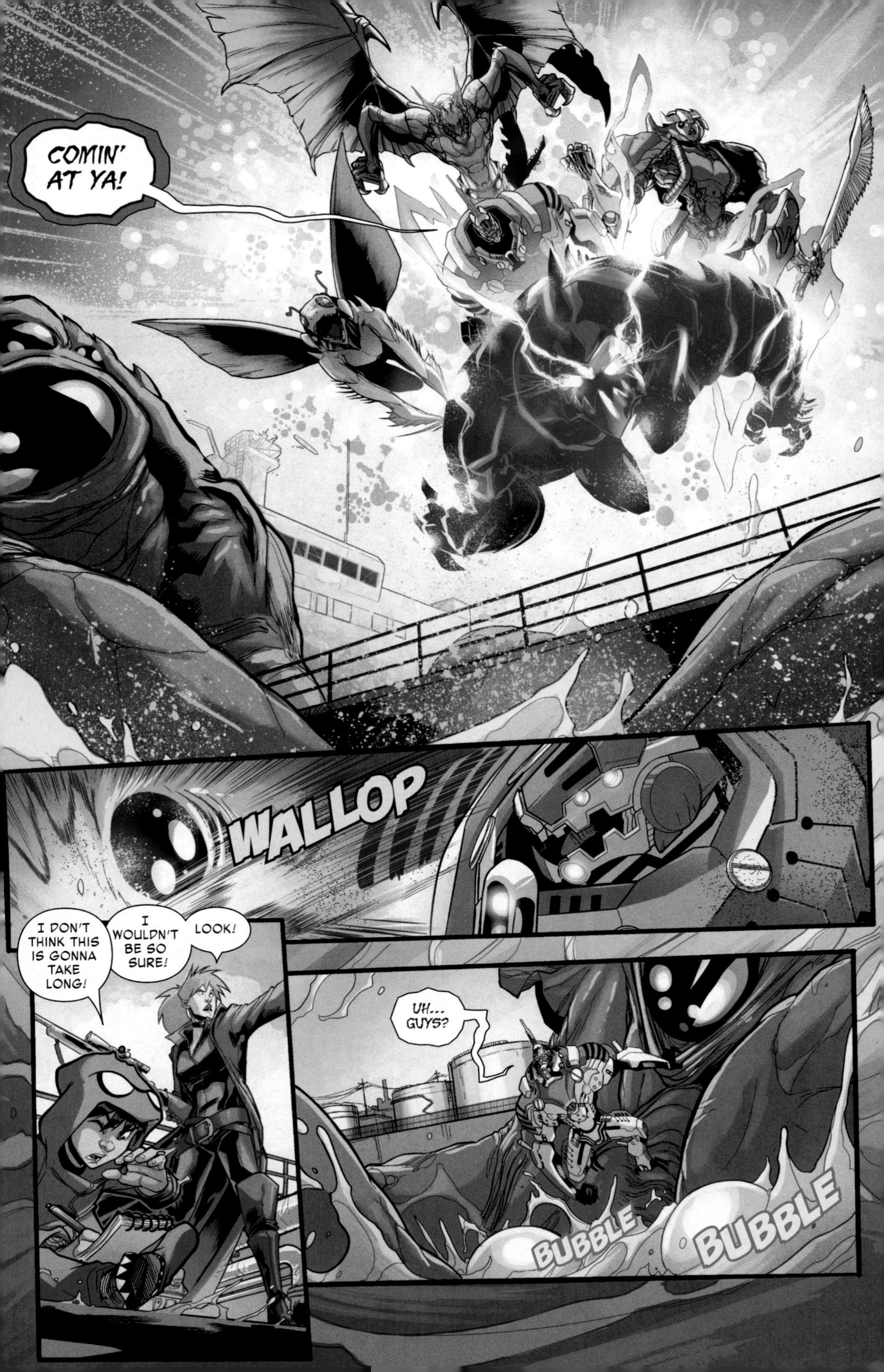
COMIN' AT YA!
WALLOP
I DON'T THINK THIS IS GONNA TAKE LONG!
I WOULDN'T BE SO SURE!
LOOK!
UH... GUYS?
BUBBLE
BUBBLE

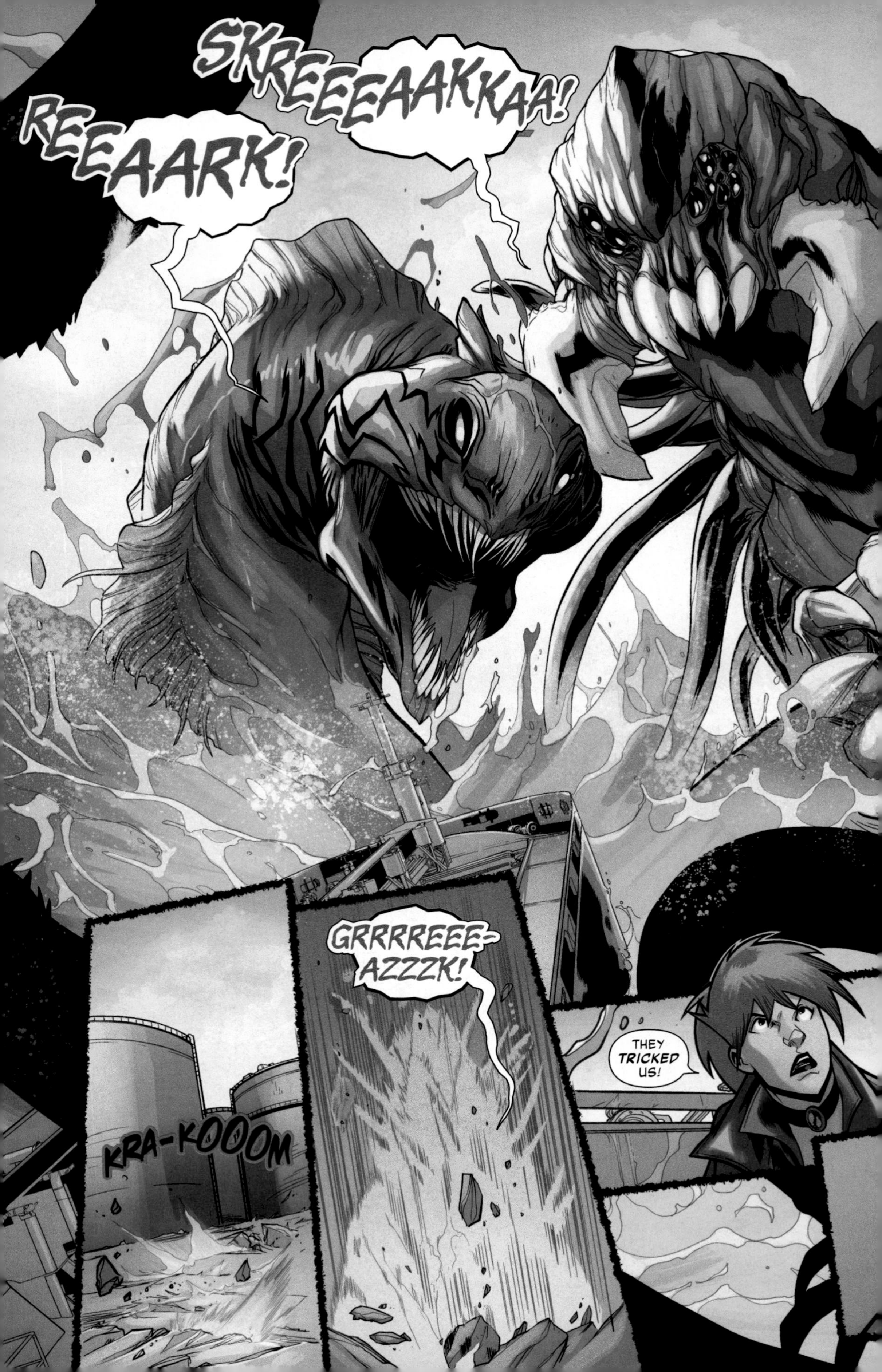
SKREEEEAAKKAA!
REEEAARK!
GRRRREEE-
AZZZK!
KRA-KOOOM
THEY TRICKED US!

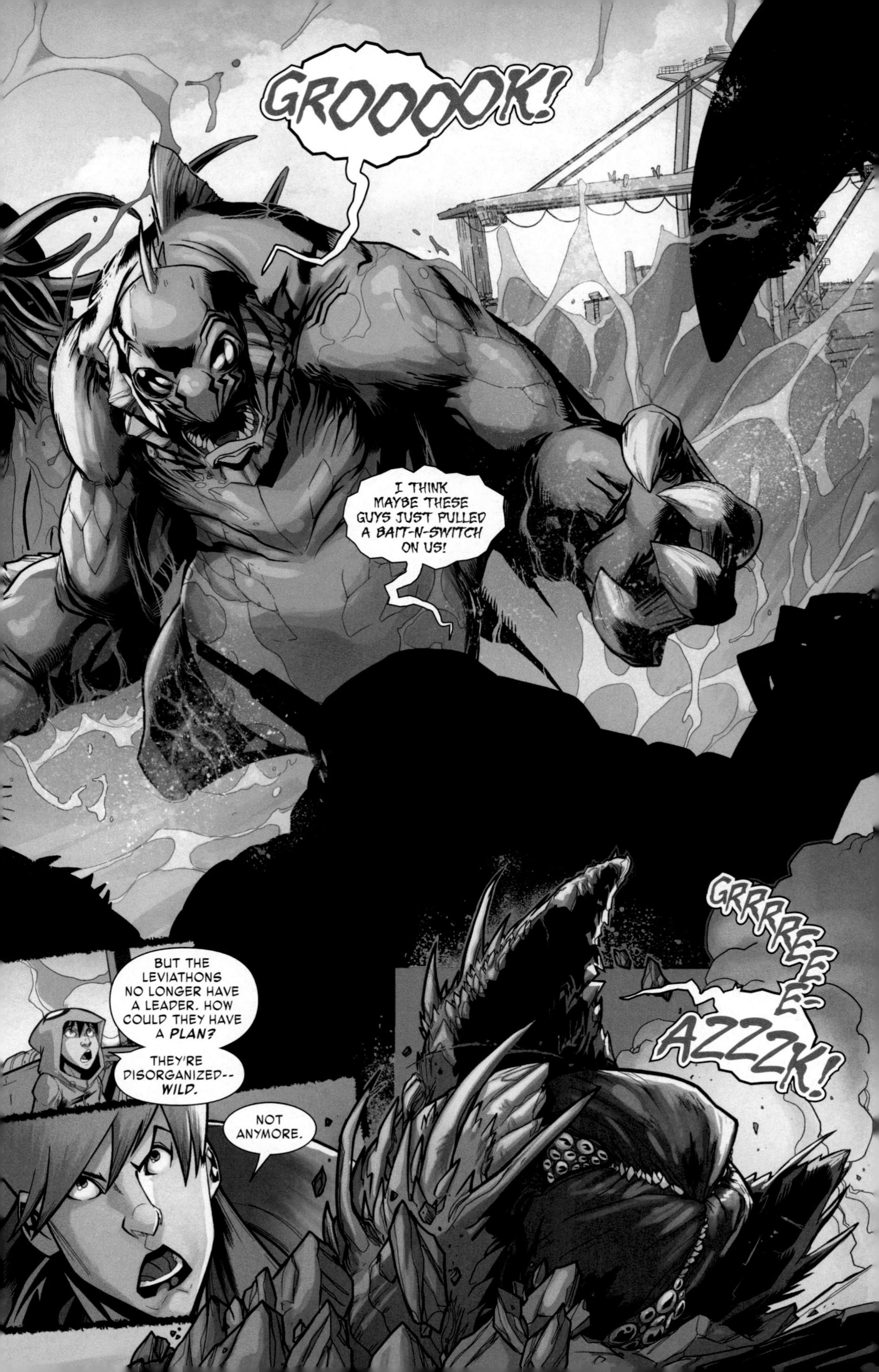
GROOOOK!
I THINK MAYBE THESE GUYS JUST PULLED A BAIT-N-SWITCH ON US!
GRRRREEE-E-AZZZK!
BUT THE LEVIATHONS NO LONGER HAVE A LEADER. HOW COULD THEY HAVE A PLAN?
THEY'RE DISORGANIZED-- WILD.
NOT ANYMORE.

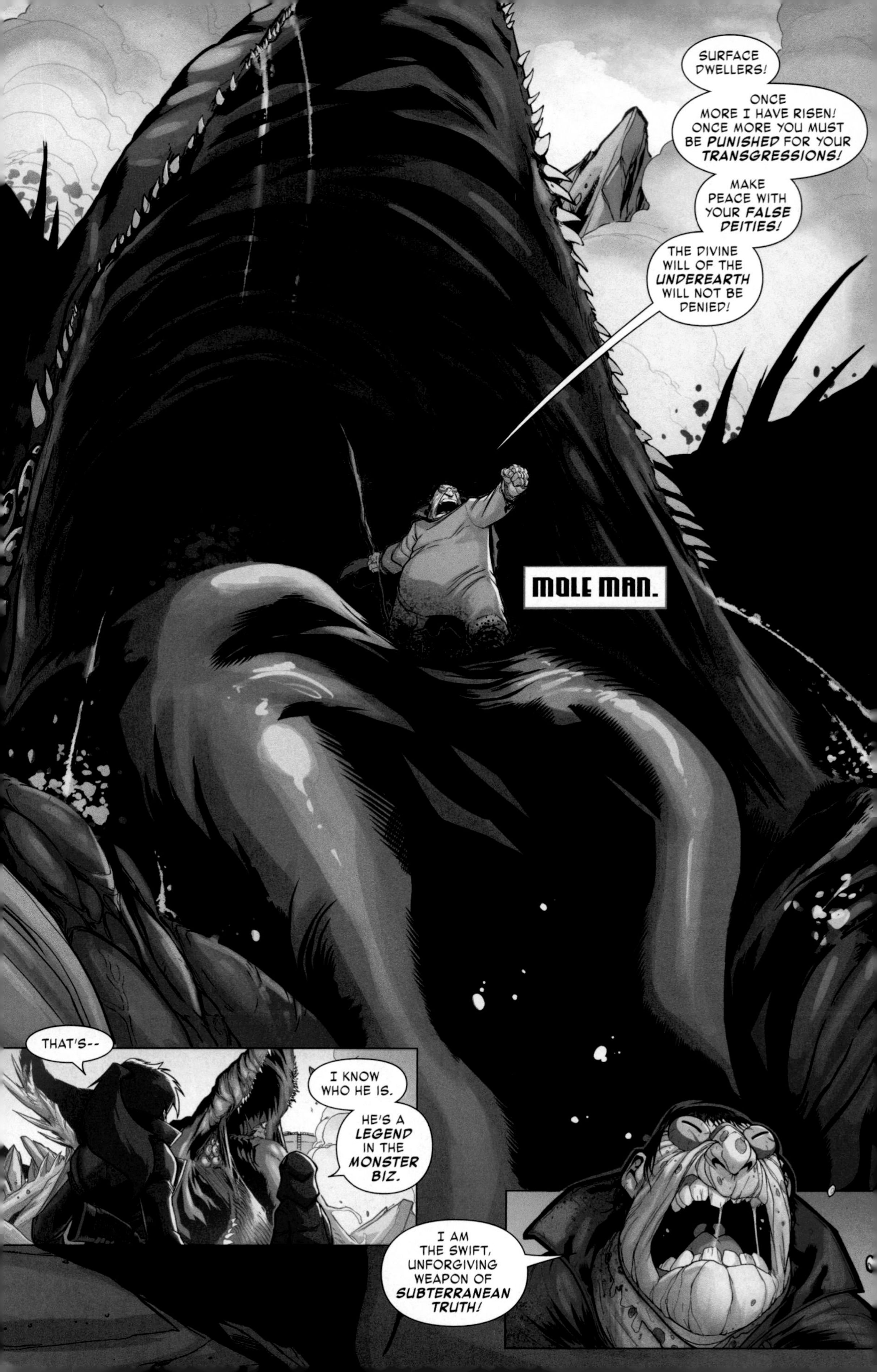

SURFACE DWELLERS!
ONCE MORE I HAVE RISEN! ONCE MORE YOU MUST BE PUNISHED FOR YOUR TRANSGRESSIONS!
MAKE PEACE WITH YOUR FALSE DEITIES!
THE DIVINE WILL OF THE UNDEREARTH WILL NOT BE DENIED!
MOLE MAN.
THAT'S--
I KNOW WHO HE IS.
HE'S A LEGEND IN THE MONSTER BIZ.
I AM THE SWIFT, UNFORGIVING WEAPON OF SUBTERRANEAN TRUTH!

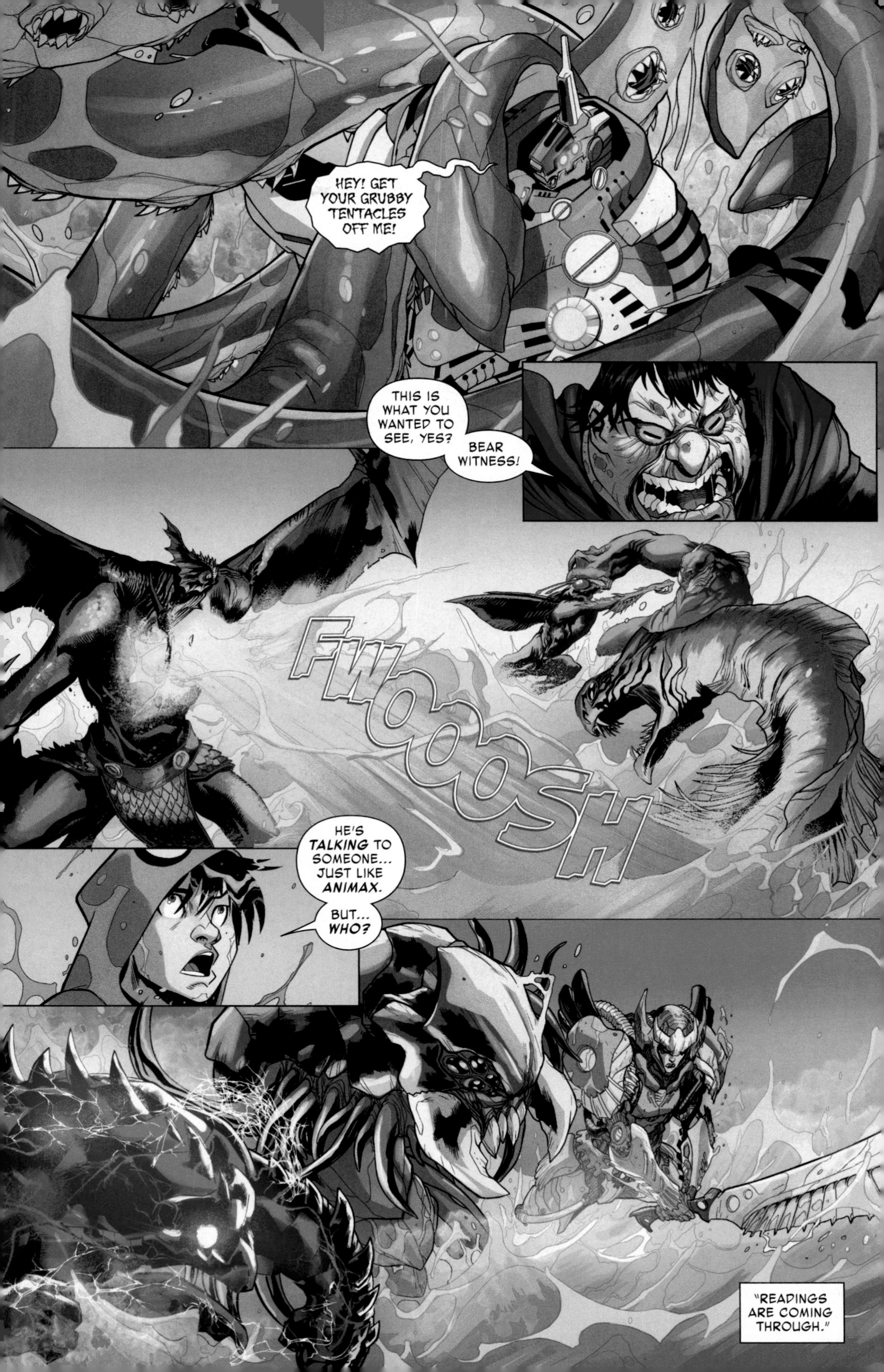
HEY! GET YOUR GRUBBY TENTACLES OFF ME!
THIS IS WHAT YOU WANTED TO SEE, YES?
BEAR WITNESS!
FWOOOOSH
HE'S TALKING TO SOMEONE... JUST LIKE ANIMAX.
BUT... WHO?
"READINGS ARE COMING THROUGH."

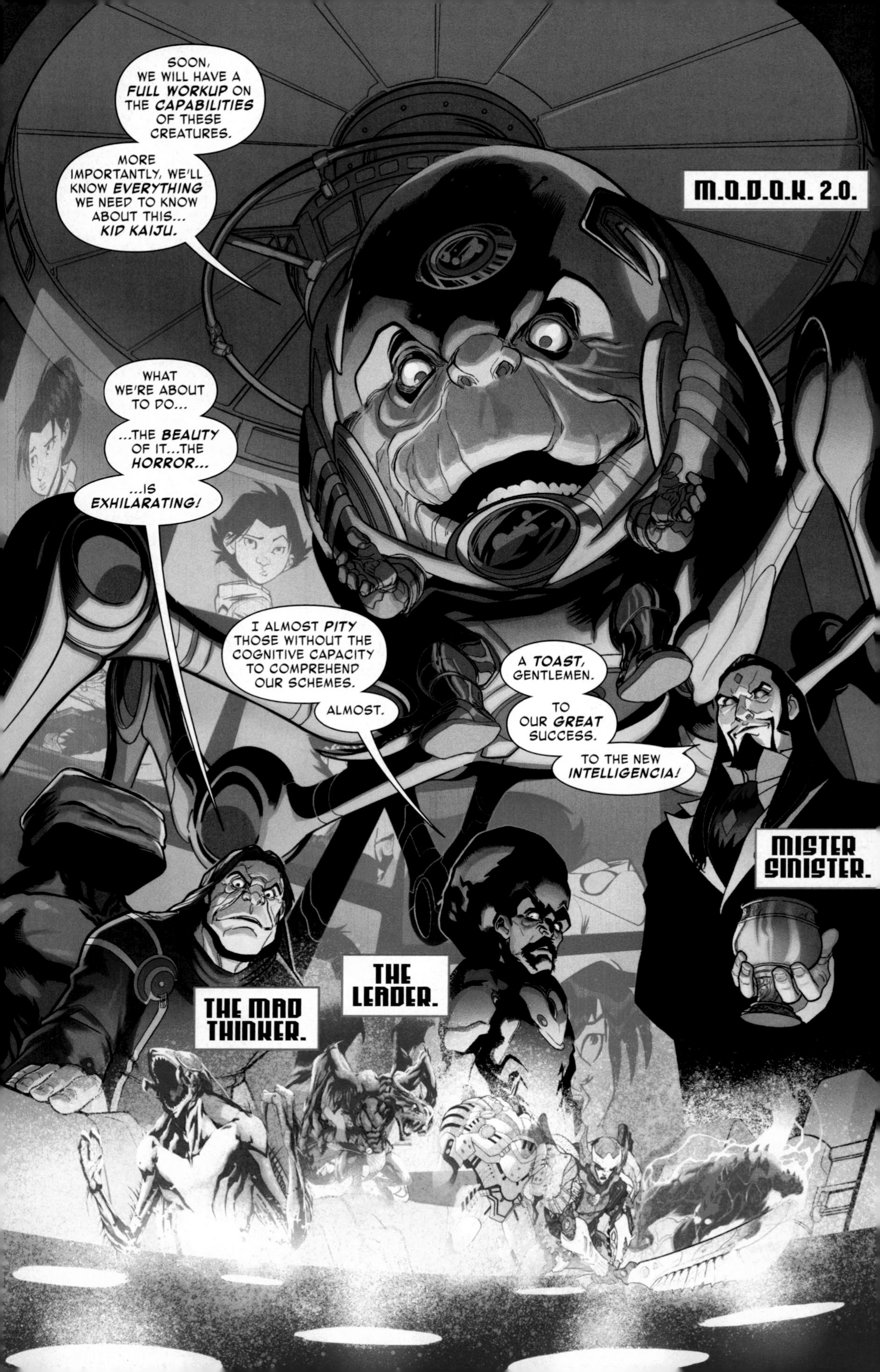

SOON, WE WILL HAVE A *FULL WORKUP* ON THE *CAPABILITIES* OF THESE CREATURES.
MORE IMPORTANTLY, WE'LL KNOW *EVERYTHING* WE NEED TO KNOW ABOUT THIS... *KID KAIJU.*
M.O.D.O.K. 2.0.
WHAT WE'RE ABOUT TO DO...
...THE *BEAUTY* OF IT...THE *HORROR...*
...IS *EXHILARATING!*
I ALMOST *PITY* THOSE WITHOUT THE COGNITIVE CAPACITY TO COMPREHEND OUR SCHEMES.
ALMOST.
A *TOAST,* GENTLEMEN.
TO OUR *GREAT* SUCCESS.
TO THE NEW *INTELLIGENCIA!*
MISTER SINISTER.
THE MAD THINKER.
THE LEADER.

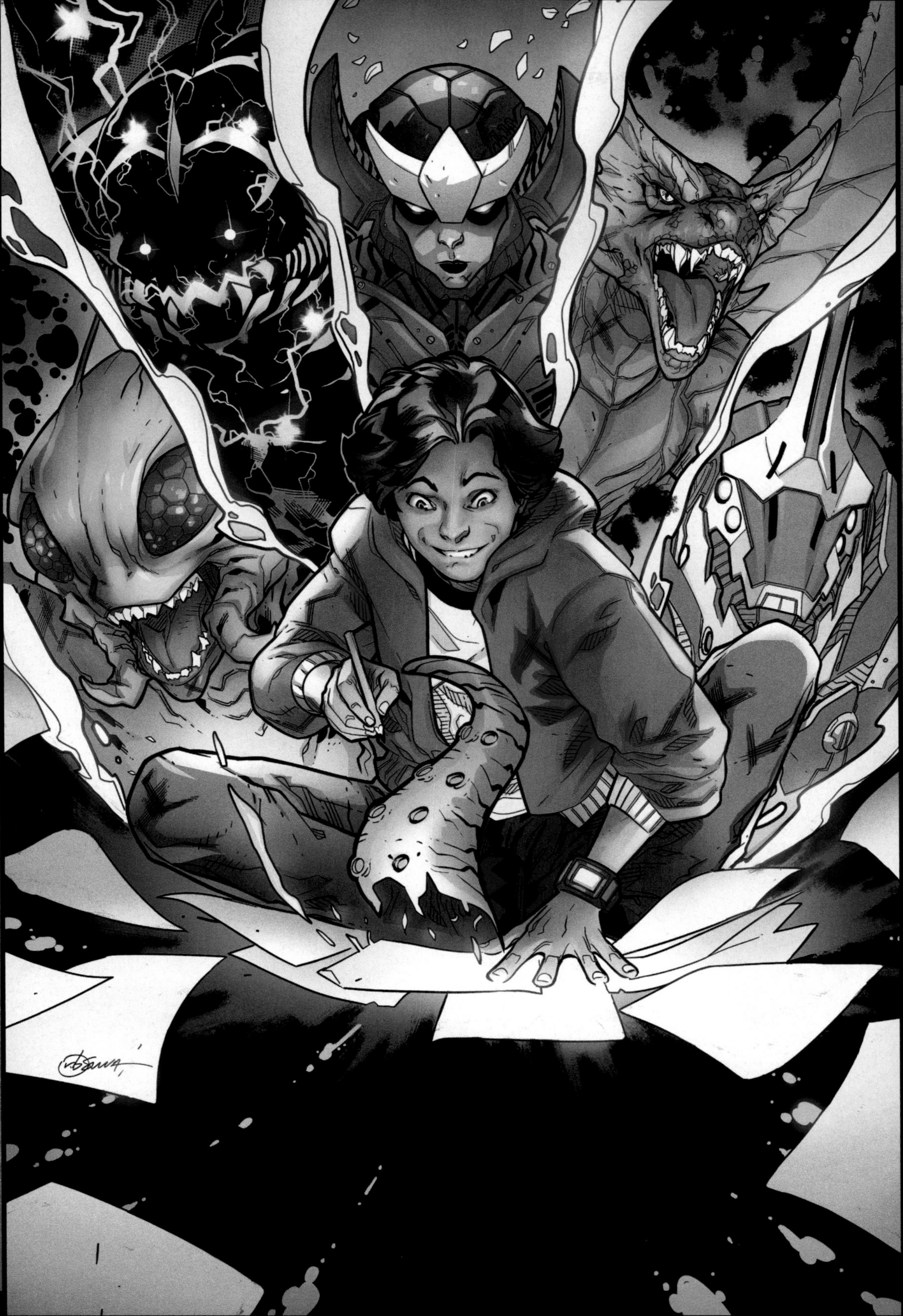

#1 VARIANT BY
R.B. SILVA & JASON KEITH

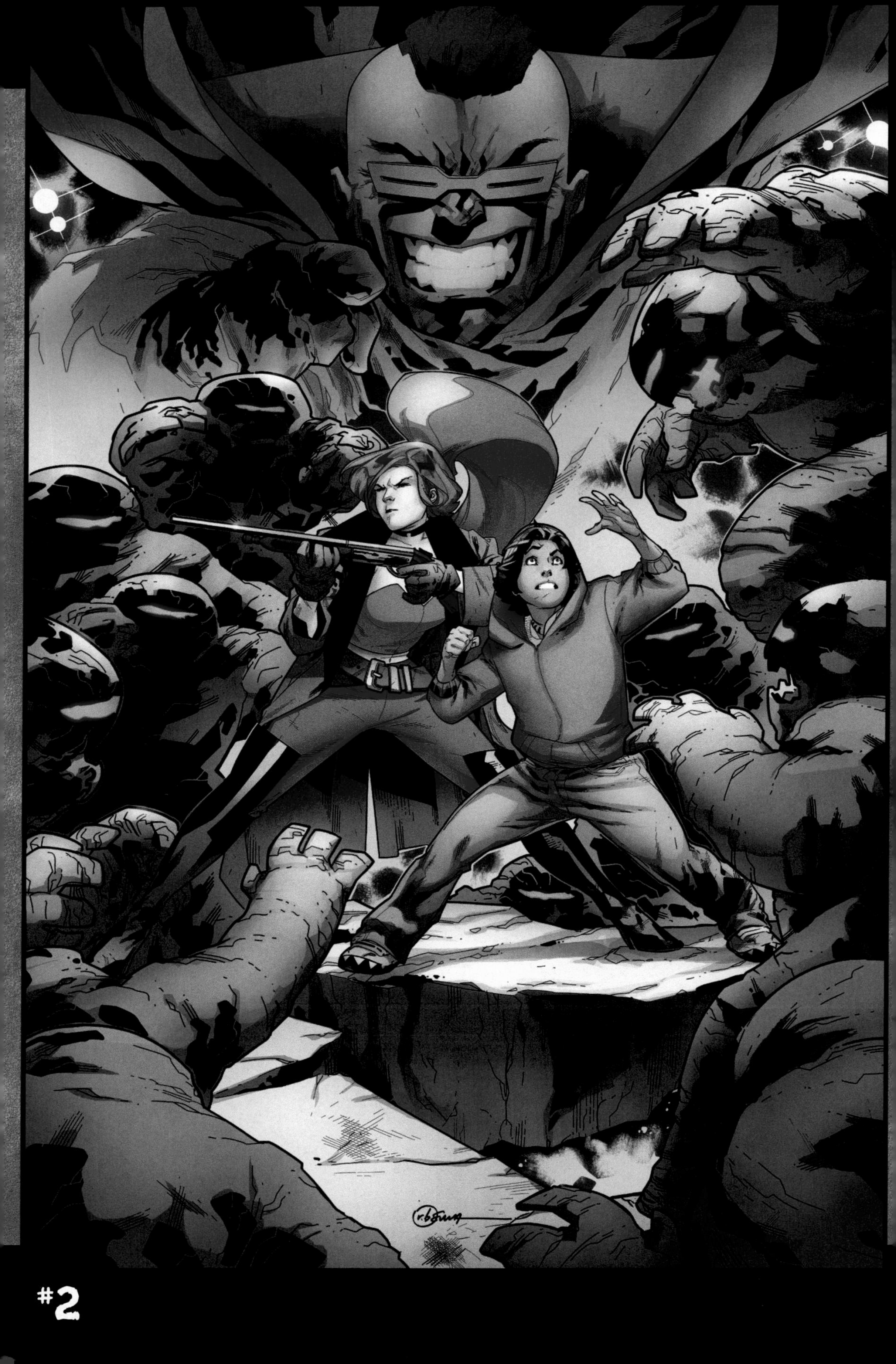

#2

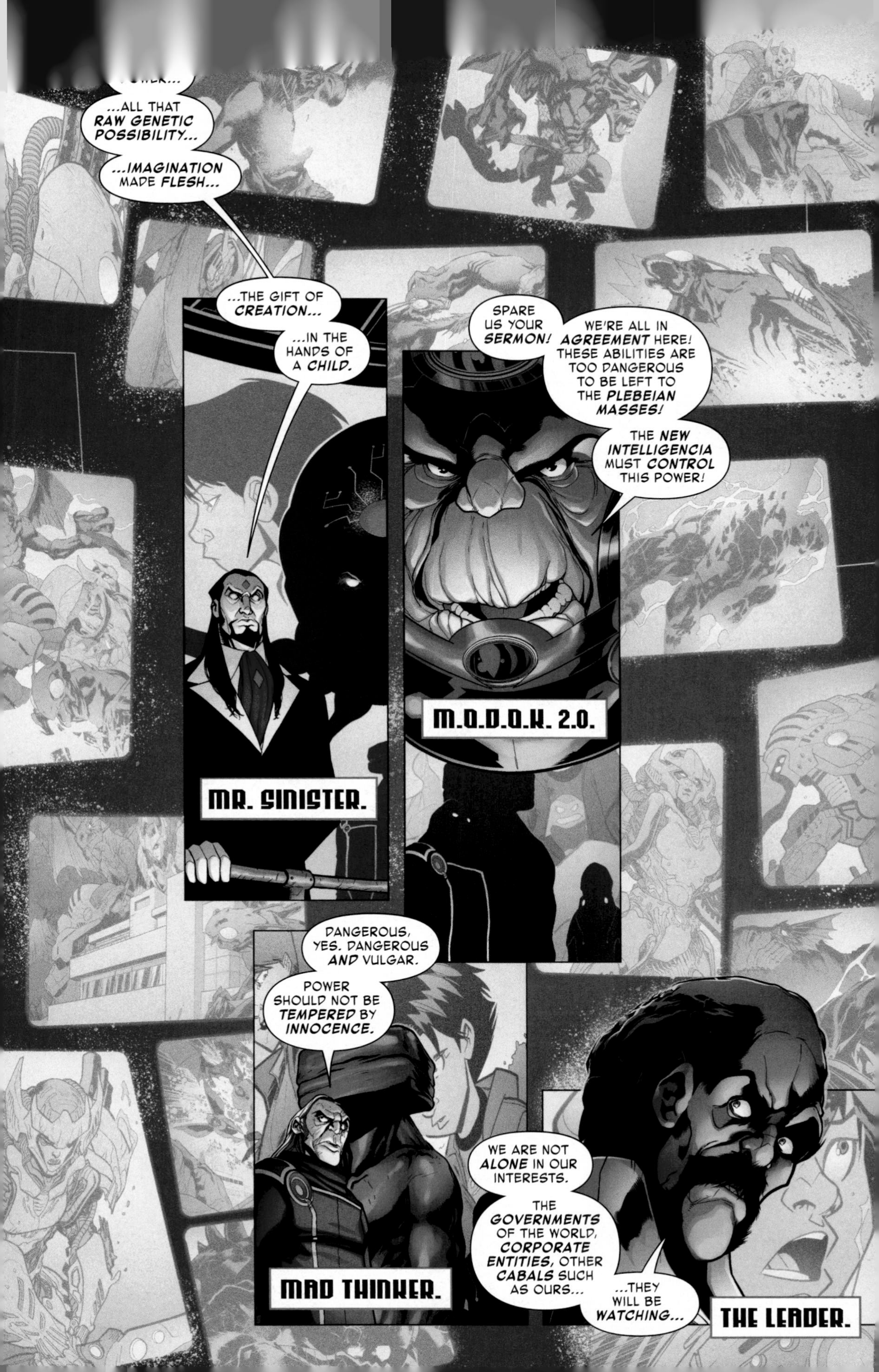

...ALL THAT RAW GENETIC POSSIBILITY...
...IMAGINATION MADE FLESH...
...THE GIFT OF CREATION...
...IN THE HANDS OF A CHILD.
MR. SINISTER.
SPARE US YOUR SERMON!
WE'RE ALL IN AGREEMENT HERE! THESE ABILITIES ARE TOO DANGEROUS TO BE LEFT TO THE PLEBEIAN MASSES!
THE NEW INTELLIGENCIA MUST CONTROL THIS POWER!
M.O.D.O.K. 2.0.
DANGEROUS, YES. DANGEROUS AND VULGAR.
POWER SHOULD NOT BE TEMPERED BY INNOCENCE.
MAD THINKER.
WE ARE NOT ALONE IN OUR INTERESTS.
THE GOVERNMENTS OF THE WORLD, CORPORATE ENTITIES, OTHER CABALS SUCH AS OURS...
...THEY WILL BE WATCHING...
THE LEADER.

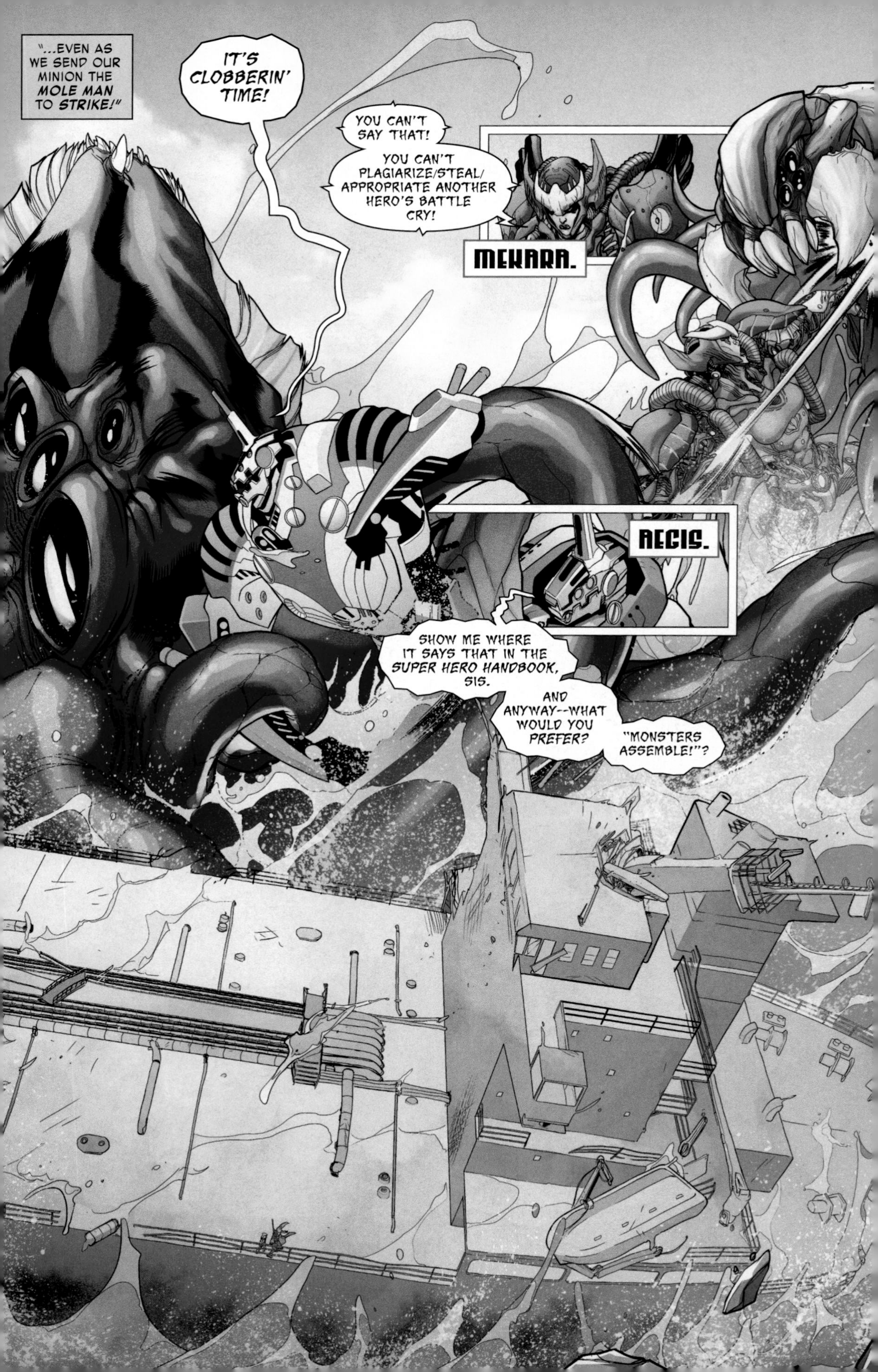
"...EVEN AS WE SEND OUR MINION THE MOLE MAN TO STRIKE!"
IT'S CLOBBERIN' TIME!
YOU CAN'T SAY THAT!
YOU CAN'T PLAGIARIZE/STEAL/ APPROPRIATE ANOTHER HERO'S BATTLE CRY!
MEKARA.
REGIS.
SHOW ME WHERE IT SAYS THAT IN THE SUPER HERO HANDBOOK, SIS.
AND ANYWAY--WHAT WOULD YOU PREFER?
"MONSTERS ASSEMBLE!"?

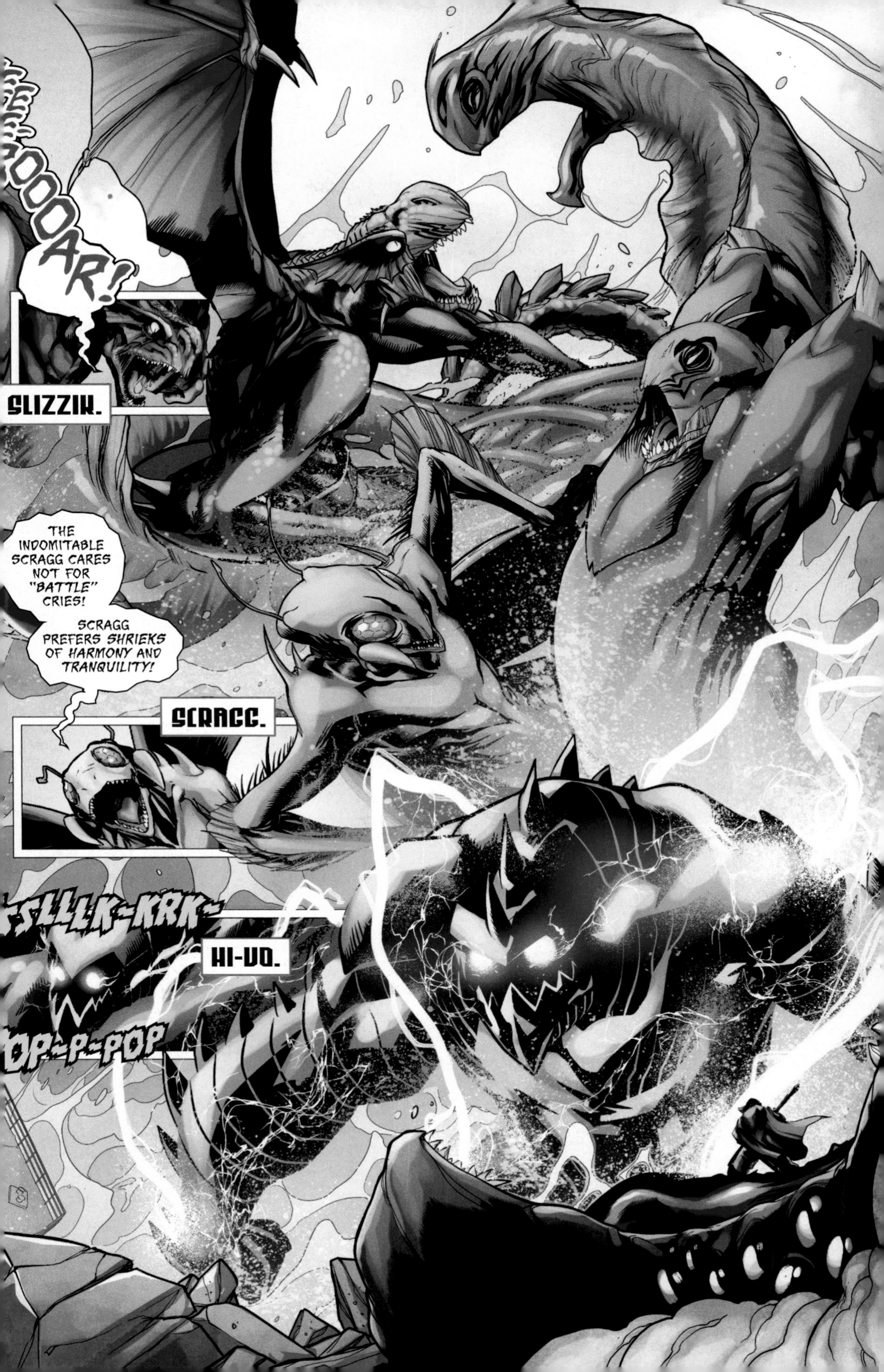

...OOOAR!
SLIZZIK.
THE INDOMITABLE SCRAGG CARES NOT FOR "BATTLE" CRIES!
SCRAGG PREFERS SHRIEKS OF HARMONY AND TRANQUILITY!
SCRAGG.
SLLLK-KRK-
HI-VO.
OP-P-POP

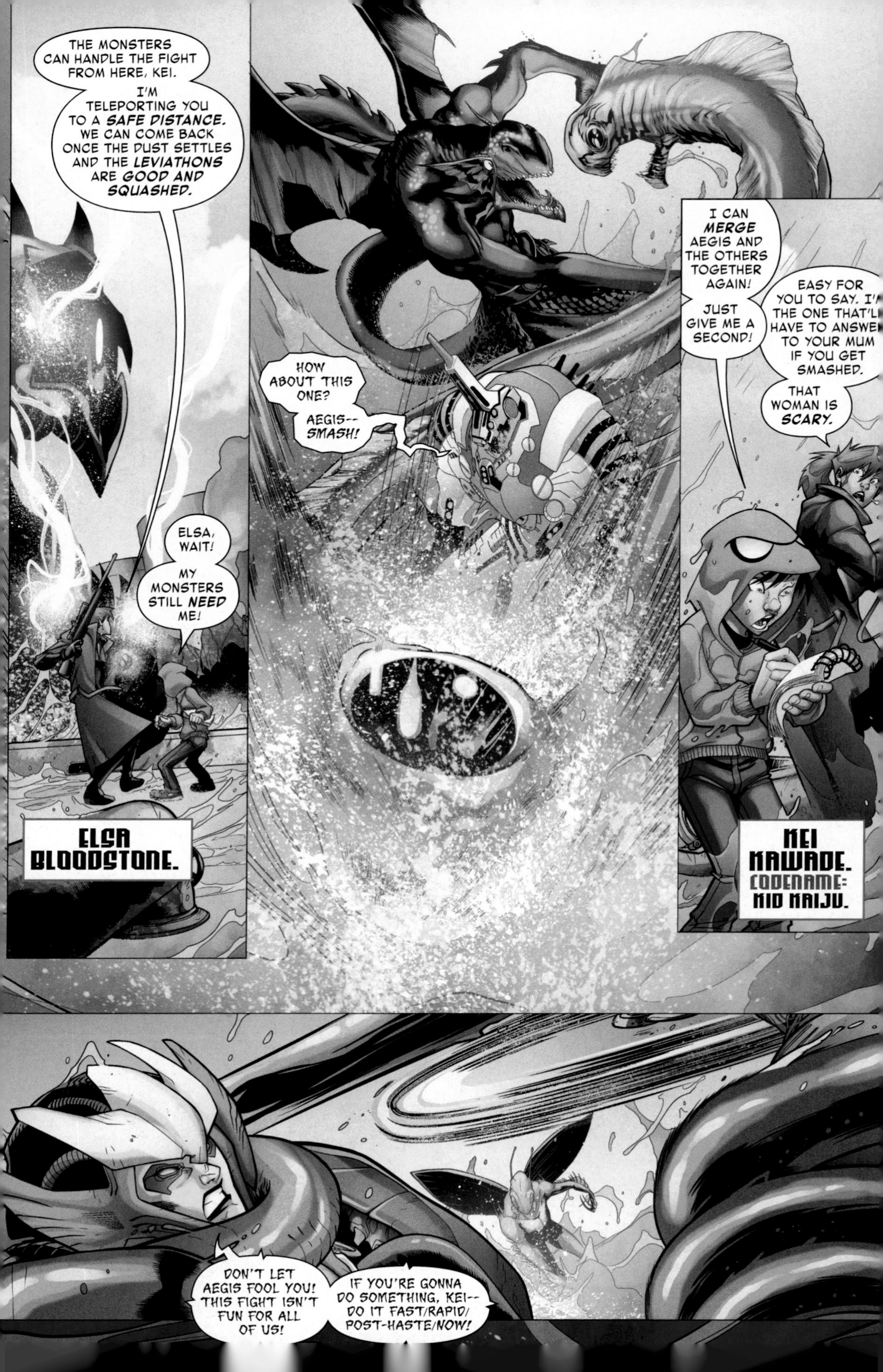
THE MONSTERS CAN HANDLE THE FIGHT FROM HERE, KEI.
I'M TELEPORTING YOU TO A SAFE DISTANCE. WE CAN COME BACK ONCE THE DUST SETTLES AND THE LEVIATHONS ARE GOOD AND SQUASHED.
ELSA, WAIT!
MY MONSTERS STILL NEED ME!
ELSA BLOODSTONE.
HOW ABOUT THIS ONE?
AEGIS-- SMASH!
I CAN MERGE AEGIS AND THE OTHERS TOGETHER AGAIN!
JUST GIVE ME A SECOND!
EASY FOR YOU TO SAY. I'M THE ONE THAT'LL HAVE TO ANSWER TO YOUR MUM IF YOU GET SMASHED.
THAT WOMAN IS SCARY.
KEI KAWADE. CODENAME: KID KAIJU.
DON'T LET AEGIS FOOL YOU! THIS FIGHT ISN'T FUN FOR ALL OF US!
IF YOU'RE GONNA DO SOMETHING, KEI-- DO IT FAST/RAPID/ POST-HASTE/NOW!

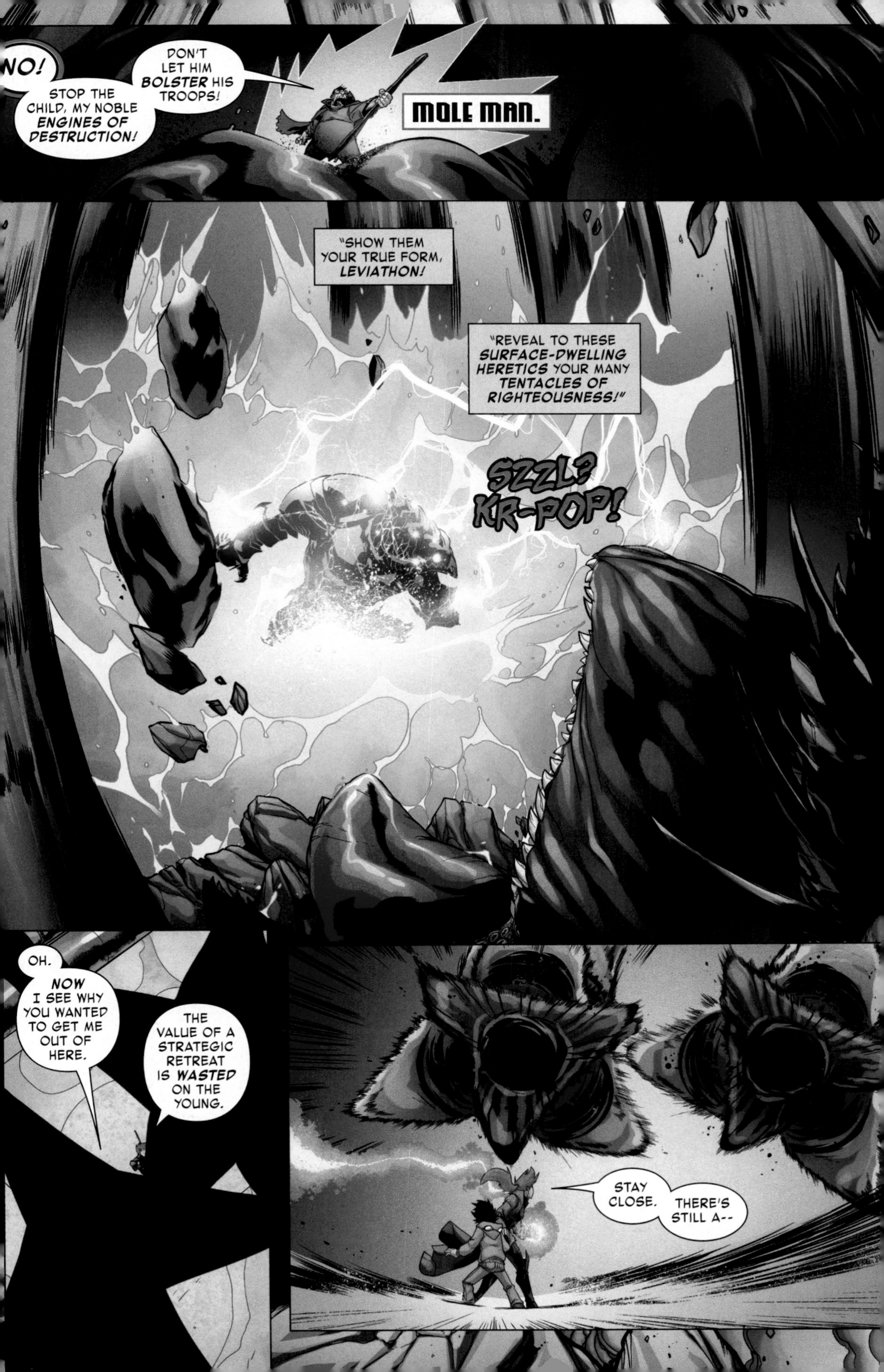
NO!
STOP THE CHILD, MY NOBLE ENGINES OF DESTRUCTION!
DON'T LET HIM BOLSTER HIS TROOPS!
MOLE MAN.
"SHOW THEM YOUR TRUE FORM, LEVIATHON!
"REVEAL TO THESE SURFACE-DWELLING HERETICS YOUR MANY TENTACLES OF RIGHTEOUSNESS!"
SZZL? KR-POP!
OH.
NOW I SEE WHY YOU WANTED TO GET ME OUT OF HERE.
THE VALUE OF A STRATEGIC RETREAT IS WASTED ON THE YOUNG.
STAY CLOSE.
THERE'S STILL A--

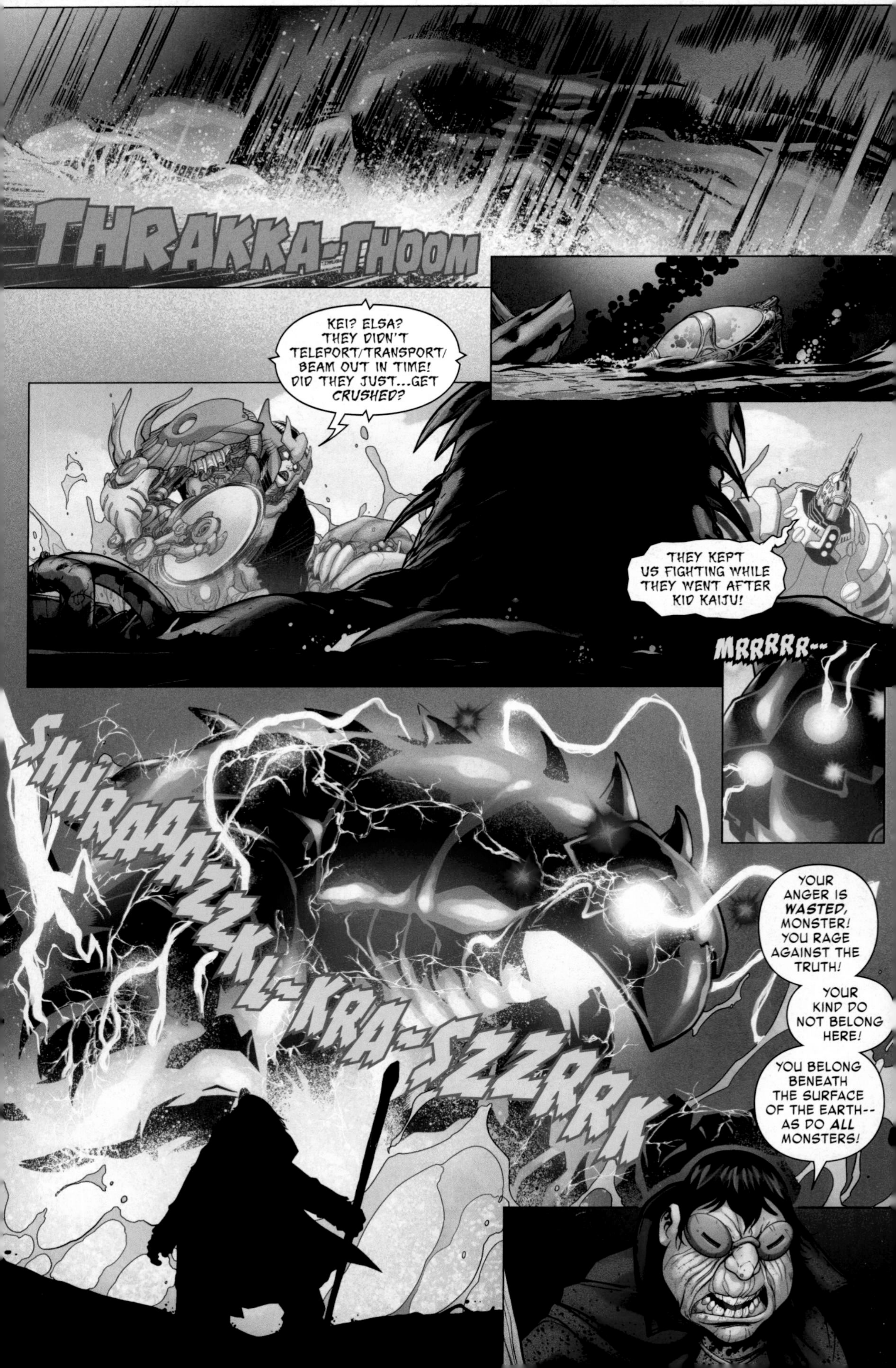
THRAKKA-THOOM
KEI? ELSA? THEY DIDN'T TELEPORT/TRANSPORT/ BEAM OUT IN TIME! DID THEY JUST...GET CRUSHED?
THEY KEPT US FIGHTING WHILE THEY WENT AFTER KID KAIJU!
MRRRRR--
SHHRAAAZZKL-KRA-SZZRRK
YOUR ANGER IS WASTED, MONSTER! YOU RAGE AGAINST THE TRUTH!
YOUR KIND DO NOT BELONG HERE!
YOU BELONG BENEATH THE SURFACE OF THE EARTH-- AS DO ALL MONSTERS!

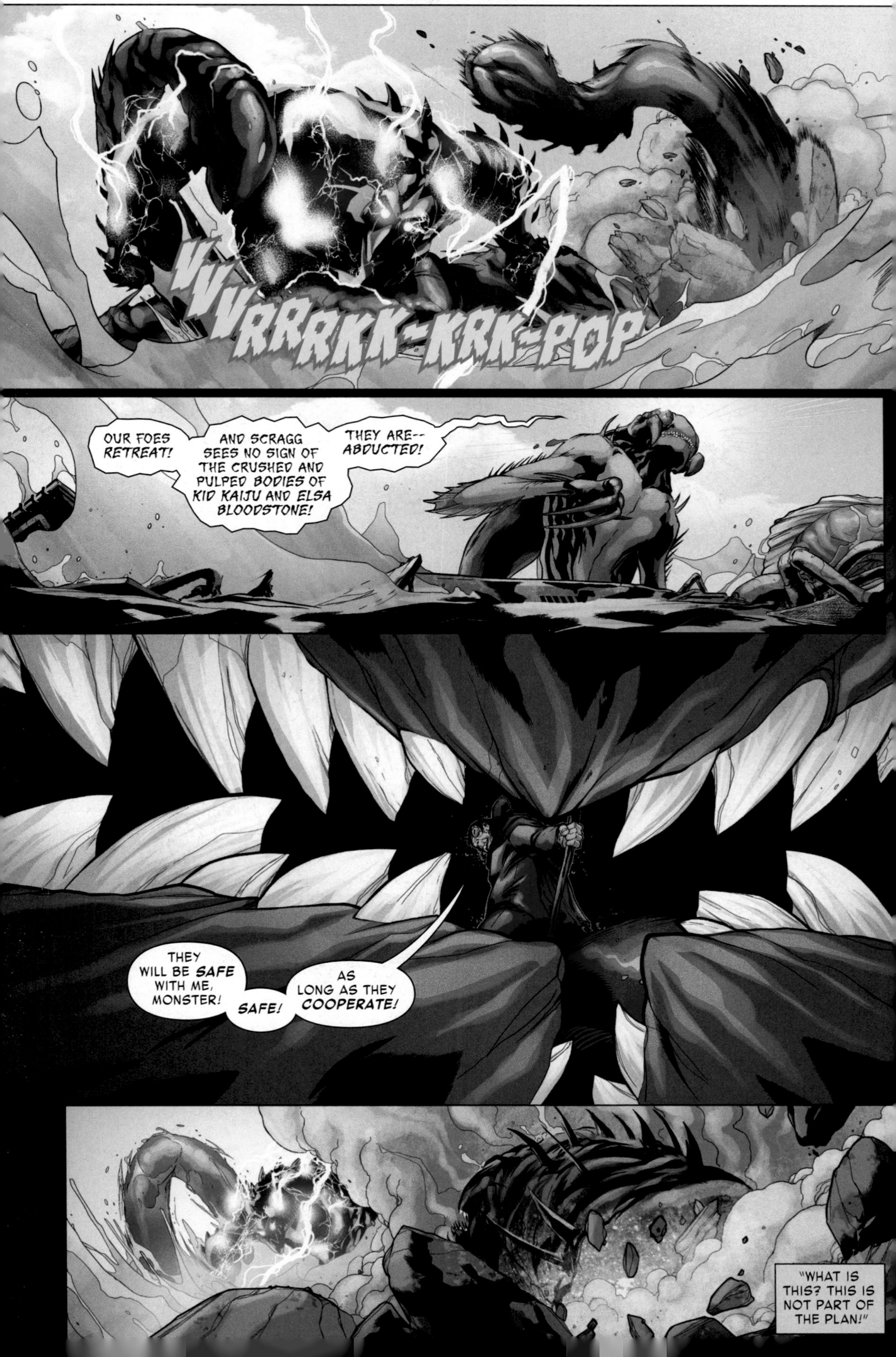
VVVRRRKK-KRK-POP
OUR FOES RETREAT!
AND SCRAGG SEES NO SIGN OF THE CRUSHED AND PULPED BODIES OF KID KAIJU AND ELSA BLOODSTONE!
THEY ARE-- ABDUCTED!
THEY WILL BE SAFE WITH ME, MONSTER!
SAFE!
AS LONG AS THEY COOPERATE!
"WHAT IS THIS? THIS IS NOT PART OF THE PLAN!"

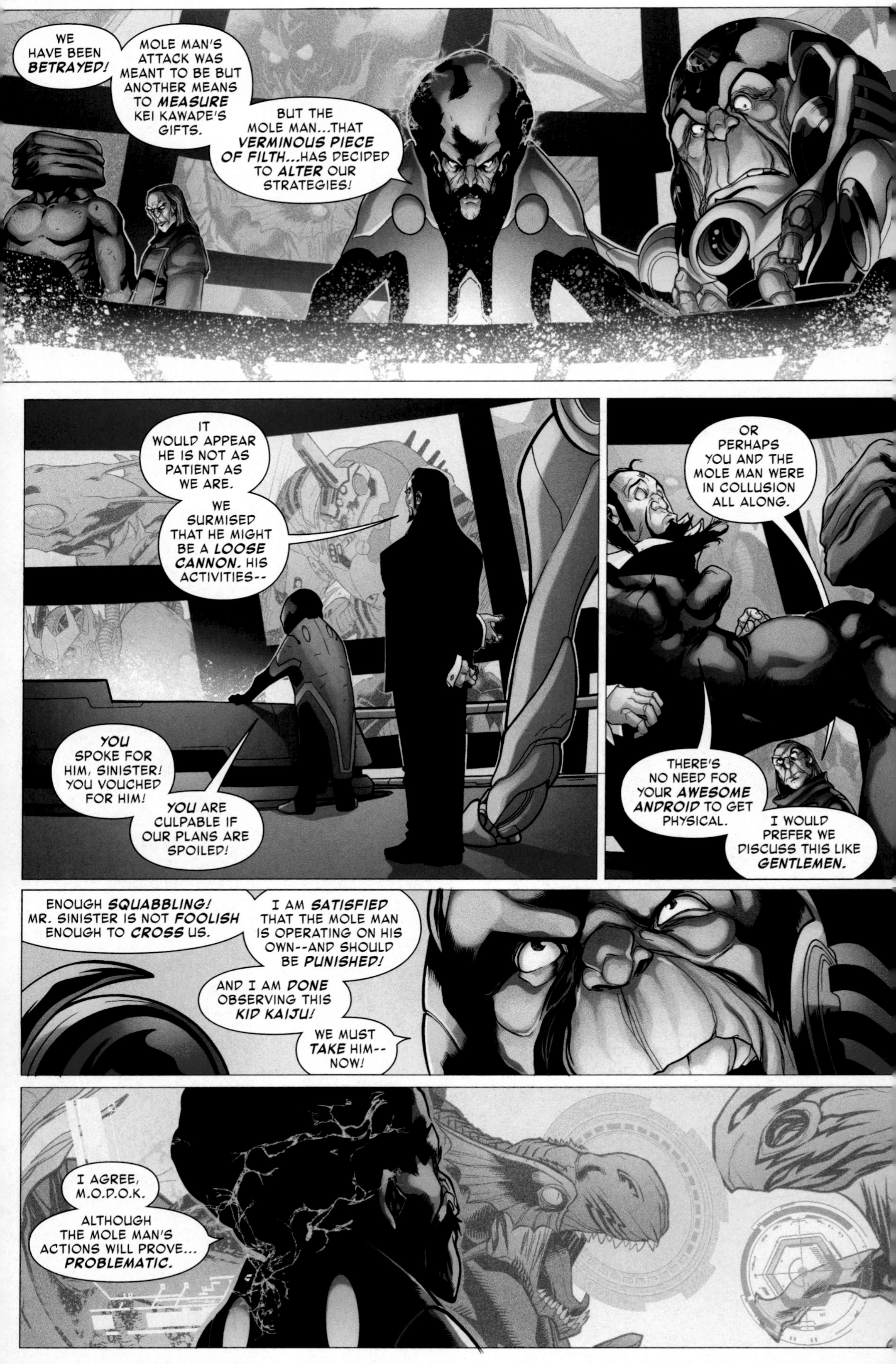
WE HAVE BEEN BETRAYED!
MOLE MAN'S ATTACK WAS MEANT TO BE BUT ANOTHER MEANS TO MEASURE KEI KAWADE'S GIFTS.
BUT THE MOLE MAN...THAT VERMINOUS PIECE OF FILTH...HAS DECIDED TO ALTER OUR STRATEGIES!
IT WOULD APPEAR HE IS NOT AS PATIENT AS WE ARE.
WE SURMISED THAT HE MIGHT BE A LOOSE CANNON. HIS ACTIVITIES--
YOU SPOKE FOR HIM, SINISTER! YOU VOUCHED FOR HIM!
YOU ARE CULPABLE IF OUR PLANS ARE SPOILED!
OR PERHAPS YOU AND THE MOLE MAN WERE IN COLLUSION ALL ALONG.
THERE'S NO NEED FOR YOUR AWESOME ANDROID TO GET PHYSICAL.
I WOULD PREFER WE DISCUSS THIS LIKE GENTLEMEN.
ENOUGH SQUABBLING! MR. SINISTER IS NOT FOOLISH ENOUGH TO CROSS US.
I AM SATISFIED THAT THE MOLE MAN IS OPERATING ON HIS OWN--AND SHOULD BE PUNISHED!
AND I AM DONE OBSERVING THIS KID KAIJU!
WE MUST TAKE HIM--NOW!
I AGREE, M.O.D.O.K.
ALTHOUGH THE MOLE MAN'S ACTIONS WILL PROVE... PROBLEMATIC.

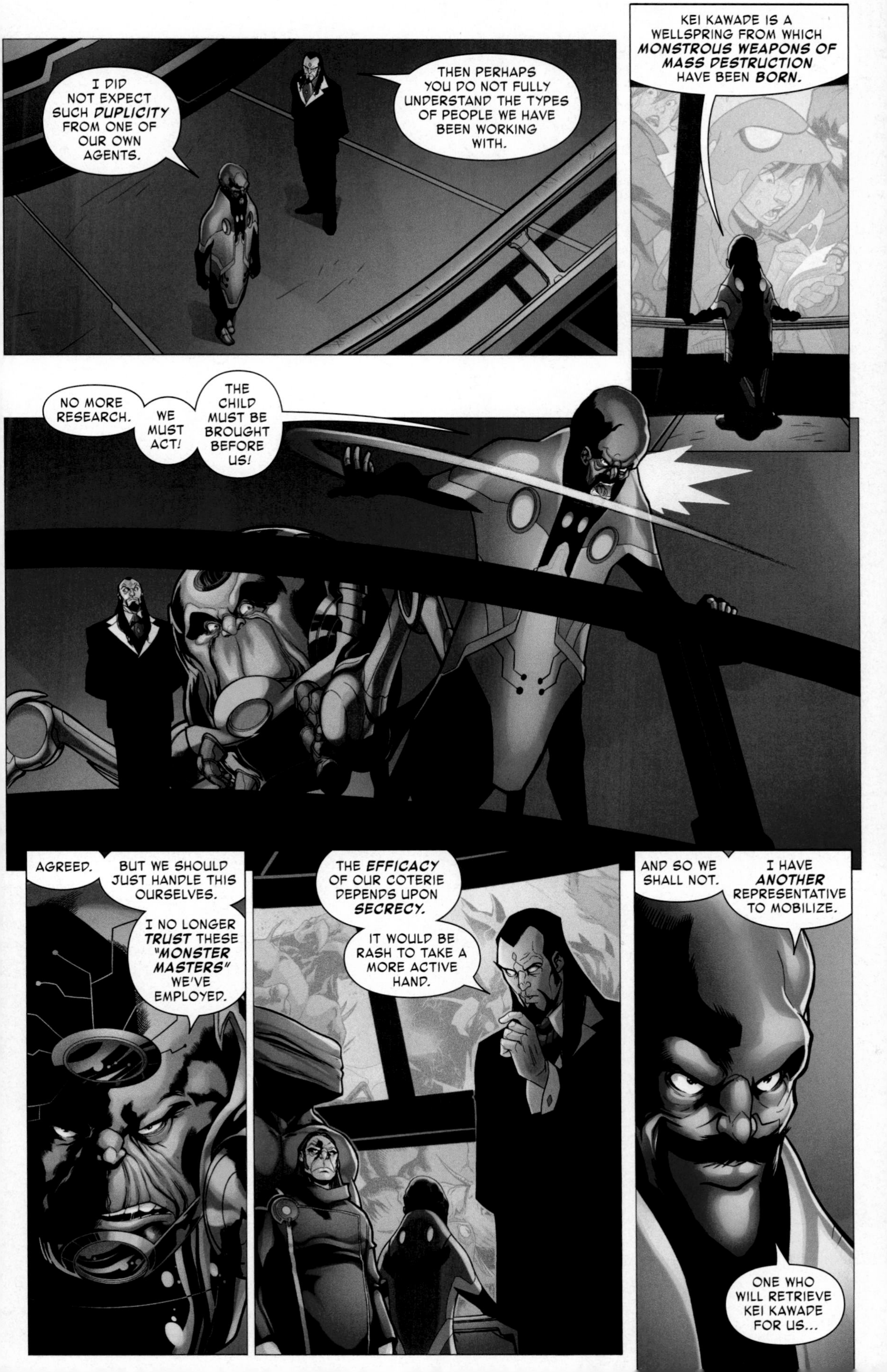
I DID NOT EXPECT SUCH DUPLICITY FROM ONE OF OUR OWN AGENTS.
THEN PERHAPS YOU DO NOT FULLY UNDERSTAND THE TYPES OF PEOPLE WE HAVE BEEN WORKING WITH.
KEI KAWADE IS A WELLSPRING FROM WHICH MONSTROUS WEAPONS OF MASS DESTRUCTION HAVE BEEN BORN.
NO MORE RESEARCH.
WE MUST ACT!
THE CHILD MUST BE BROUGHT BEFORE US!
AGREED.
BUT WE SHOULD JUST HANDLE THIS OURSELVES.
I NO LONGER TRUST THESE "MONSTER MASTERS" WE'VE EMPLOYED.
THE EFFICACY OF OUR COTERIE DEPENDS UPON SECRECY.
IT WOULD BE RASH TO TAKE A MORE ACTIVE HAND.
AND SO WE SHALL NOT.
I HAVE ANOTHER REPRESENTATIVE TO MOBILIZE.
ONE WHO WILL RETRIEVE KEI KAWADE FOR US...

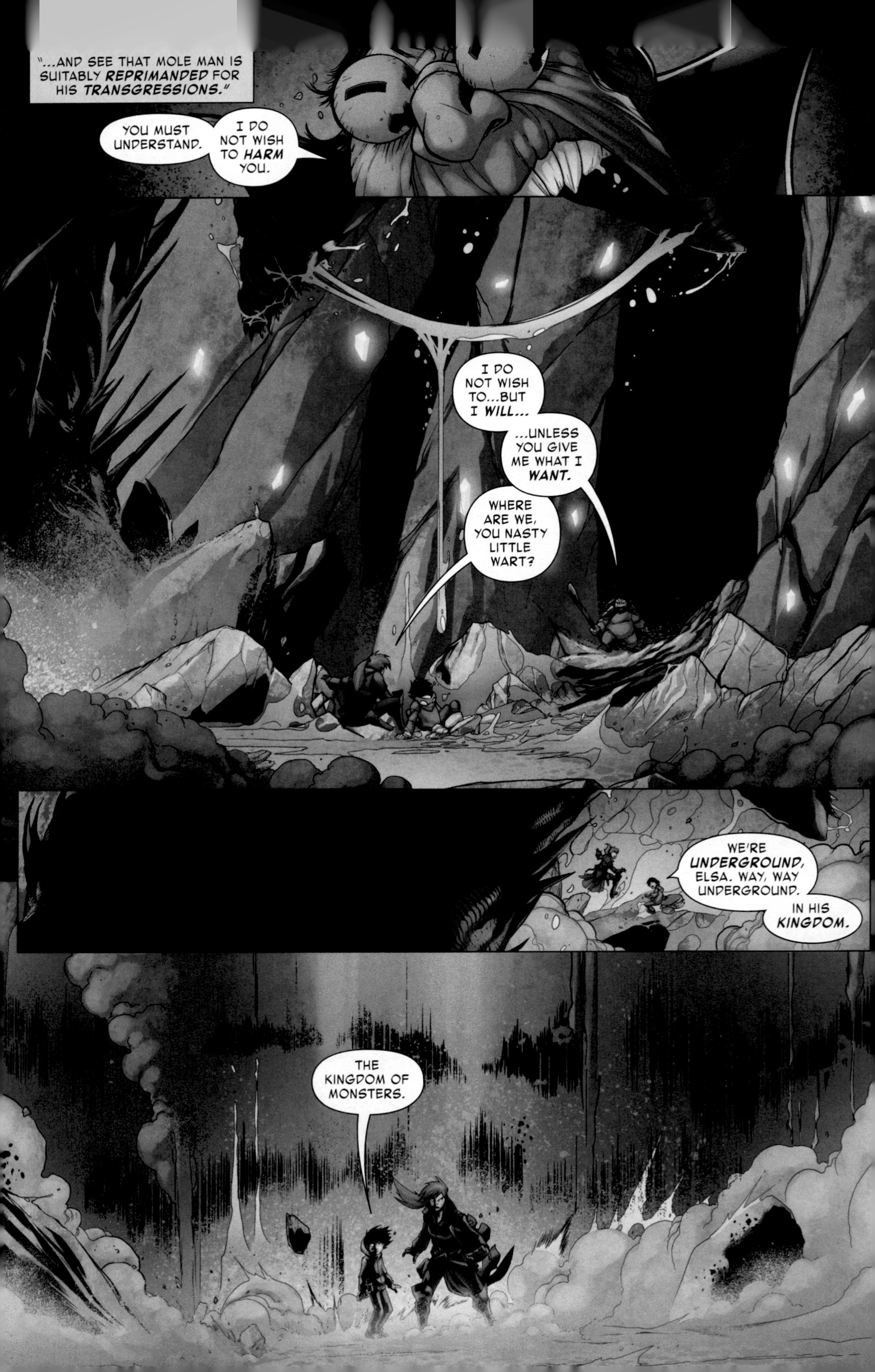
"...AND SEE THAT MOLE MAN IS SUITABLY REPRIMANDED FOR HIS TRANSGRESSIONS."
YOU MUST UNDERSTAND.
I DO NOT WISH TO HARM YOU.
I DO NOT WISH TO...BUT I WILL...
...UNLESS YOU GIVE ME WHAT I WANT.
WHERE ARE WE, YOU NASTY LITTLE WART?
WE'RE UNDERGROUND, ELSA. WAY, WAY UNDERGROUND.
IN HIS KINGDOM.
THE KINGDOM OF MONSTERS.

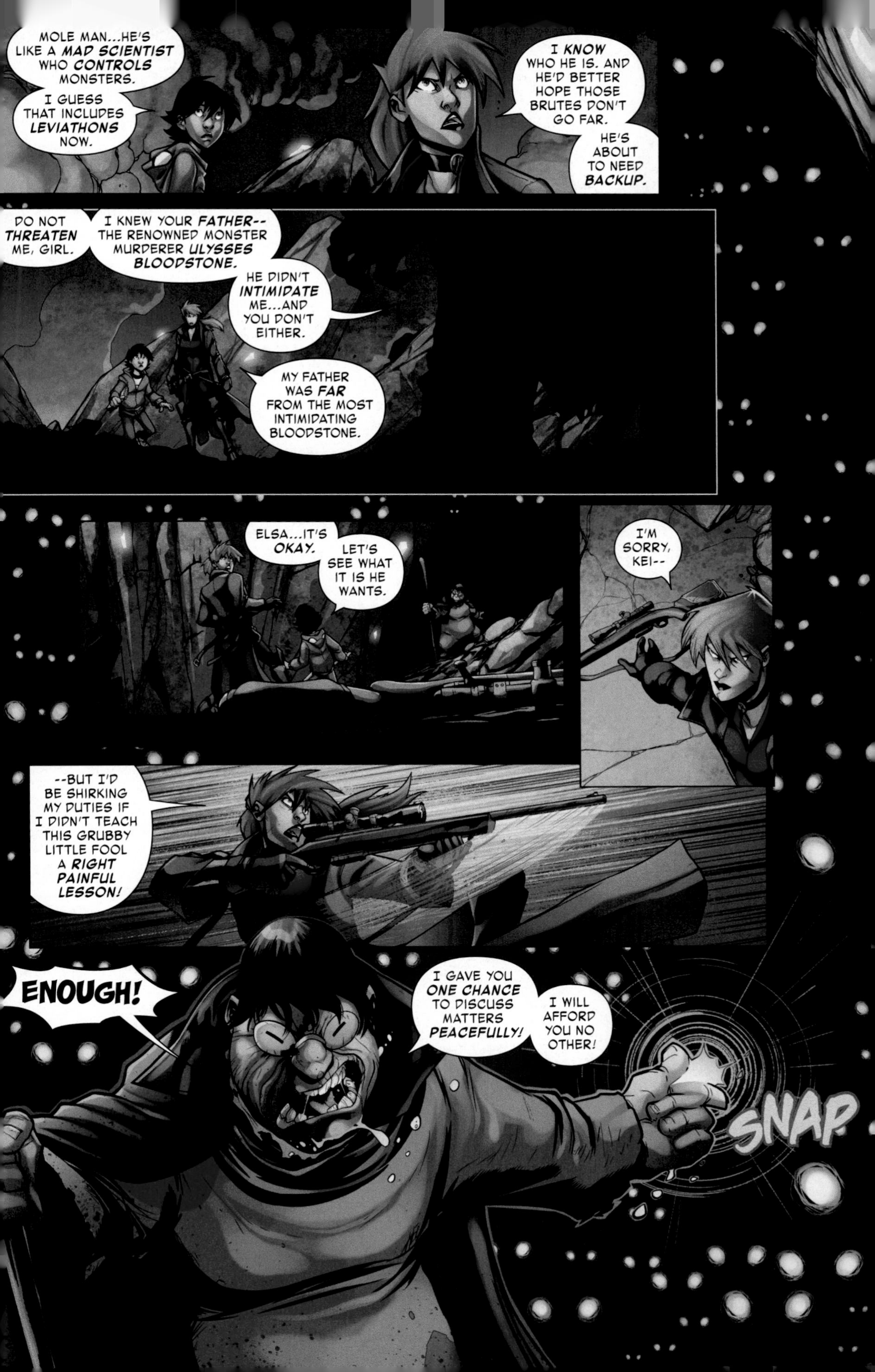
MOLE MAN...HE'S LIKE A MAD SCIENTIST WHO CONTROLS MONSTERS.
I GUESS THAT INCLUDES LEVIATHONS NOW.
I KNOW WHO HE IS. AND HE'D BETTER HOPE THOSE BRUTES DON'T GO FAR.
HE'S ABOUT TO NEED BACKUP.
DO NOT THREATEN ME, GIRL.
I KNEW YOUR FATHER-- THE RENOWNED MONSTER MURDERER ULYSSES BLOODSTONE.
HE DIDN'T INTIMIDATE ME...AND YOU DON'T EITHER.
MY FATHER WAS FAR FROM THE MOST INTIMIDATING BLOODSTONE.
ELSA...IT'S OKAY.
LET'S SEE WHAT IT IS HE WANTS.
I'M SORRY, KEI--
--BUT I'D BE SHIRKING MY DUTIES IF I DIDN'T TEACH THIS GRUBBY LITTLE FOOL A RIGHT PAINFUL LESSON!
ENOUGH!
I GAVE YOU ONE CHANCE TO DISCUSS MATTERS PEACEFULLY!
I WILL AFFORD YOU NO OTHER!
SNAP

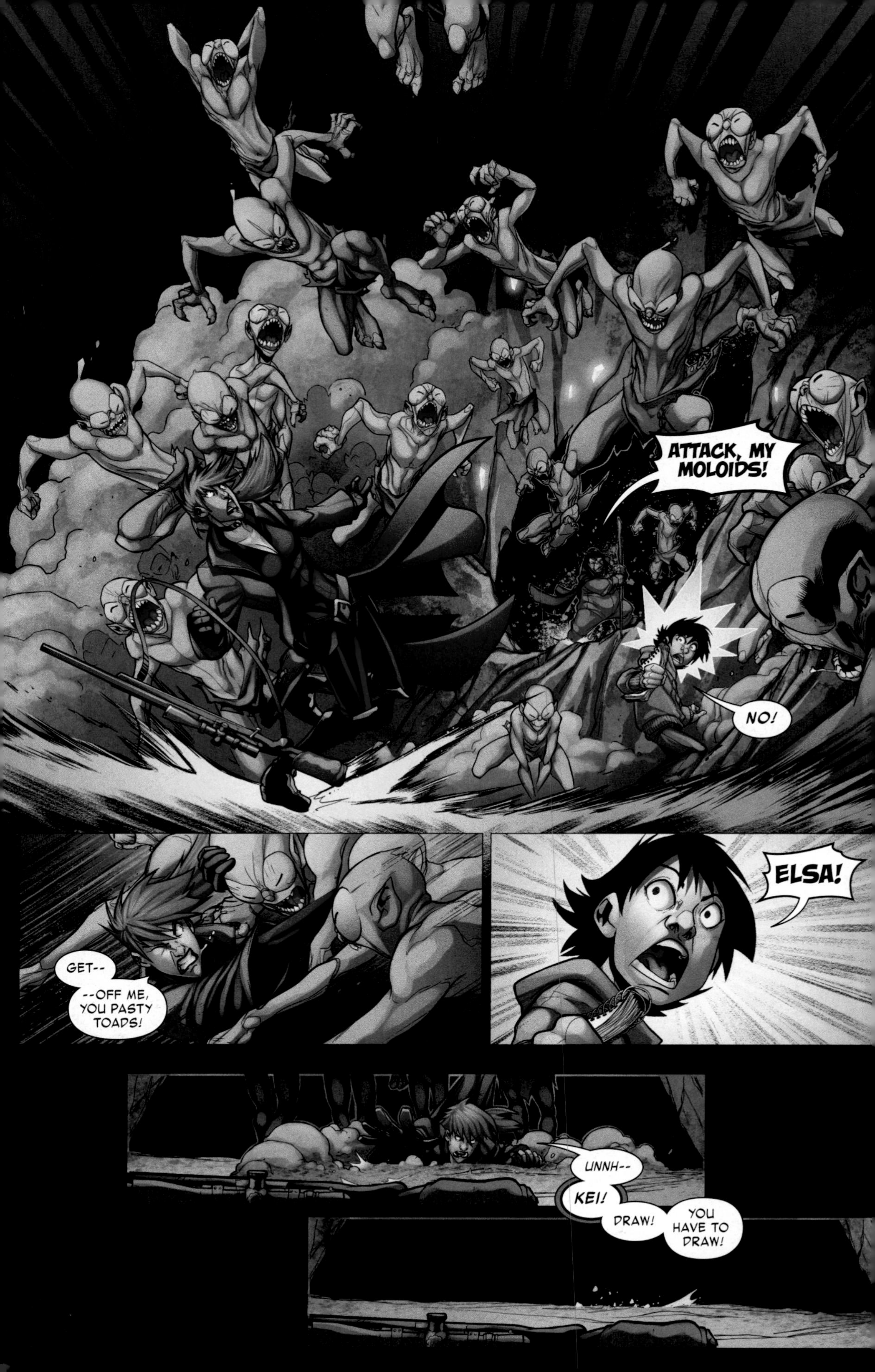
ATTACK, MY MOLOIDS!
NO!
GET--
--OFF ME, YOU PASTY TOADS!
ELSA!
UNNH--
KEI!
DRAW!
YOU HAVE TO DRAW!

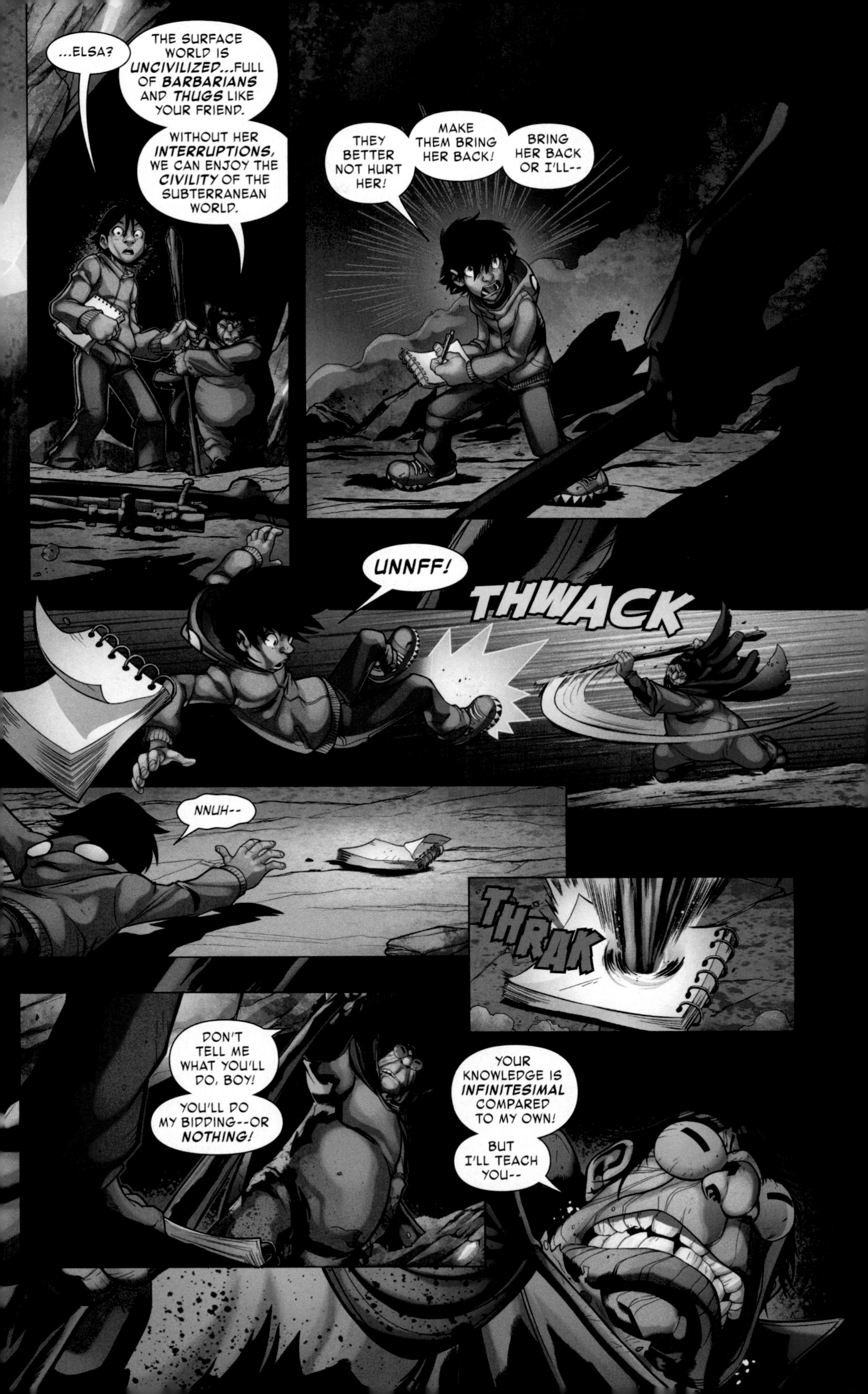
...ELSA?
THE SURFACE WORLD IS UNCIVILIZED...FULL OF BARBARIANS AND THUGS LIKE YOUR FRIEND.
WITHOUT HER INTERRUPTIONS, WE CAN ENJOY THE CIVILITY OF THE SUBTERRANEAN WORLD.
THEY BETTER NOT HURT HER!
MAKE THEM BRING HER BACK!
BRING HER BACK OR I'LL--
UNNFF!
THWACK
NNUH--
THRAK
DON'T TELL ME WHAT YOU'LL DO, BOY!
YOU'LL DO MY BIDDING--OR NOTHING!
YOUR KNOWLEDGE IS INFINITESIMAL COMPARED TO MY OWN!
BUT I'LL TEACH YOU--

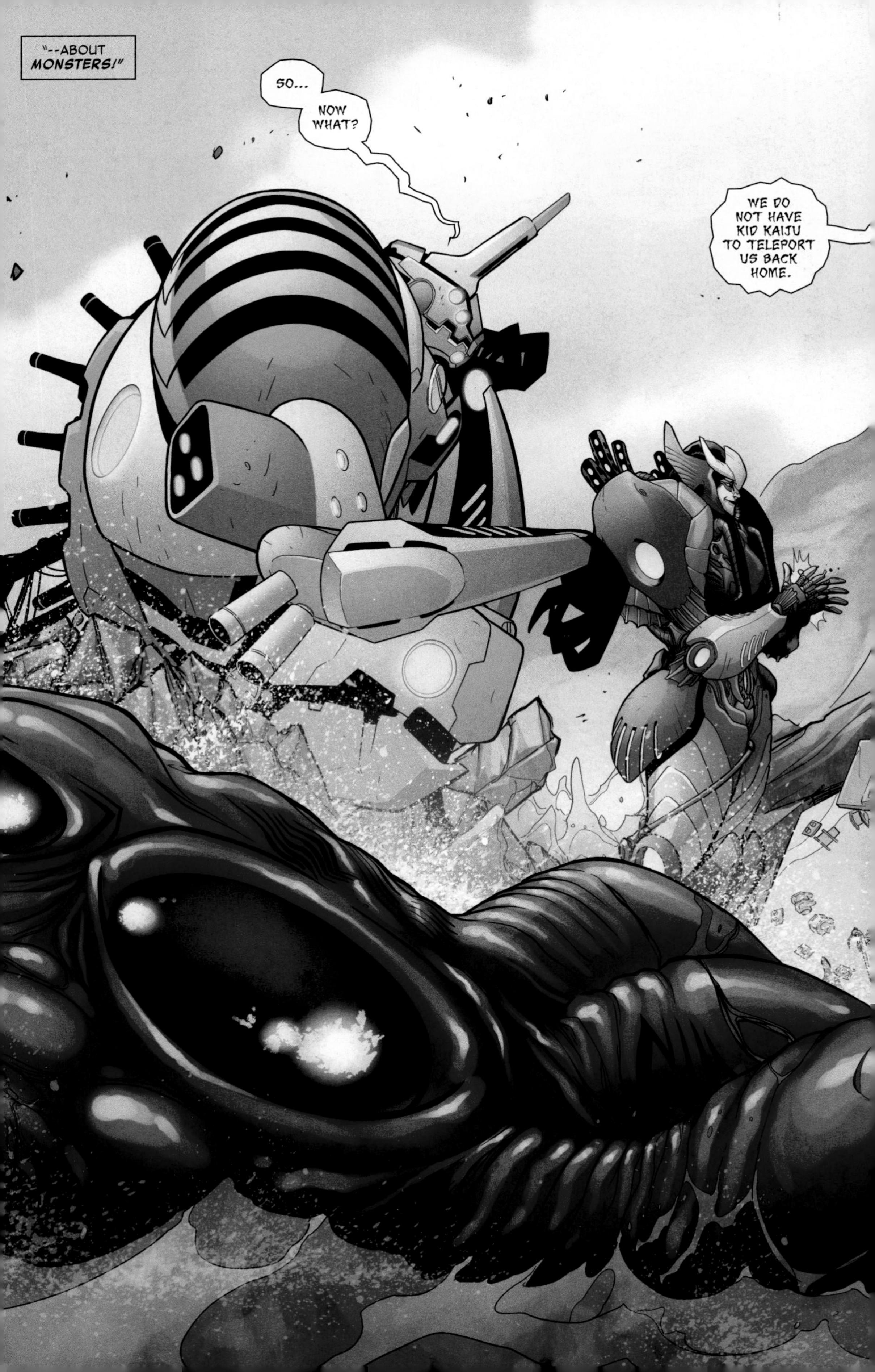
"--ABOUT MONSTERS!"
SO...
NOW WHAT?
WE DO NOT HAVE KID KAIJU TO TELEPORT US BACK HOME.

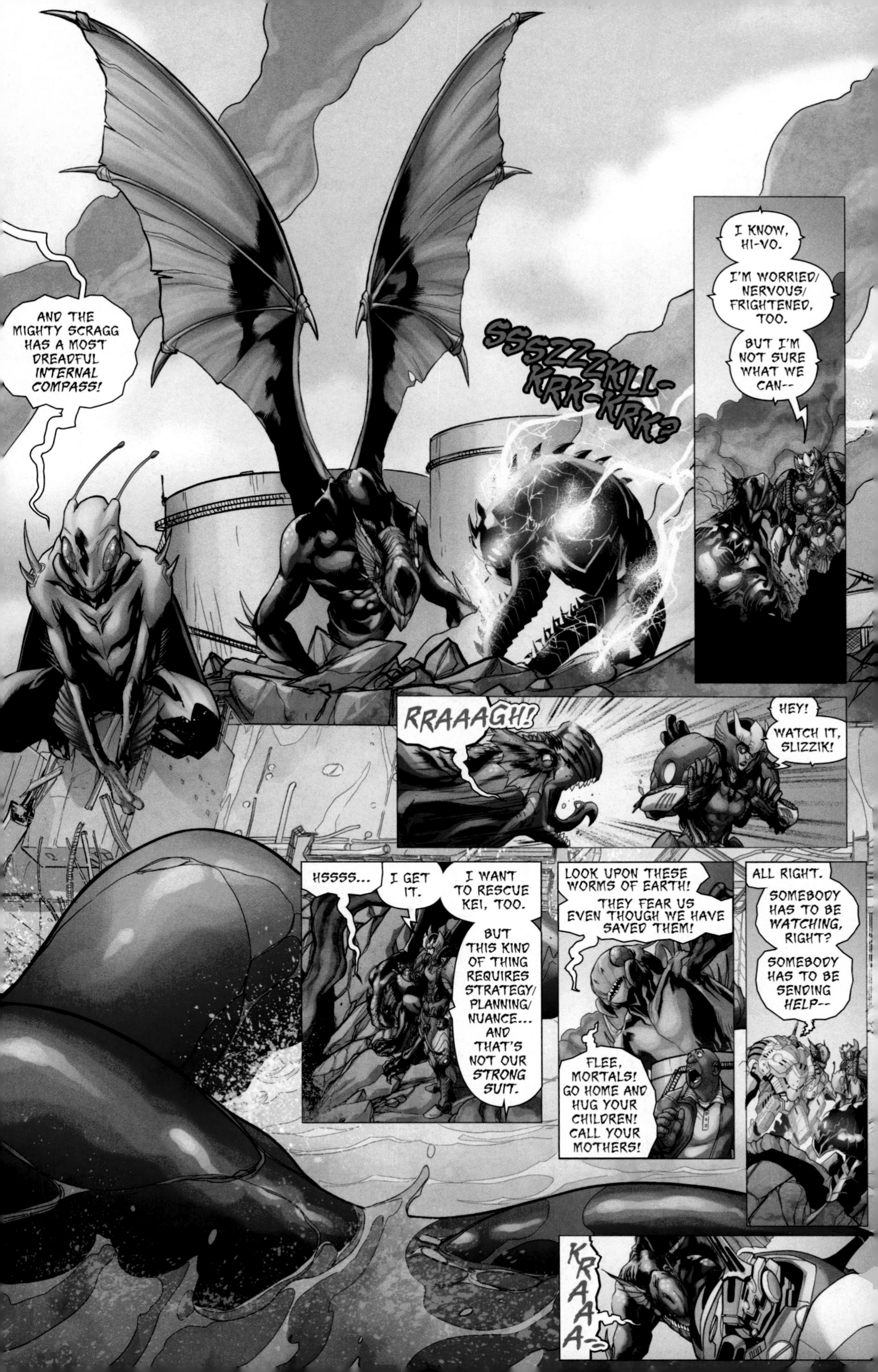
AND THE MIGHTY SCRAGG HAS A MOST DREADFUL INTERNAL COMPASS!
SSSZZZZKLL-KRK-KRK?
I KNOW, HI-VO.
I'M WORRIED/ NERVOUS/ FRIGHTENED, TOO.
BUT I'M NOT SURE WHAT WE CAN--
RRAAAGH!
HEY!
WATCH IT, SLIZZIK!
HSSSS...
I GET IT.
I WANT TO RESCUE KEI, TOO.
BUT THIS KIND OF THING REQUIRES STRATEGY/ PLANNING/ NUANCE... AND THAT'S NOT OUR STRONG SUIT.
LOOK UPON THESE WORMS OF EARTH!
THEY FEAR US EVEN THOUGH WE HAVE SAVED THEM!
FLEE, MORTALS! GO HOME AND HUG YOUR CHILDREN! CALL YOUR MOTHERS!
ALL RIGHT.
SOMEBODY HAS TO BE WATCHING, RIGHT?
SOMEBODY HAS TO BE SENDING HELP--
KRAAAA--

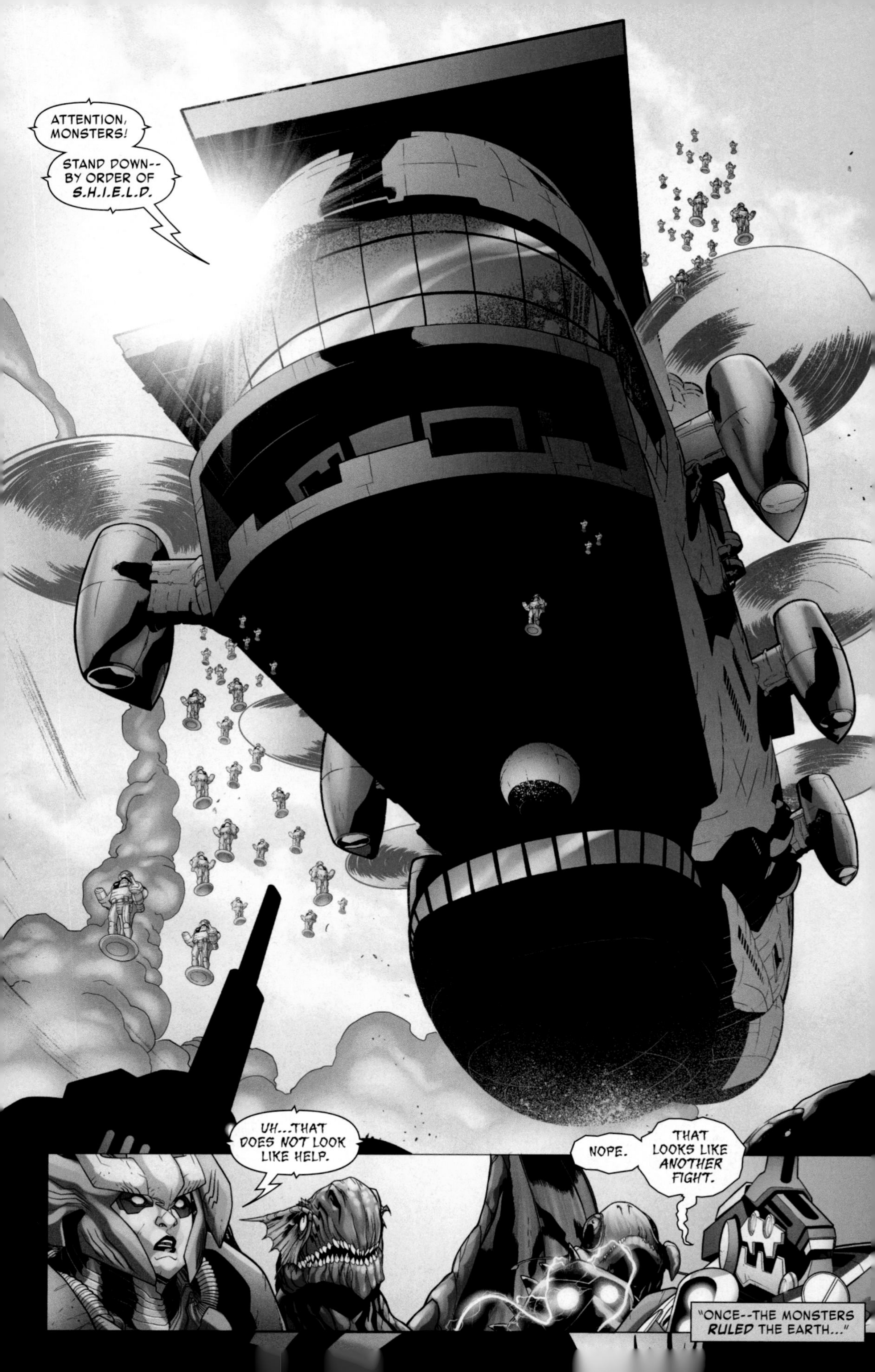
ATTENTION, MONSTERS!
STAND DOWN-- BY ORDER OF S.H.I.E.L.D.
UH...THAT DOES NOT LOOK LIKE HELP.
NOPE.
THAT LOOKS LIKE ANOTHER FIGHT.
"ONCE--THE MONSTERS RULED THE EARTH..."

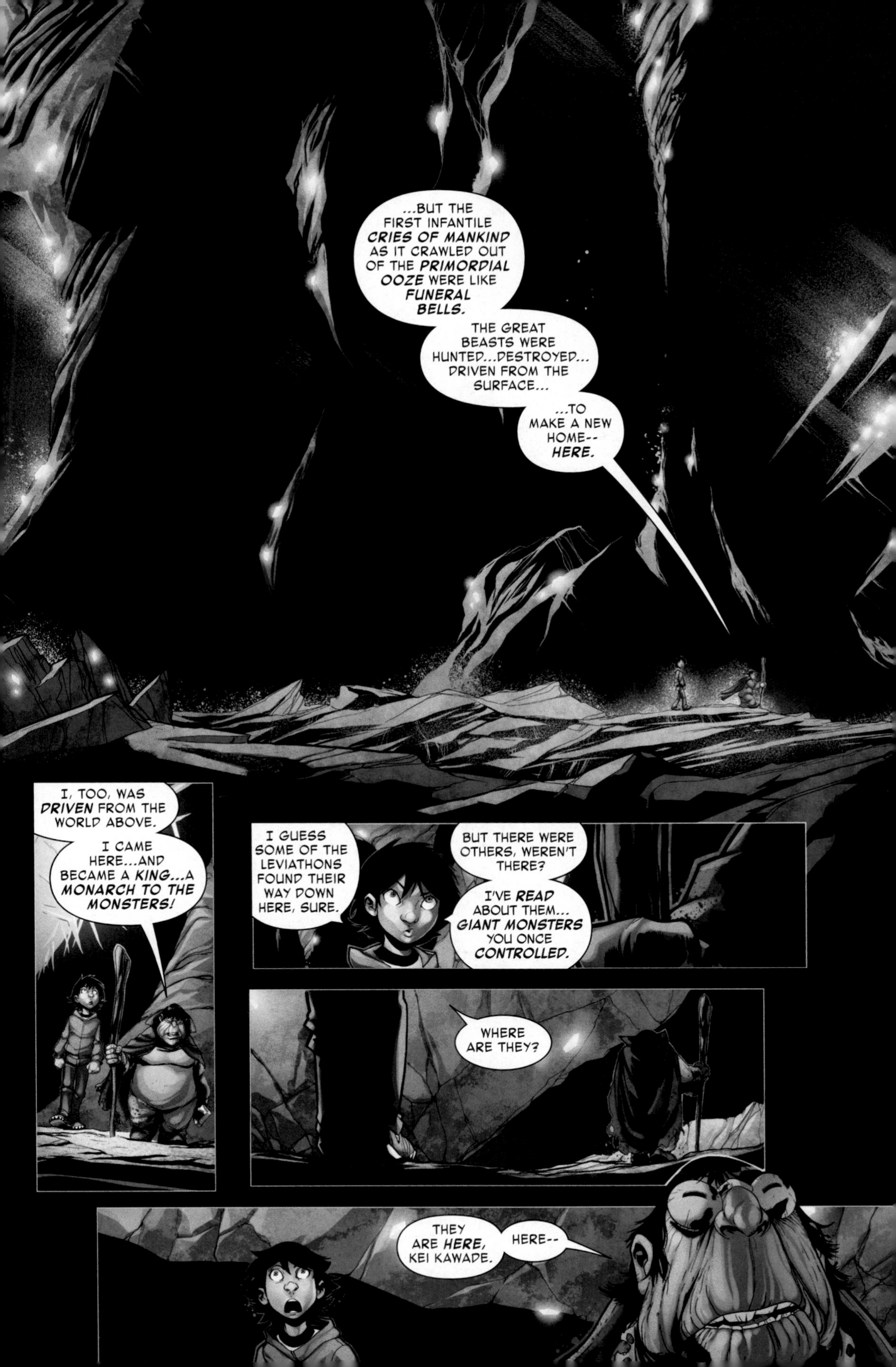
...BUT THE FIRST INFANTILE CRIES OF MANKIND AS IT CRAWLED OUT OF THE PRIMORDIAL OOZE WERE LIKE FUNERAL BELLS.
THE GREAT BEASTS WERE HUNTED...DESTROYED... DRIVEN FROM THE SURFACE...
...TO MAKE A NEW HOME-- HERE.
I, TOO, WAS DRIVEN FROM THE WORLD ABOVE.
I CAME HERE...AND BECAME A KING...A MONARCH TO THE MONSTERS!
I GUESS SOME OF THE LEVIATHONS FOUND THEIR WAY DOWN HERE, SURE.
BUT THERE WERE OTHERS, WEREN'T THERE?
I'VE READ ABOUT THEM... GIANT MONSTERS YOU ONCE CONTROLLED.
WHERE ARE THEY?
THEY ARE HERE, KEI KAWADE.
HERE--

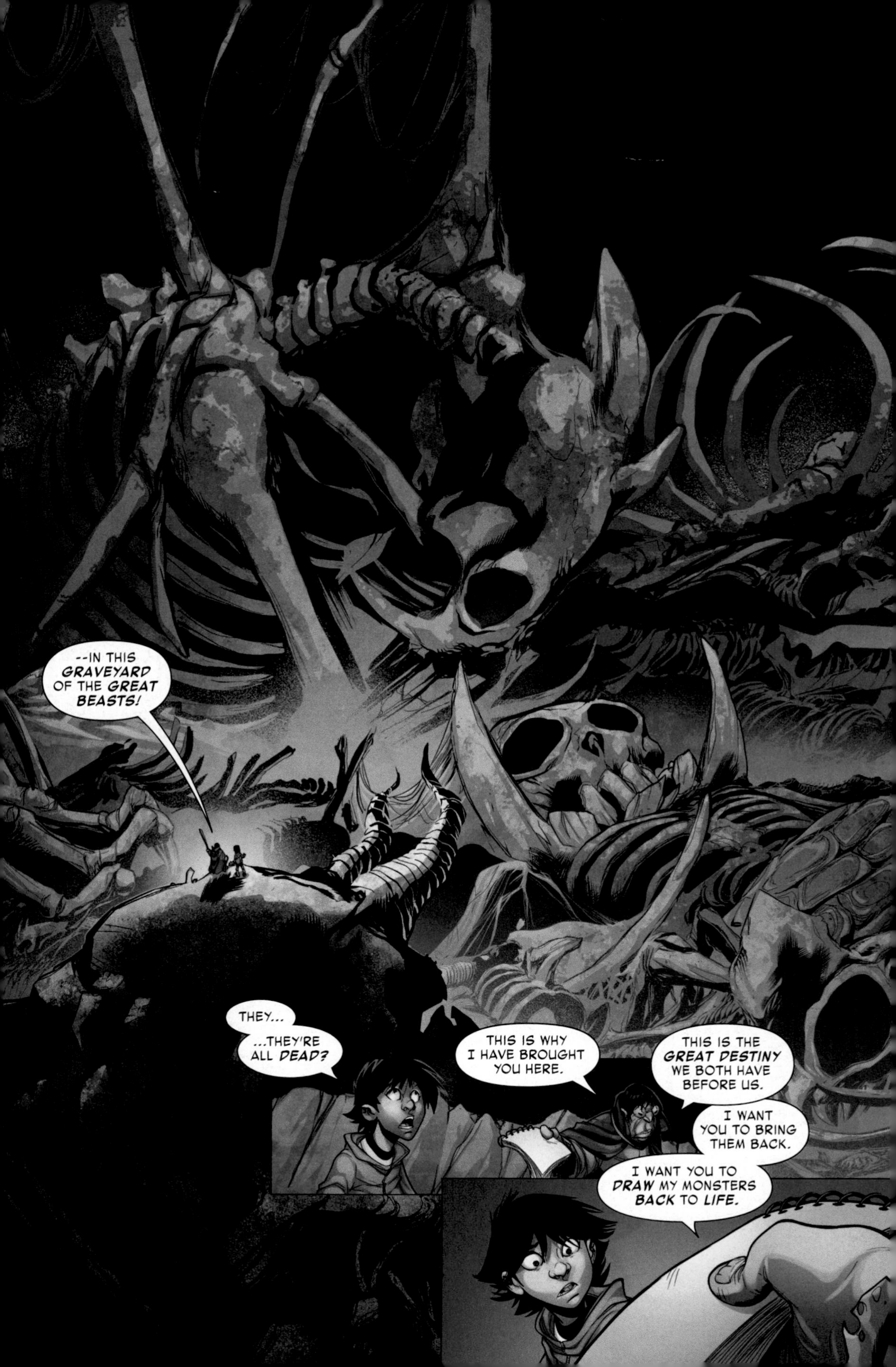
--IN THIS GRAVEYARD OF THE GREAT BEASTS!
THEY...
...THEY'RE ALL DEAD?
THIS IS WHY I HAVE BROUGHT YOU HERE.
THIS IS THE GREAT DESTINY WE BOTH HAVE BEFORE US.
I WANT YOU TO BRING THEM BACK.
I WANT YOU TO DRAW MY MONSTERS BACK TO LIFE.

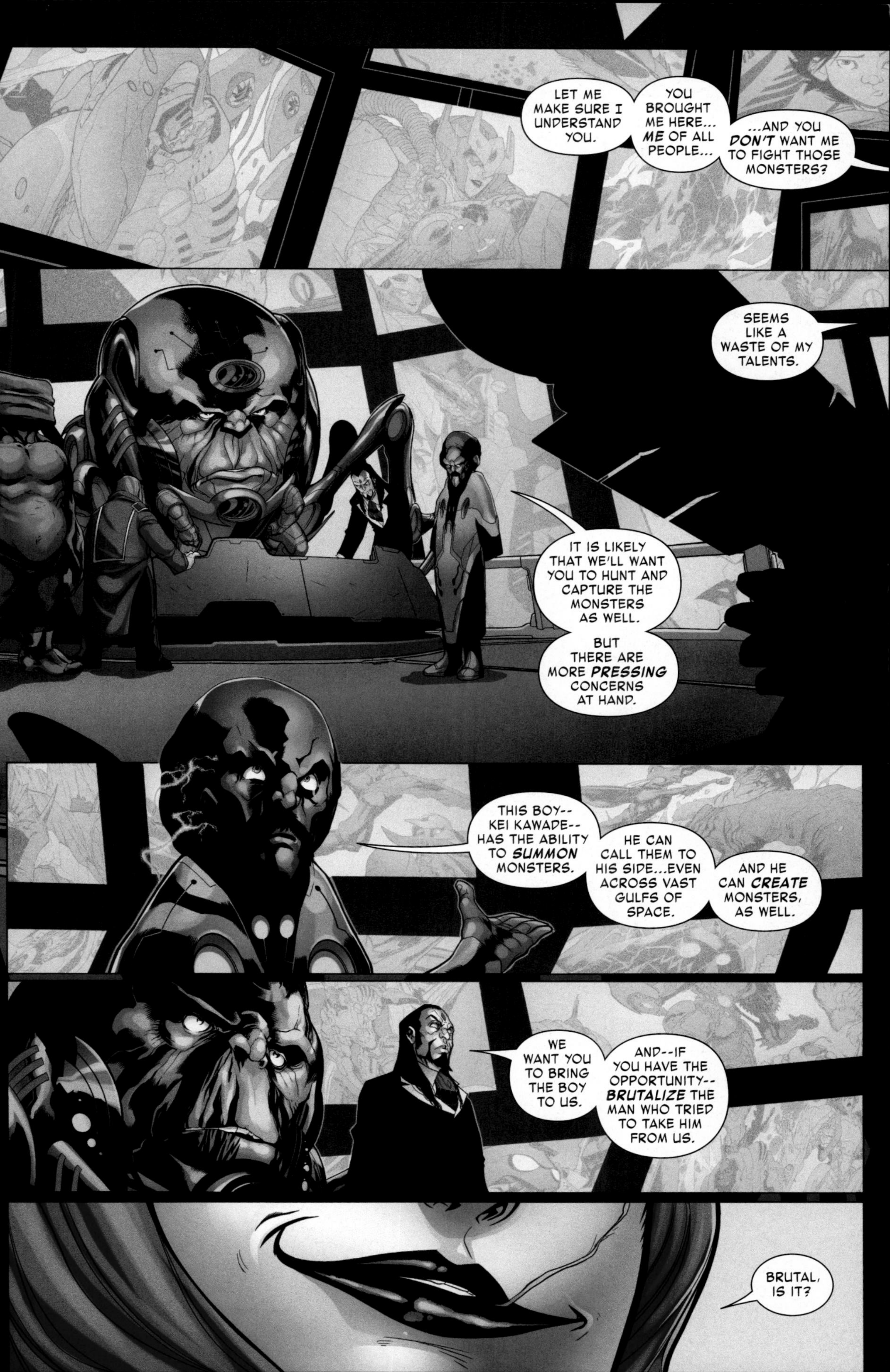
LET ME MAKE SURE I UNDERSTAND YOU.
YOU BROUGHT ME HERE... *ME* OF ALL PEOPLE...
...AND YOU *DON'T* WANT ME TO FIGHT THOSE MONSTERS?
SEEMS LIKE A WASTE OF MY TALENTS.
IT IS LIKELY THAT WE'LL WANT YOU TO HUNT AND CAPTURE THE MONSTERS AS WELL.
BUT THERE ARE MORE *PRESSING* CONCERNS AT HAND.
THIS BOY--KEI KAWADE--HAS THE ABILITY TO *SUMMON* MONSTERS.
HE CAN CALL THEM TO HIS SIDE...EVEN ACROSS VAST GULFS OF SPACE.
AND HE CAN *CREATE* MONSTERS, AS WELL.
WE WANT YOU TO BRING THE BOY TO US.
AND--IF YOU HAVE THE OPPORTUNITY--*BRUTALIZE* THE MAN WHO TRIED TO TAKE HIM FROM US.
BRUTAL, IS IT?

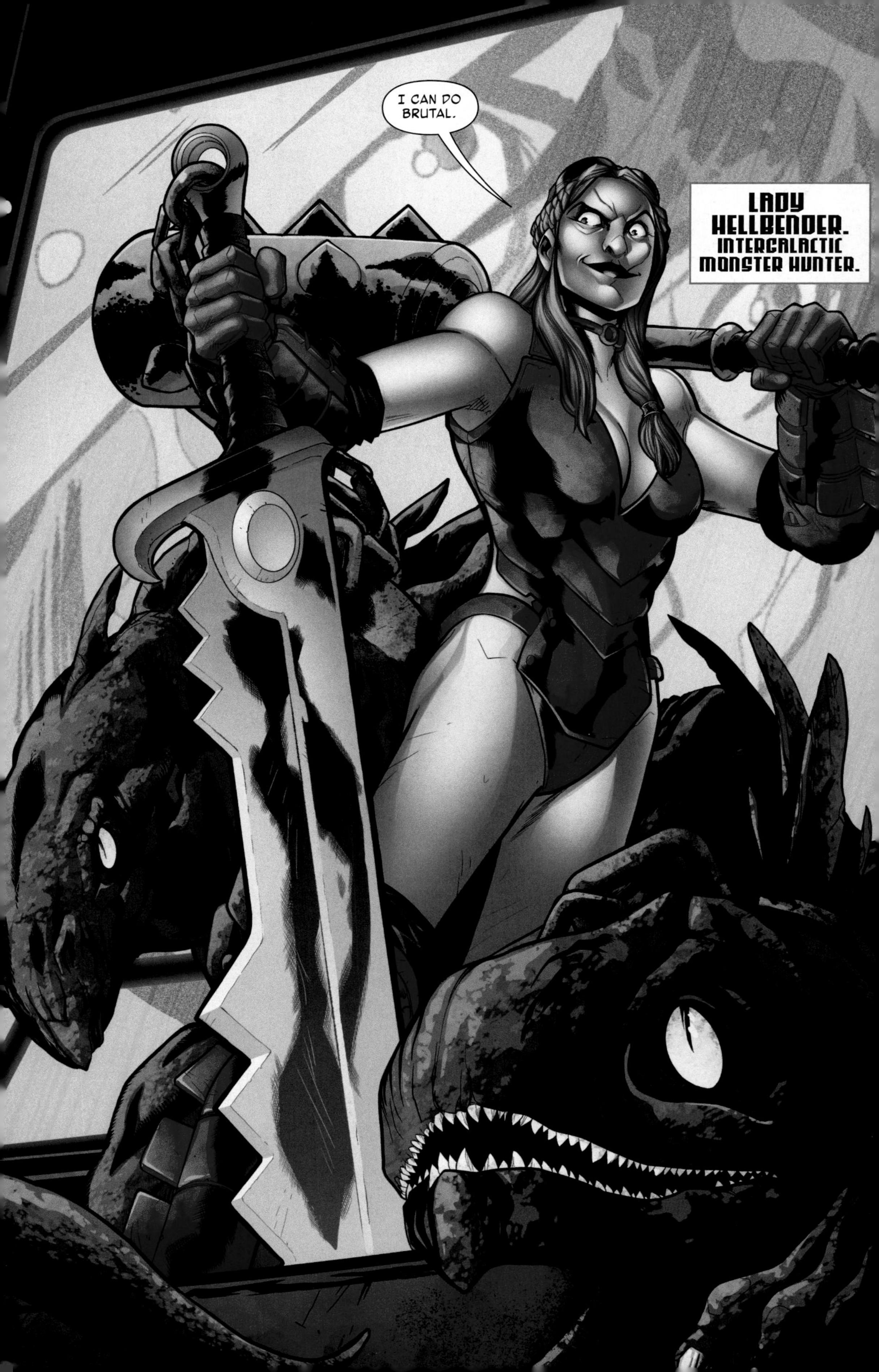
I CAN DO BRUTAL.
LADY HELLBENDER.
INTERGALACTIC MONSTER HUNTER.

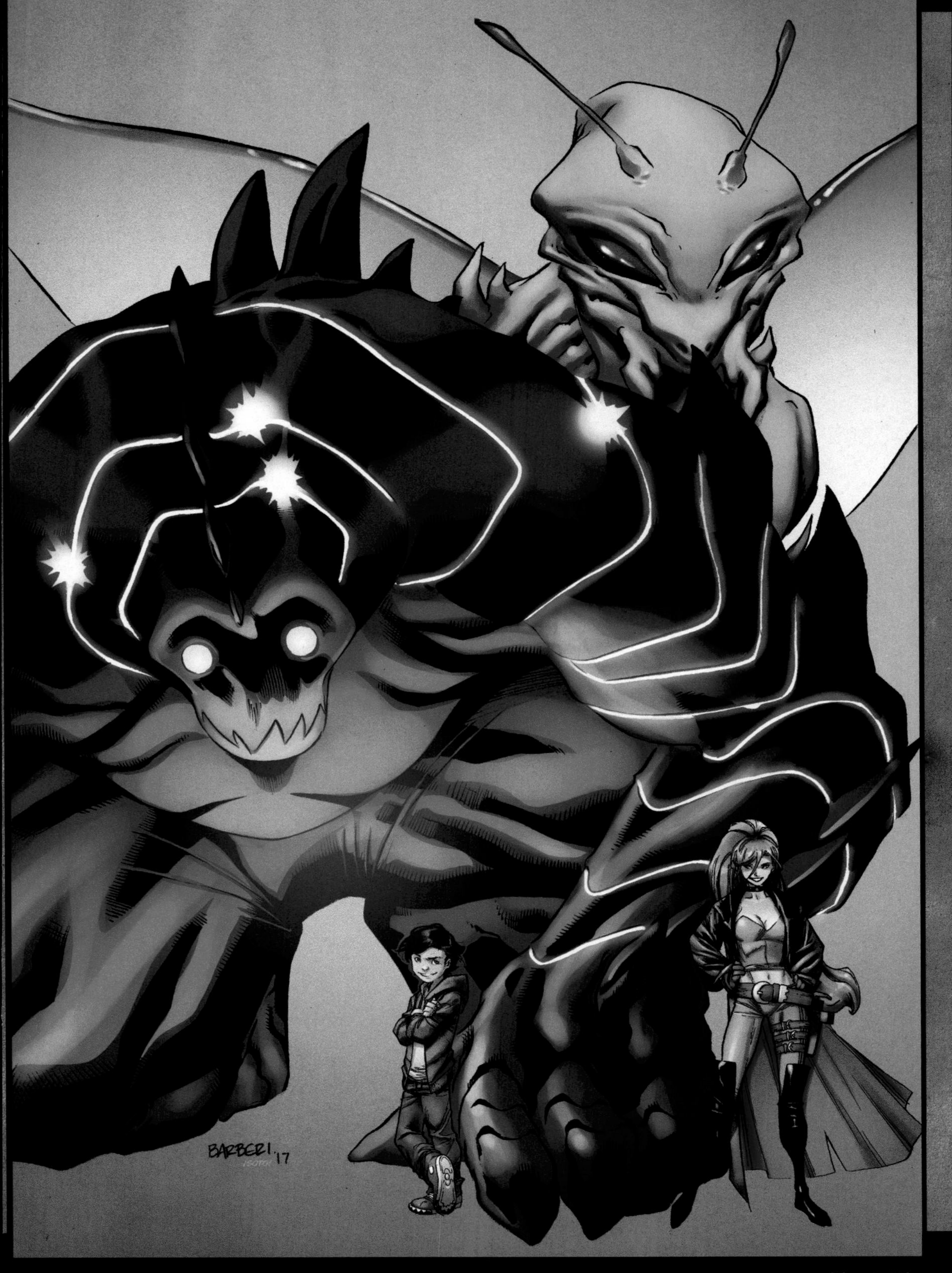
BARBERI '17

#1 VARIANT BY
CARLO BARBERI & CHRIS SOTOMAYOR

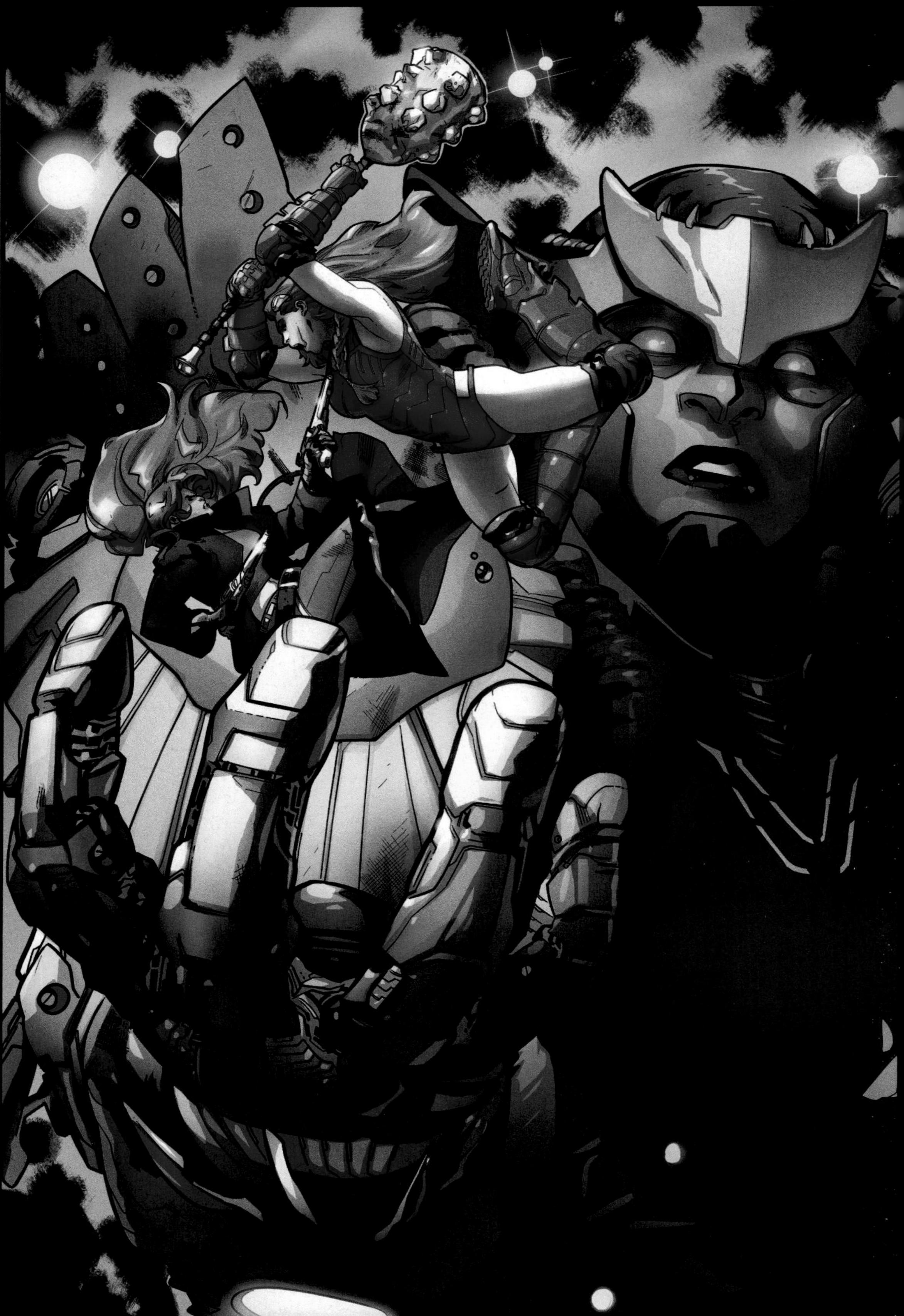

#3

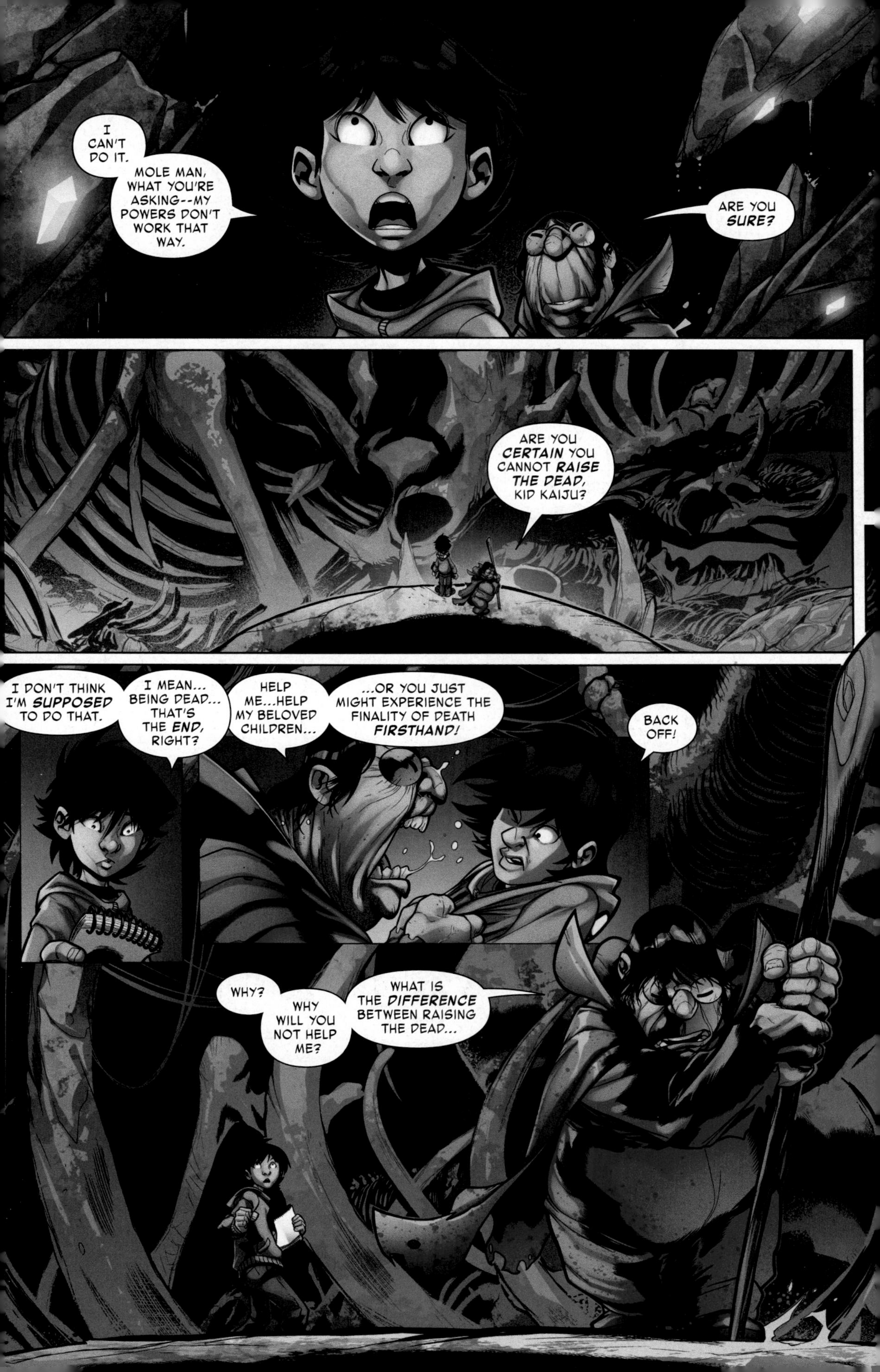
I CAN'T DO IT.
MOLE MAN, WHAT YOU'RE ASKING--MY POWERS DON'T WORK THAT WAY.
ARE YOU SURE?
ARE YOU CERTAIN YOU CANNOT RAISE THE DEAD, KID KAIJU?
I DON'T THINK I'M SUPPOSED TO DO THAT.
I MEAN... BEING DEAD... THAT'S THE END, RIGHT?
HELP ME...HELP MY BELOVED CHILDREN...
...OR YOU JUST MIGHT EXPERIENCE THE FINALITY OF DEATH FIRSTHAND!
BACK OFF!
WHY?
WHY WILL YOU NOT HELP ME?
WHAT IS THE DIFFERENCE BETWEEN RAISING THE DEAD...

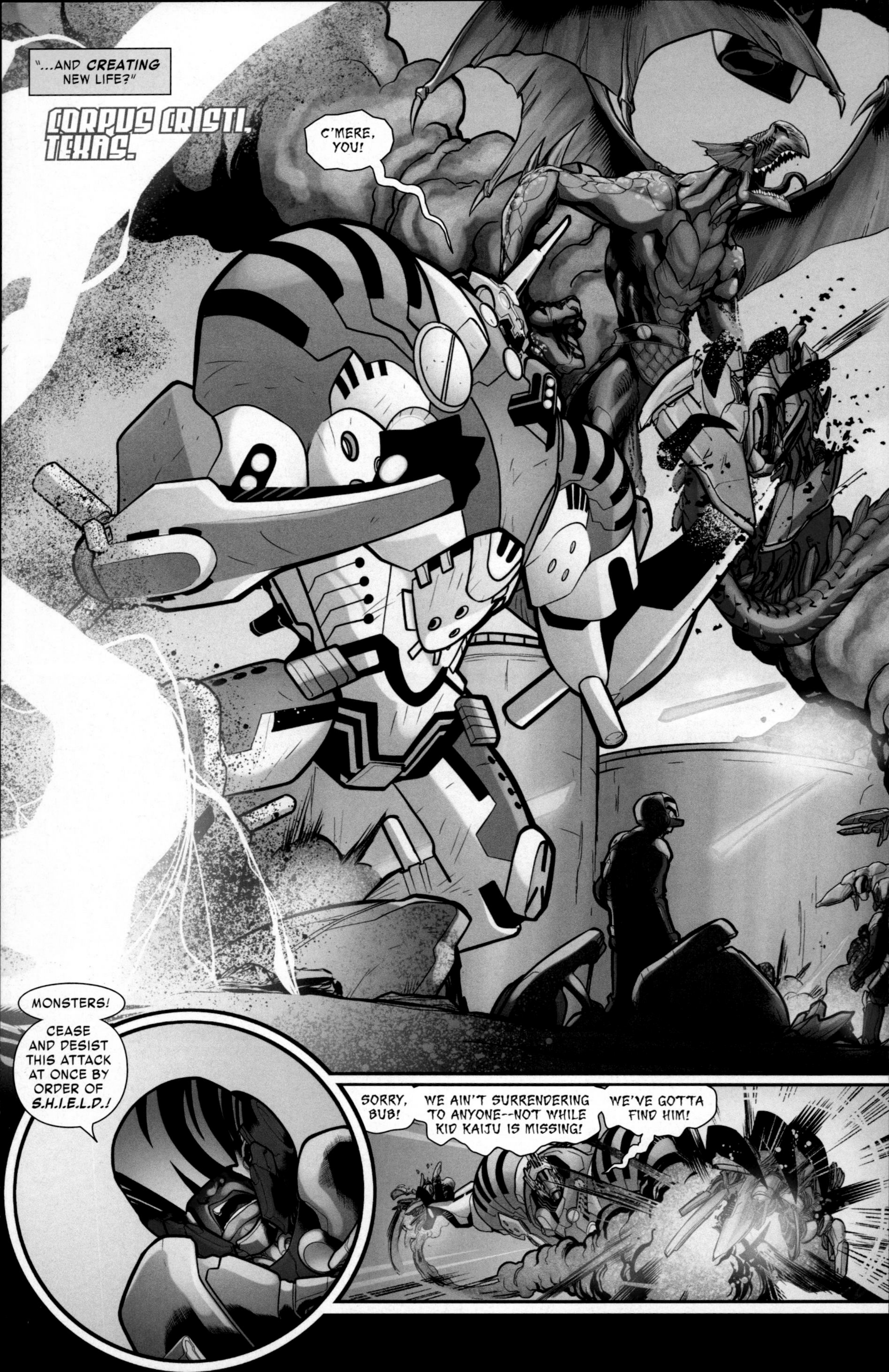
"...AND CREATING NEW LIFE?"
CORPUS CRISTI, TEXAS.
C'MERE, YOU!
MONSTERS!
CEASE AND DESIST THIS ATTACK AT ONCE BY ORDER OF S.H.I.E.L.D.!
SORRY, BUB!
WE AIN'T SURRENDERING TO ANYONE--NOT WHILE KID KAIJU IS MISSING!
WE'VE GOTTA FIND HIM!

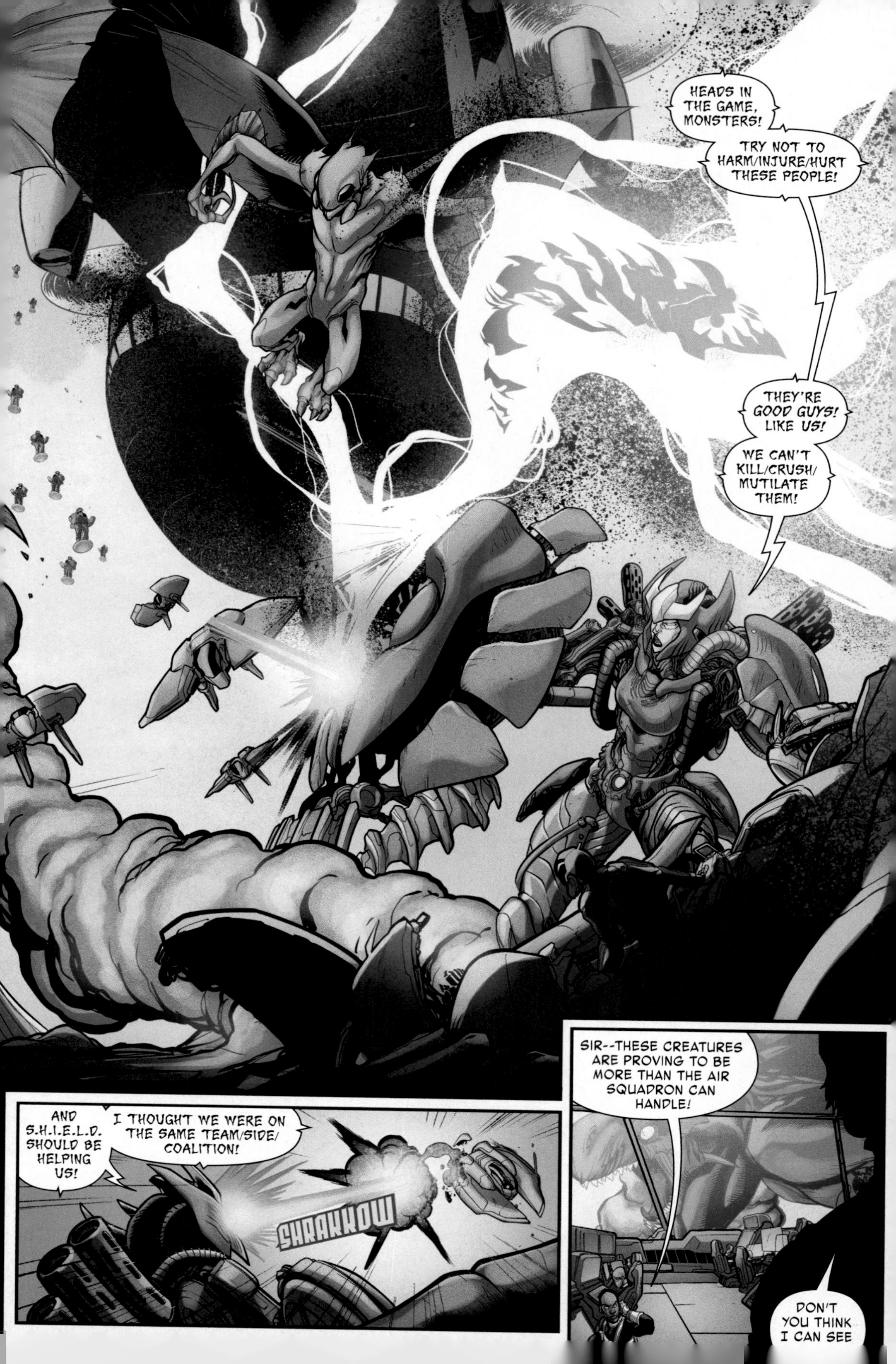
HEADS IN THE GAME, MONSTERS!
TRY NOT TO HARM/INJURE/HURT THESE PEOPLE!
THEY'RE GOOD GUYS! LIKE US!
WE CAN'T KILL/CRUSH/ MUTILATE THEM!
AND S.H.I.E.L.D. SHOULD BE HELPING US!
I THOUGHT WE WERE ON THE SAME TEAM/SIDE/ COALITION!
SHRAKKOW
SIR--THESE CREATURES ARE PROVING TO BE MORE THAN THE AIR SQUADRON CAN HANDLE!
DON'T YOU THINK I CAN SEE

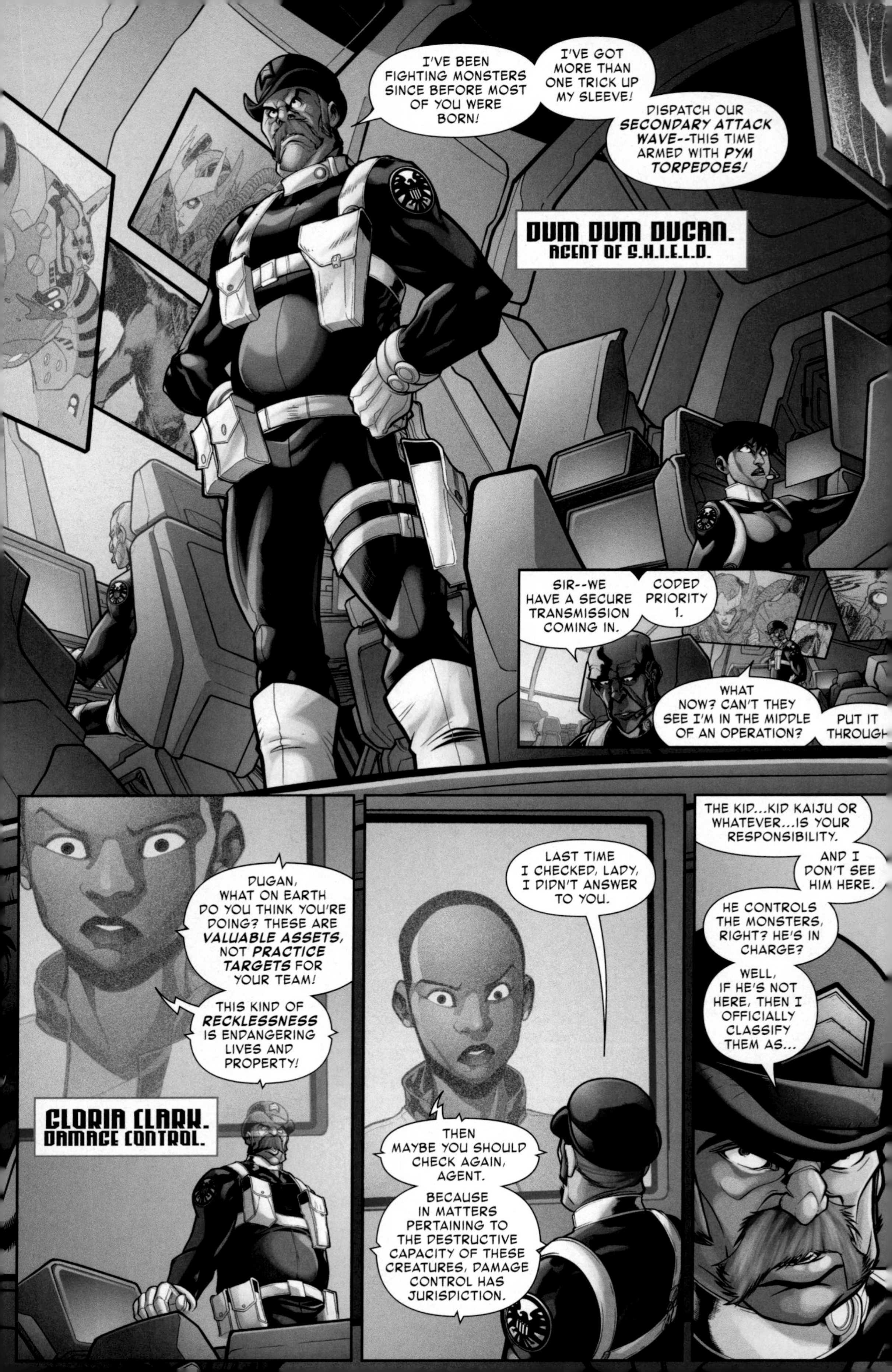
I'VE BEEN FIGHTING MONSTERS SINCE BEFORE MOST OF YOU WERE BORN!
I'VE GOT MORE THAN ONE TRICK UP MY SLEEVE!
DISPATCH OUR SECONDARY ATTACK WAVE--THIS TIME ARMED WITH PYM TORPEDOES!
DUM DUM DUGAN.
AGENT OF S.H.I.E.L.D.
SIR--WE HAVE A SECURE TRANSMISSION COMING IN.
CODED PRIORITY 1.
WHAT NOW? CAN'T THEY SEE I'M IN THE MIDDLE OF AN OPERATION?
PUT IT THROUGH
DUGAN, WHAT ON EARTH DO YOU THINK YOU'RE DOING? THESE ARE VALUABLE ASSETS, NOT PRACTICE TARGETS FOR YOUR TEAM!
THIS KIND OF RECKLESSNESS IS ENDANGERING LIVES AND PROPERTY!
GLORIA CLARK.
DAMAGE CONTROL.
LAST TIME I CHECKED, LADY, I DIDN'T ANSWER TO YOU.
THEN MAYBE YOU SHOULD CHECK AGAIN, AGENT.
BECAUSE IN MATTERS PERTAINING TO THE DESTRUCTIVE CAPACITY OF THESE CREATURES, DAMAGE CONTROL HAS JURISDICTION.
THE KID...KID KAIJU OR WHATEVER...IS YOUR RESPONSIBILITY.
AND I DON'T SEE HIM HERE.
HE CONTROLS THE MONSTERS, RIGHT? HE'S IN CHARGE?
WELL, IF HE'S NOT HERE, THEN I OFFICIALLY CLASSIFY THEM AS...

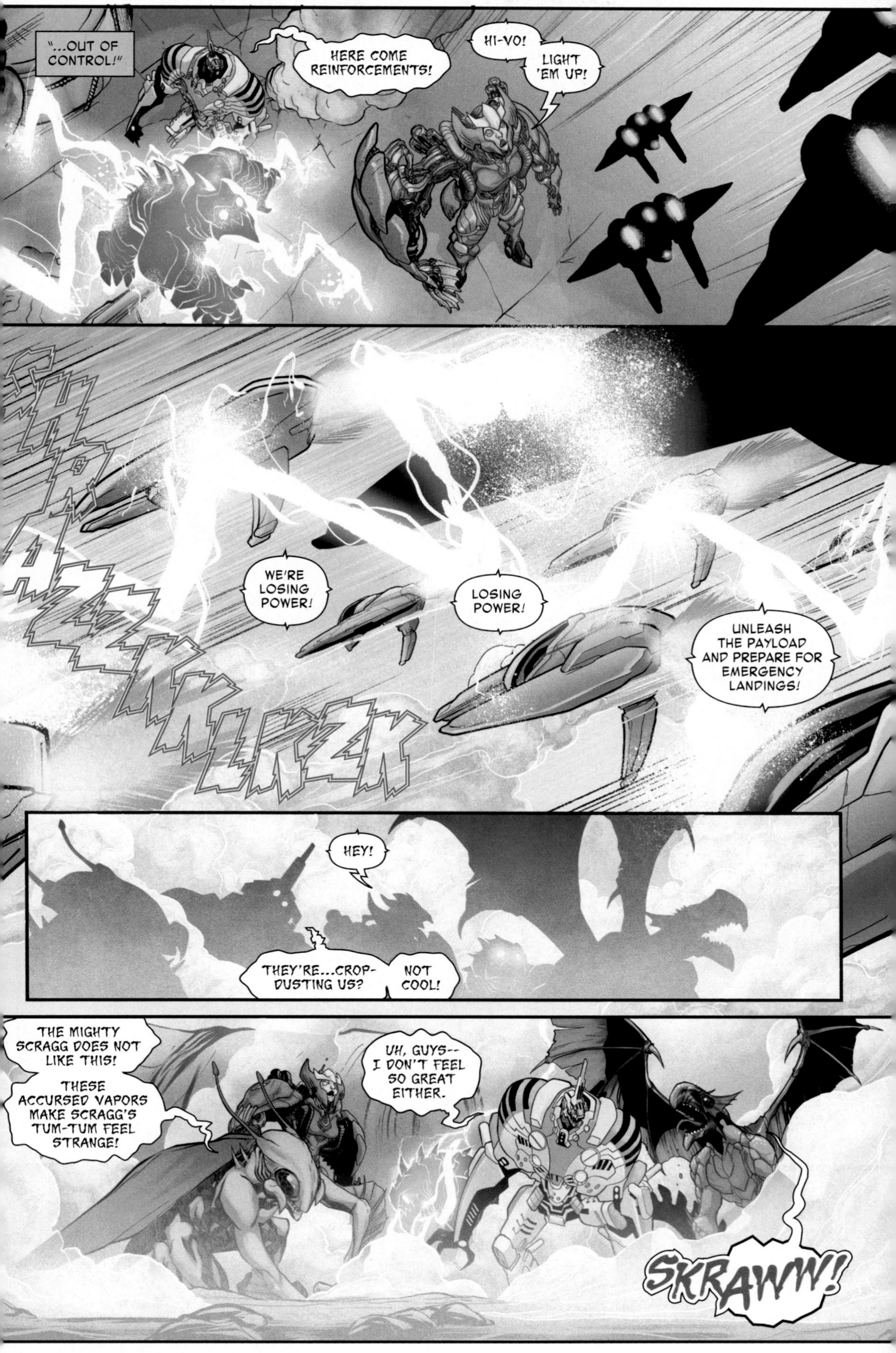
"...OUT OF CONTROL!"
HERE COME REINFORCEMENTS!
HI-YO!
LIGHT 'EM UP!
WE'RE LOSING POWER!
LOSING POWER!
UNLEASH THE PAYLOAD AND PREPARE FOR EMERGENCY LANDINGS!
HEY!
THEY'RE...CROP-DUSTING US?
NOT COOL!
THE MIGHTY SCRAGG DOES NOT LIKE THIS!
THESE ACCURSED VAPORS MAKE SCRAGG'S TUM-TUM FEEL STRANGE!
UH, GUYS-- I DON'T FEEL SO GREAT EITHER.
SKRAWW!

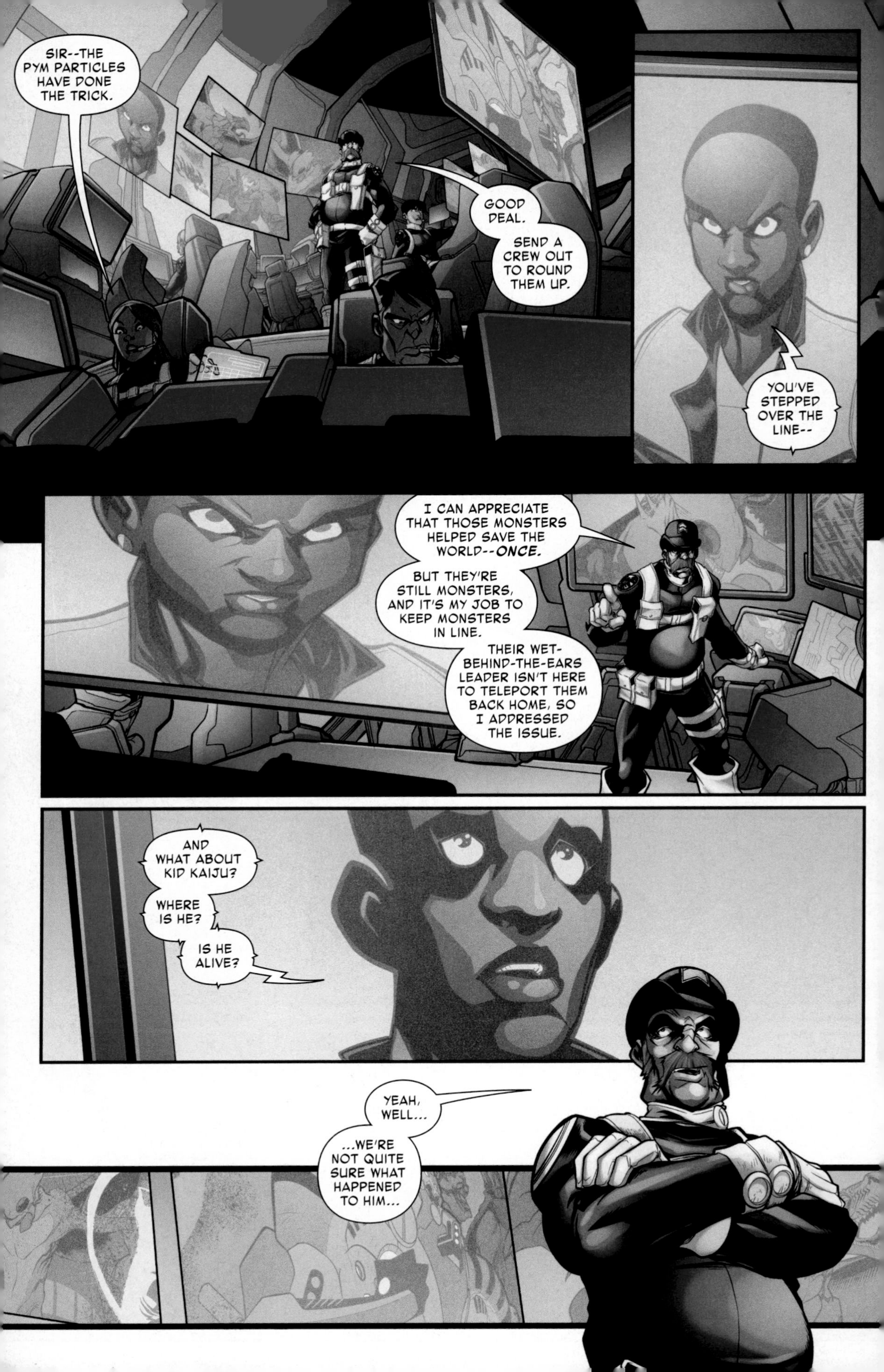
SIR--THE PYM PARTICLES HAVE DONE THE TRICK.
GOOD DEAL.
SEND A CREW OUT TO ROUND THEM UP.
YOU'VE STEPPED OVER THE LINE--
I CAN APPRECIATE THAT THOSE MONSTERS HELPED SAVE THE WORLD--ONCE.
BUT THEY'RE STILL MONSTERS, AND IT'S MY JOB TO KEEP MONSTERS IN LINE.
THEIR WET-BEHIND-THE-EARS LEADER ISN'T HERE TO TELEPORT THEM BACK HOME, SO I ADDRESSED THE ISSUE.
AND WHAT ABOUT KID KAIJU?
WHERE IS HE?
IS HE ALIVE?
YEAH, WELL...
...WE'RE NOT QUITE SURE WHAT HAPPENED TO HIM...

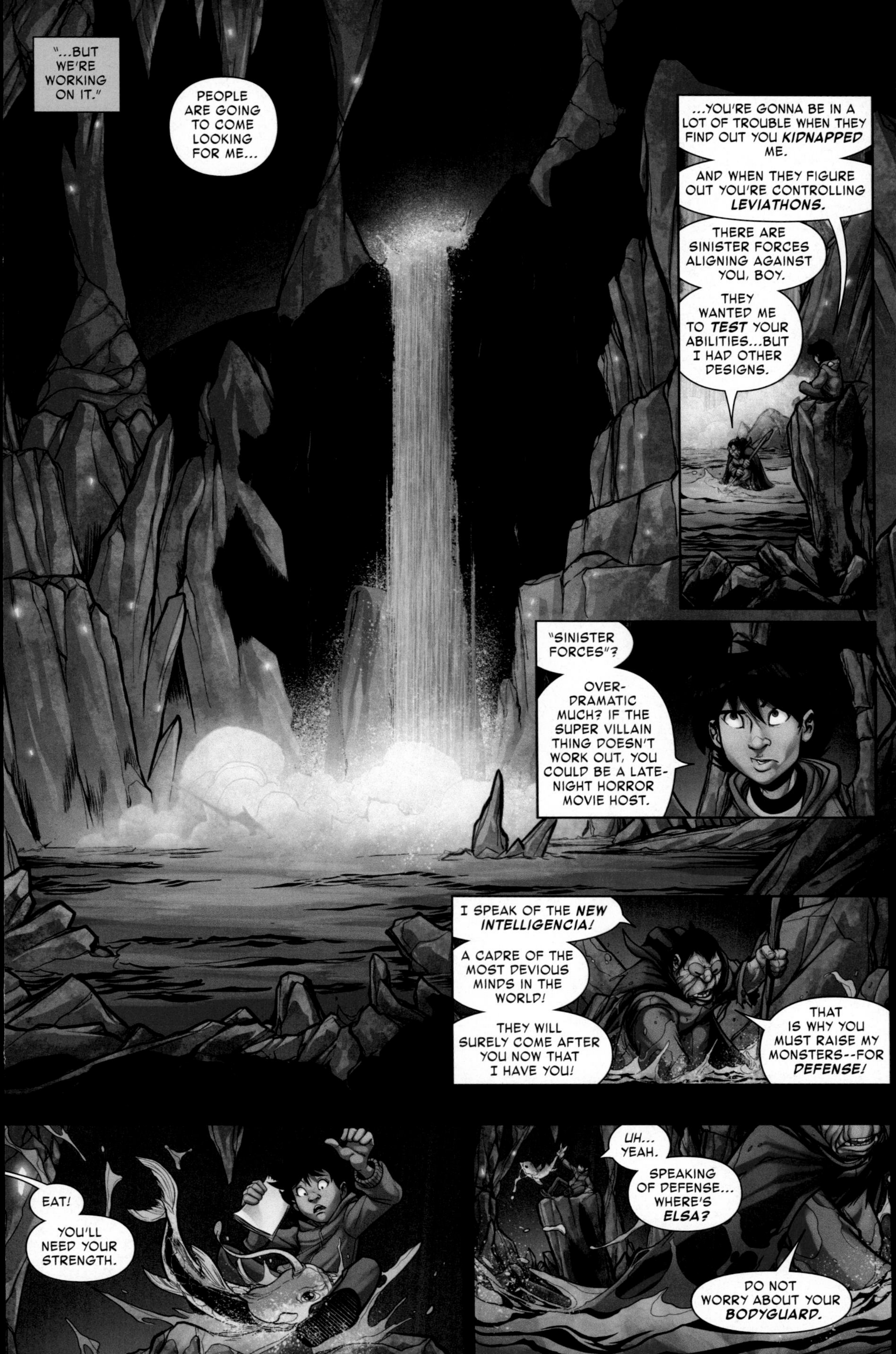
"...BUT WE'RE WORKING ON IT."
PEOPLE ARE GOING TO COME LOOKING FOR ME...
...YOU'RE GONNA BE IN A LOT OF TROUBLE WHEN THEY FIND OUT YOU KIDNAPPED ME.
AND WHEN THEY FIGURE OUT YOU'RE CONTROLLING LEVIATHONS.
THERE ARE SINISTER FORCES ALIGNING AGAINST YOU, BOY.
THEY WANTED ME TO TEST YOUR ABILITIES...BUT I HAD OTHER DESIGNS.
"SINISTER FORCES"?
OVER-DRAMATIC MUCH? IF THE SUPER VILLAIN THING DOESN'T WORK OUT, YOU COULD BE A LATE-NIGHT HORROR MOVIE HOST.
I SPEAK OF THE NEW INTELLIGENCIA!
A CADRE OF THE MOST DEVIOUS MINDS IN THE WORLD!
THEY WILL SURELY COME AFTER YOU NOW THAT I HAVE YOU!
THAT IS WHY YOU MUST RAISE MY MONSTERS--FOR DEFENSE!
EAT!
YOU'LL NEED YOUR STRENGTH.
UH... YEAH.
SPEAKING OF DEFENSE... WHERE'S ELSA?
DO NOT WORRY ABOUT YOUR BODYGUARD.

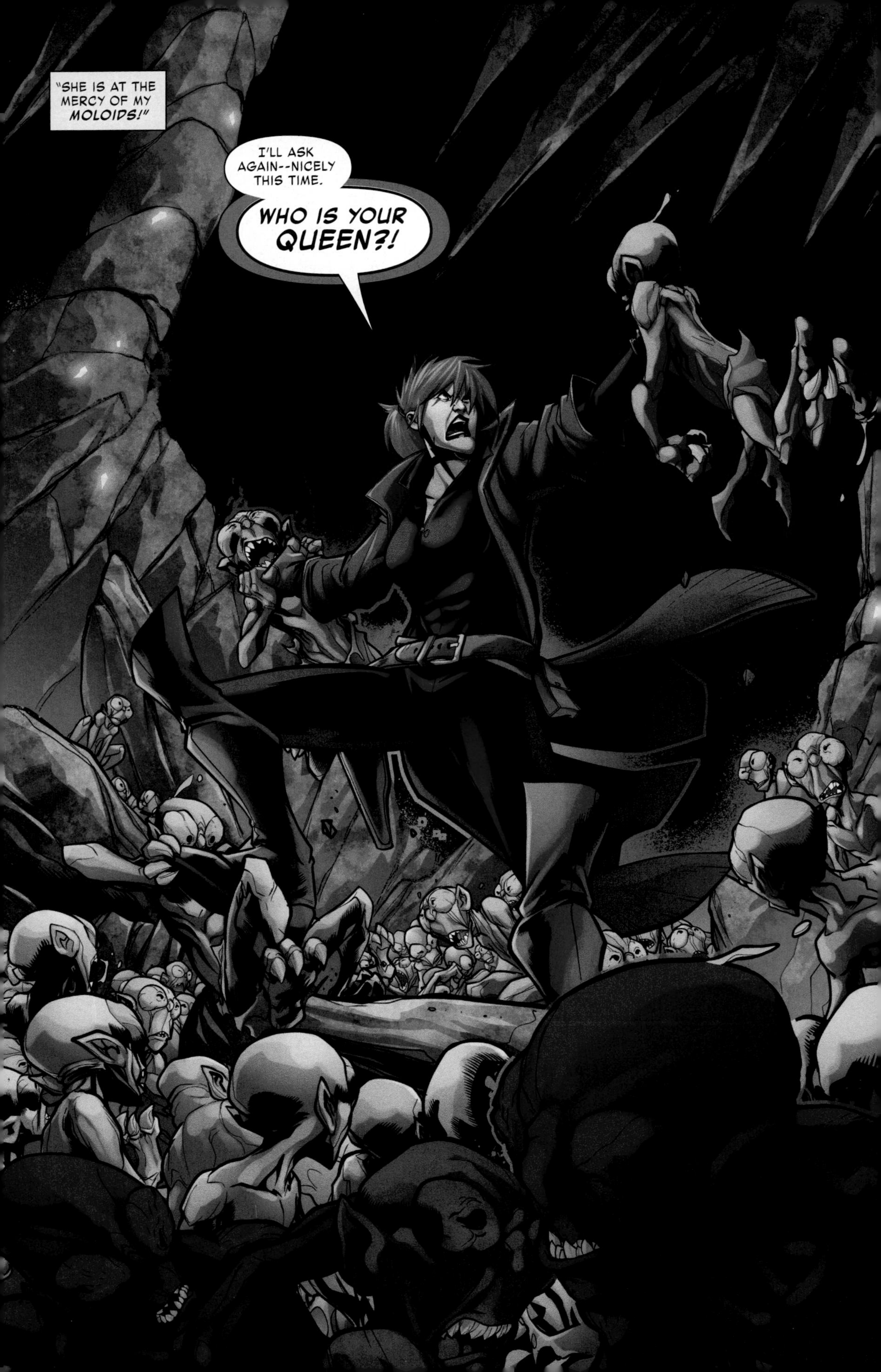
"SHE IS AT THE MERCY OF MY *MOLOIDS!*"
I'LL ASK AGAIN--NICELY THIS TIME.
WHO IS YOUR **QUEEN?!**

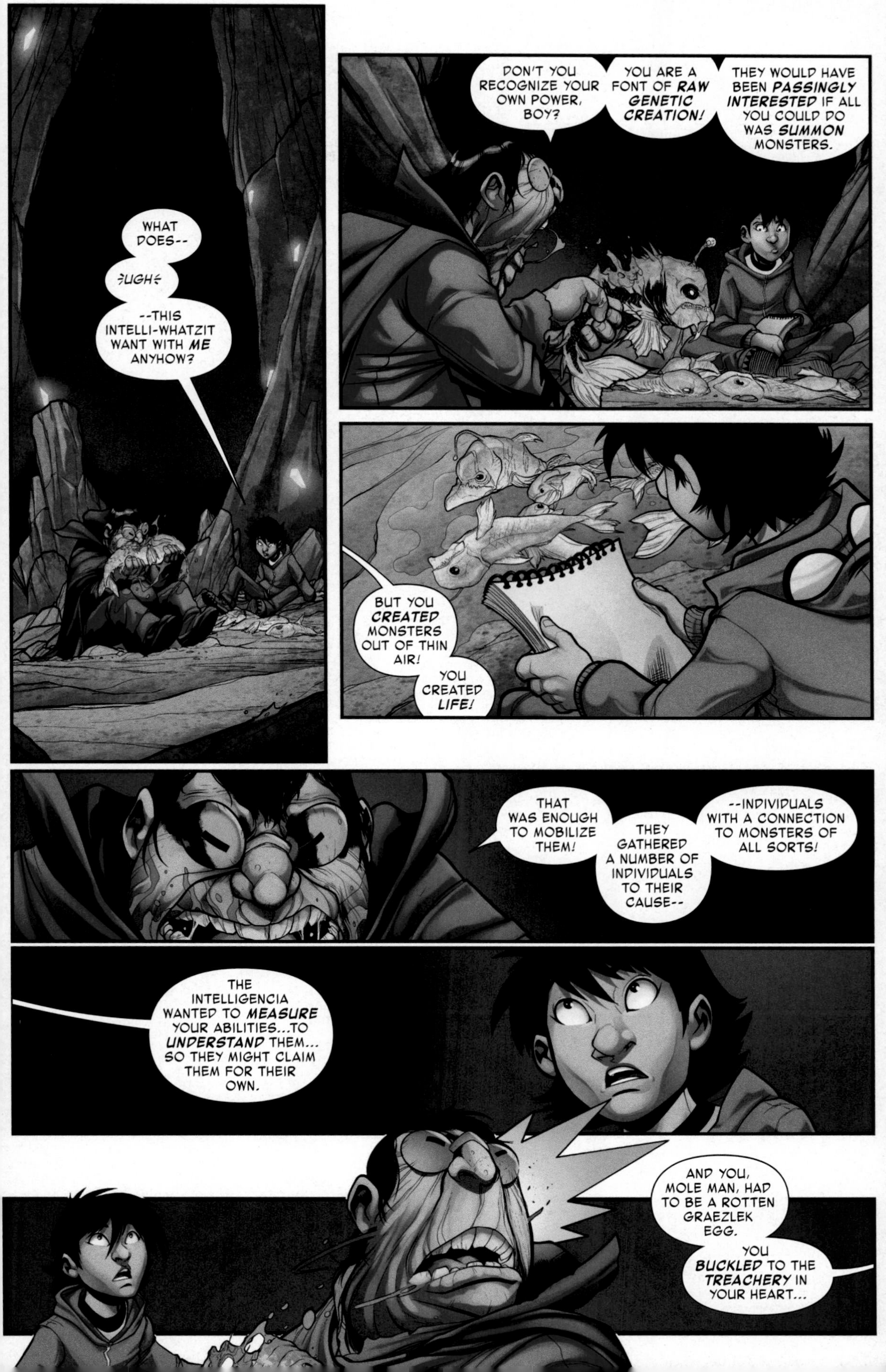

WHAT DOES--
≷UGH≶
--THIS INTELLI-WHATZIT WANT WITH *ME* ANYHOW?
DON'T YOU RECOGNIZE YOUR OWN POWER, BOY?
YOU ARE A FONT OF *RAW GENETIC CREATION!*
THEY WOULD HAVE BEEN *PASSINGLY INTERESTED* IF ALL YOU COULD DO WAS *SUMMON* MONSTERS.
BUT YOU *CREATED* MONSTERS OUT OF THIN AIR!
YOU CREATED *LIFE!*
THAT WAS ENOUGH TO MOBILIZE THEM!
THEY GATHERED A NUMBER OF INDIVIDUALS TO THEIR CAUSE--
--INDIVIDUALS WITH A CONNECTION TO MONSTERS OF ALL SORTS!
THE INTELLIGENCIA WANTED TO *MEASURE* YOUR ABILITIES...TO *UNDERSTAND* THEM... SO THEY MIGHT CLAIM THEM FOR THEIR OWN.
AND YOU, MOLE MAN, HAD TO BE A ROTTEN GRAEZLEK EGG.
YOU *BUCKLED* TO THE *TREACHERY* IN YOUR HEART...

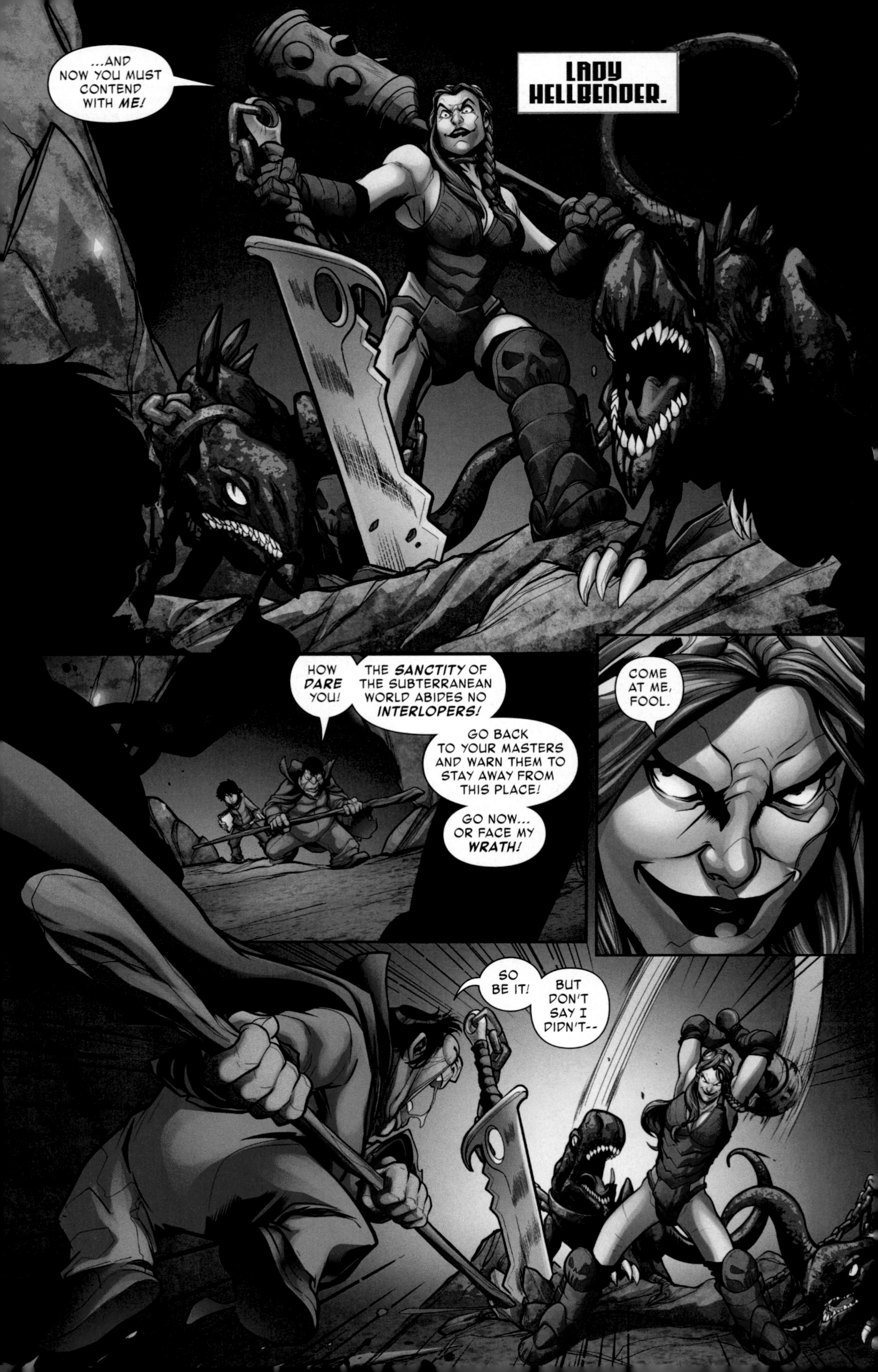
...AND NOW YOU MUST CONTEND WITH ME!
LADY HELLBENDER.
HOW DARE YOU!
THE SANCTITY OF THE SUBTERRANEAN WORLD ABIDES NO INTERLOPERS!
GO BACK TO YOUR MASTERS AND WARN THEM TO STAY AWAY FROM THIS PLACE!
GO NOW... OR FACE MY WRATH!
COME AT ME, FOOL.
SO BE IT!
BUT DON'T SAY I DIDN'T--

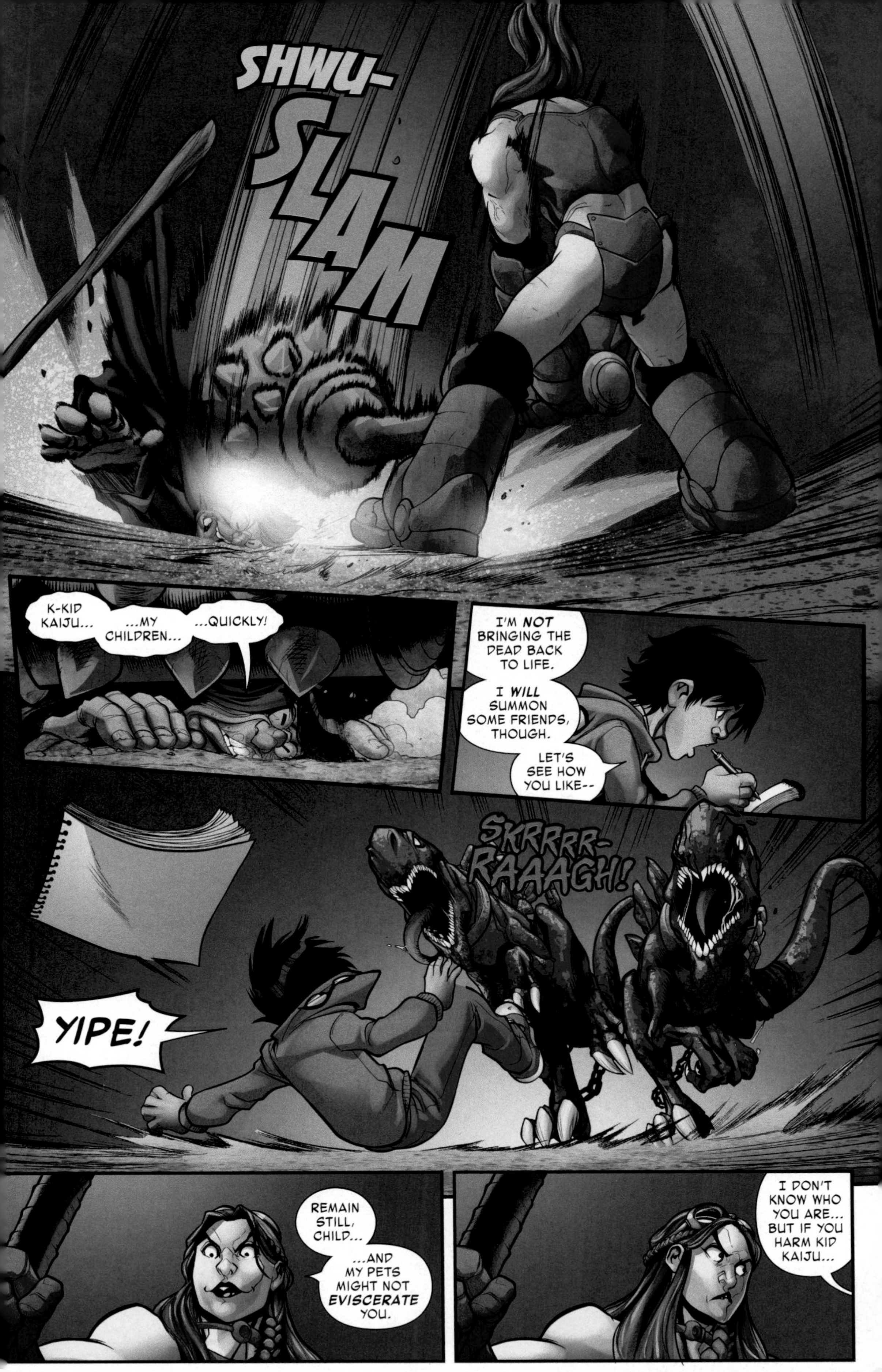
SHWU-SLAM
K-KID KAIJU...
...MY CHILDREN...
...QUICKLY!
I'M NOT BRINGING THE DEAD BACK TO LIFE.
I WILL SUMMON SOME FRIENDS, THOUGH.
LET'S SEE HOW YOU LIKE--
SKRRRR-RAAAGH!
YIPE!
REMAIN STILL, CHILD...
...AND MY PETS MIGHT NOT EVISCERATE YOU.
I DON'T KNOW WHO YOU ARE... BUT IF YOU HARM KID KAIJU...

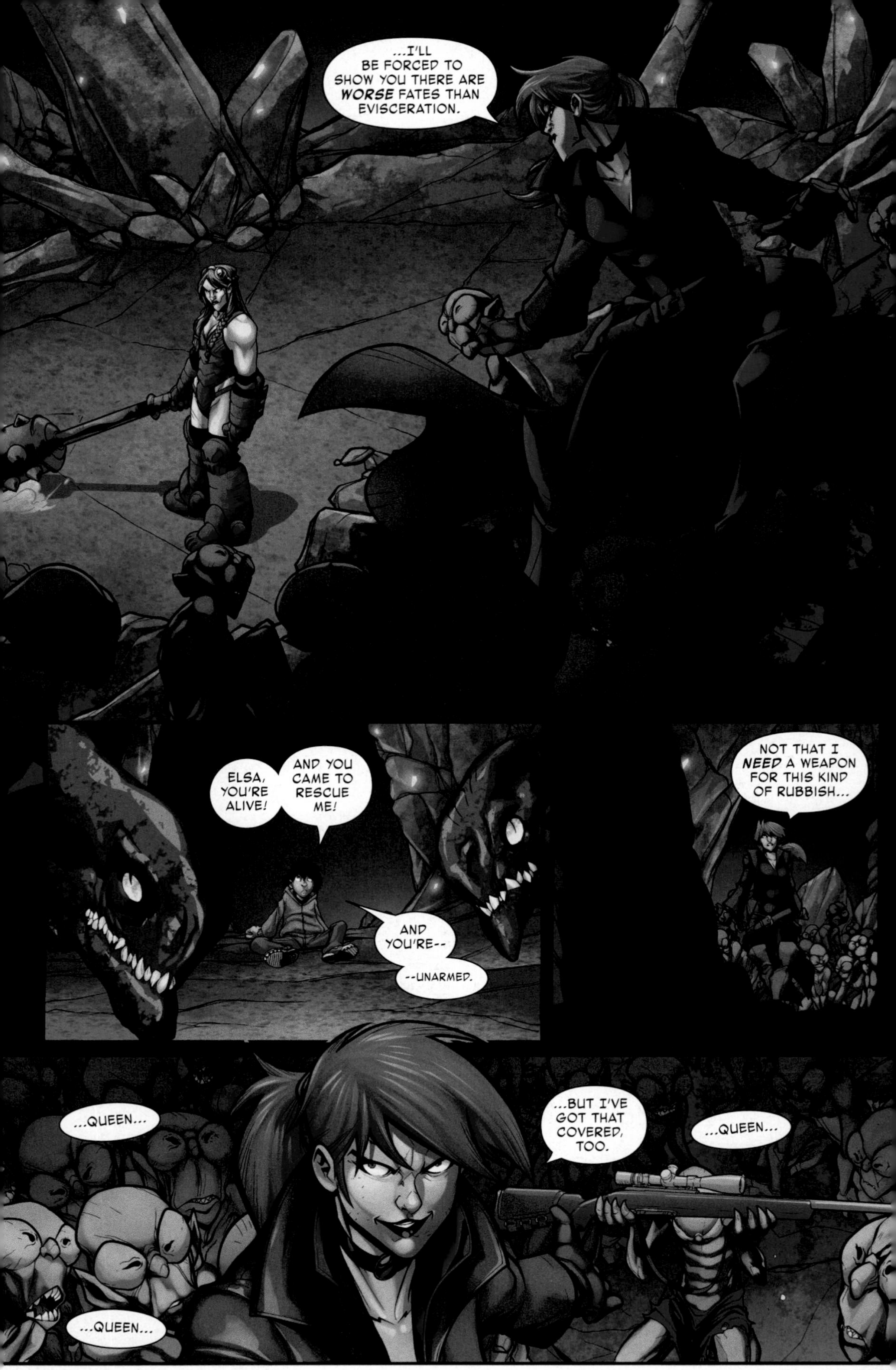
...I'LL BE FORCED TO SHOW YOU THERE ARE WORSE FATES THAN EVISCERATION.
ELSA, YOU'RE ALIVE!
AND YOU CAME TO RESCUE ME!
AND YOU'RE--
--UNARMED.
NOT THAT I NEED A WEAPON FOR THIS KIND OF RUBBISH...
...QUEEN...
...BUT I'VE GOT THAT COVERED, TOO.
...QUEEN...
...QUEEN...

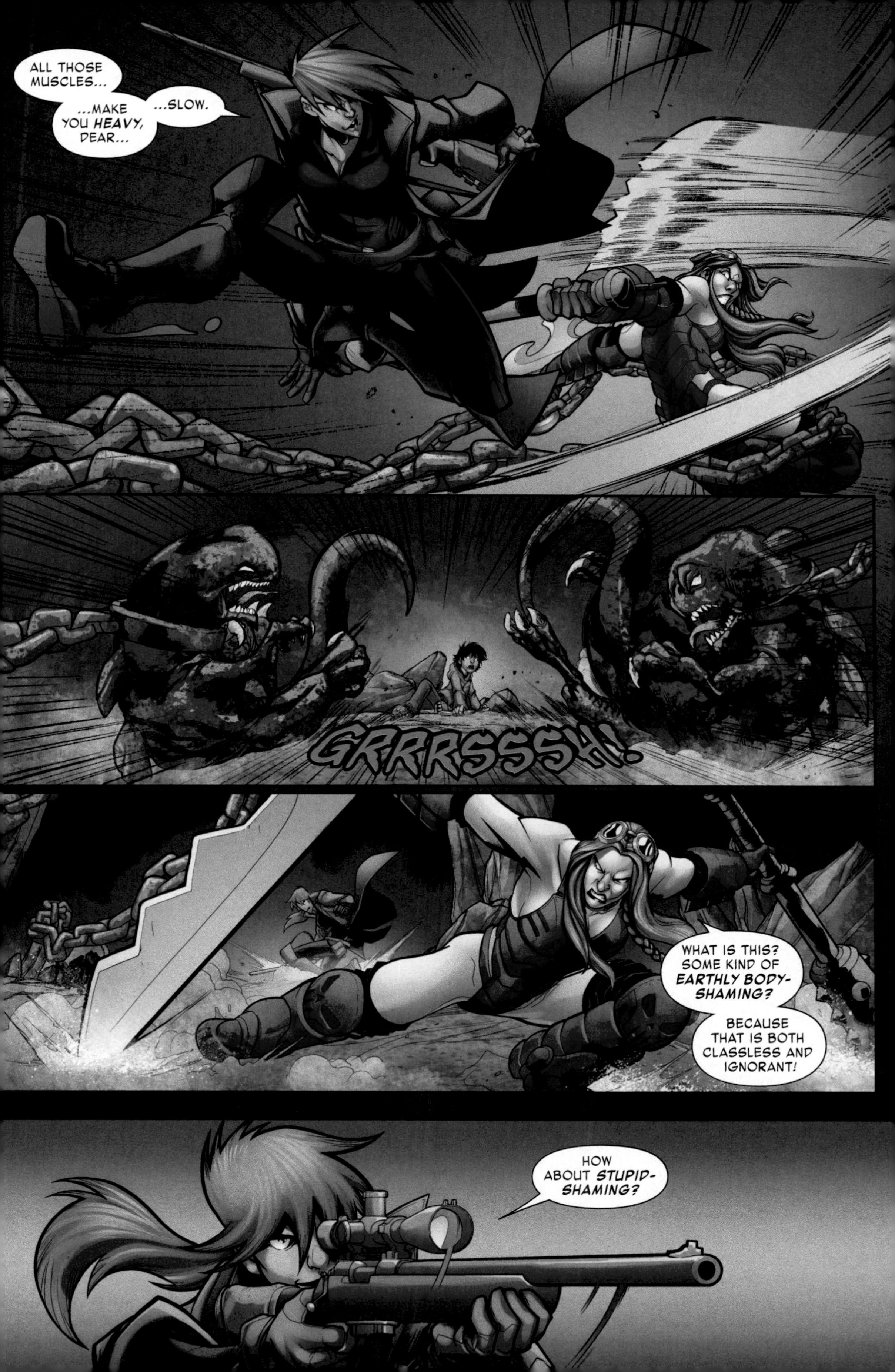

ALL THOSE MUSCLES...
...MAKE YOU *HEAVY,* DEAR...
...SLOW.
GRRRSSSH!
WHAT IS THIS? SOME KIND OF *EARTHLY BODY-SHAMING?*
BECAUSE THAT IS BOTH CLASSLESS AND IGNORANT!
HOW ABOUT *STUPID-SHAMING?*

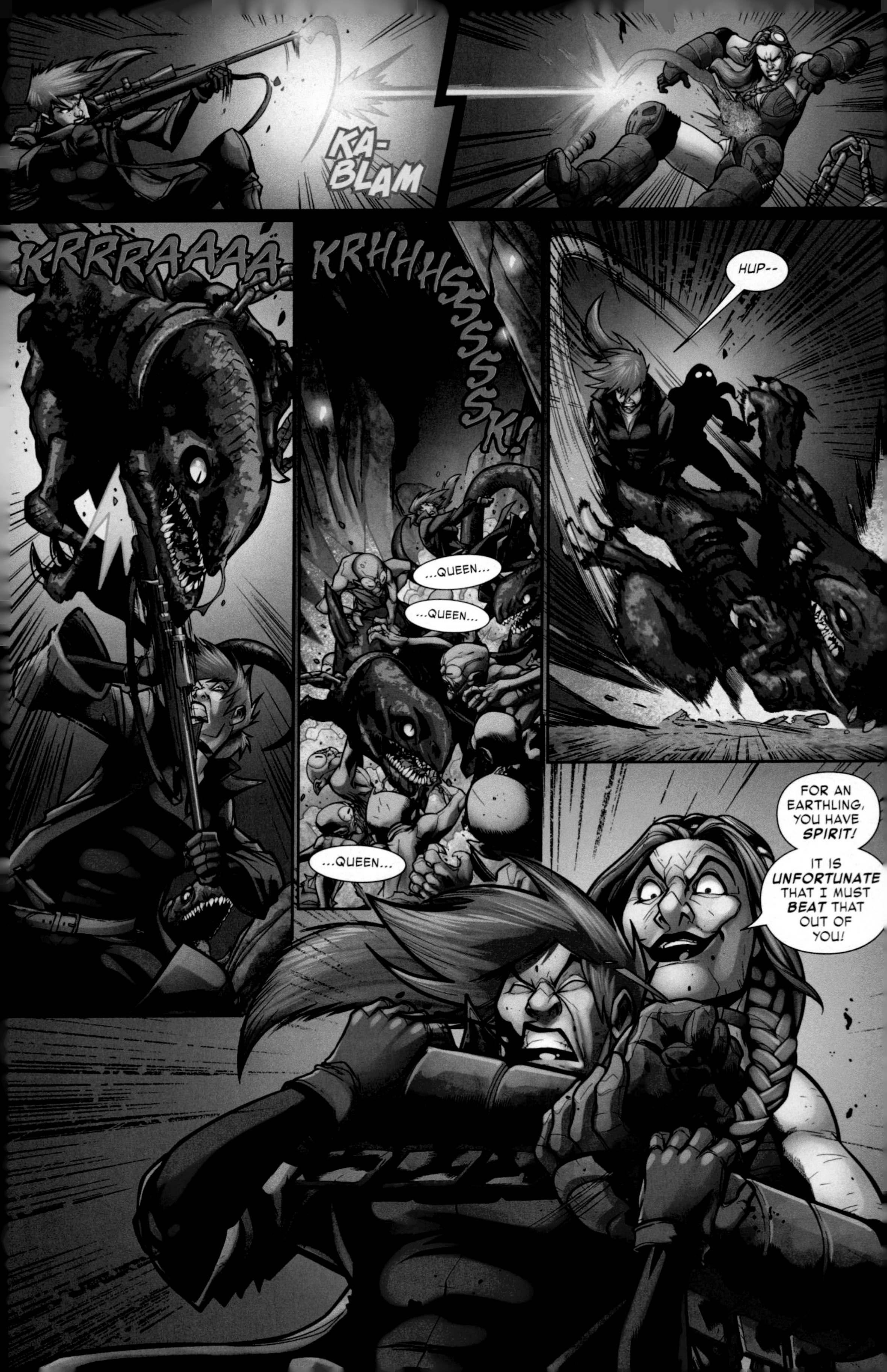
KA-BLAM
KRRRAAAA
KRHHHSSSSSK!
...QUEEN...
...QUEEN...
...QUEEN...
HUP--
FOR AN EARTHLING, YOU HAVE SPIRIT!
IT IS UNFORTUNATE THAT I MUST BEAT THAT OUT OF YOU!

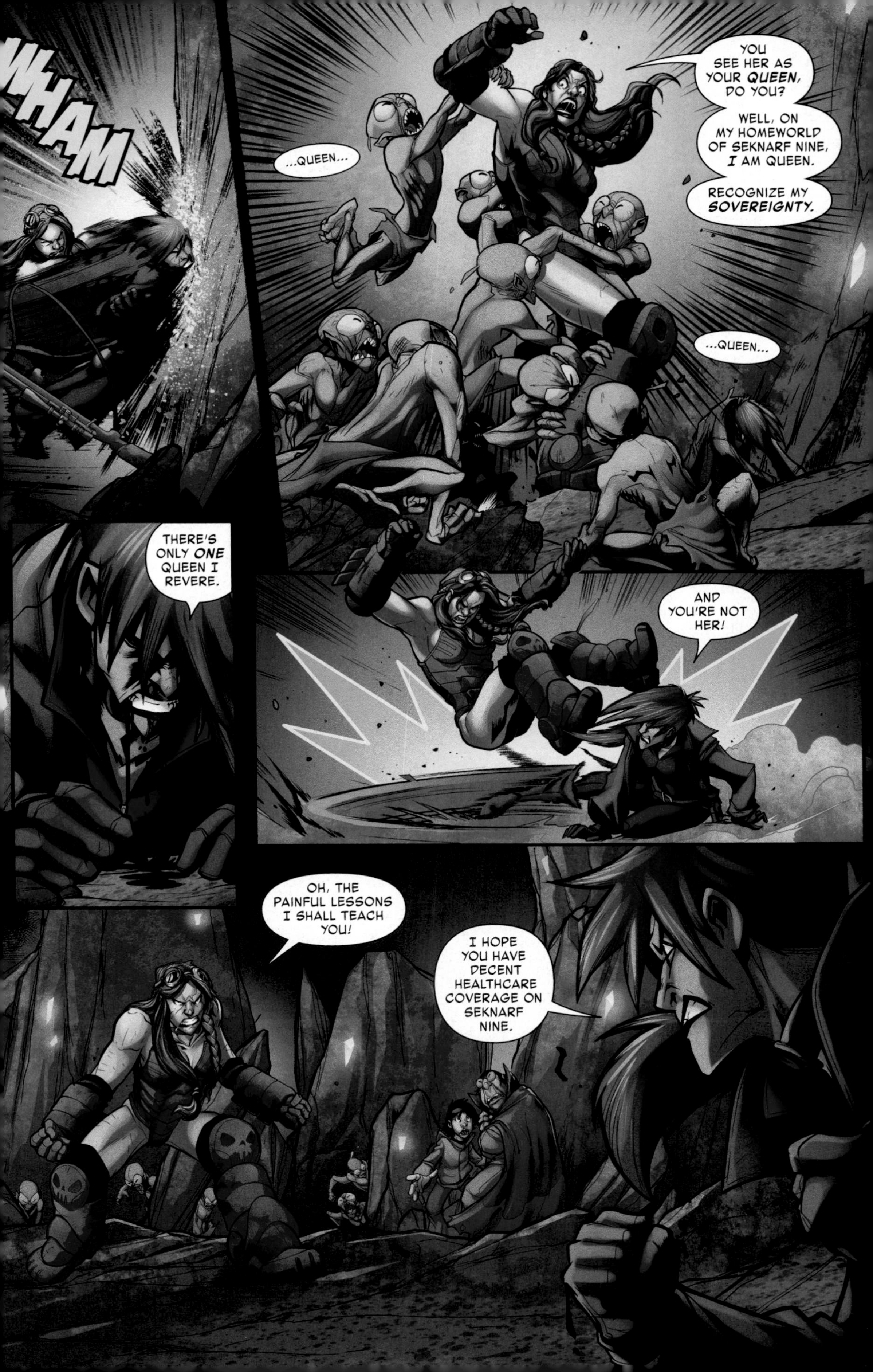
WHAM
...QUEEN...
YOU SEE HER AS YOUR QUEEN, DO YOU?
WELL, ON MY HOMEWORLD OF SEKNARF NINE, I AM QUEEN.
RECOGNIZE MY SOVEREIGNTY.
...QUEEN...
THERE'S ONLY ONE QUEEN I REVERE.
AND YOU'RE NOT HER!
OH, THE PAINFUL LESSONS I SHALL TEACH YOU!
I HOPE YOU HAVE DECENT HEALTHCARE COVERAGE ON SEKNARF NINE.

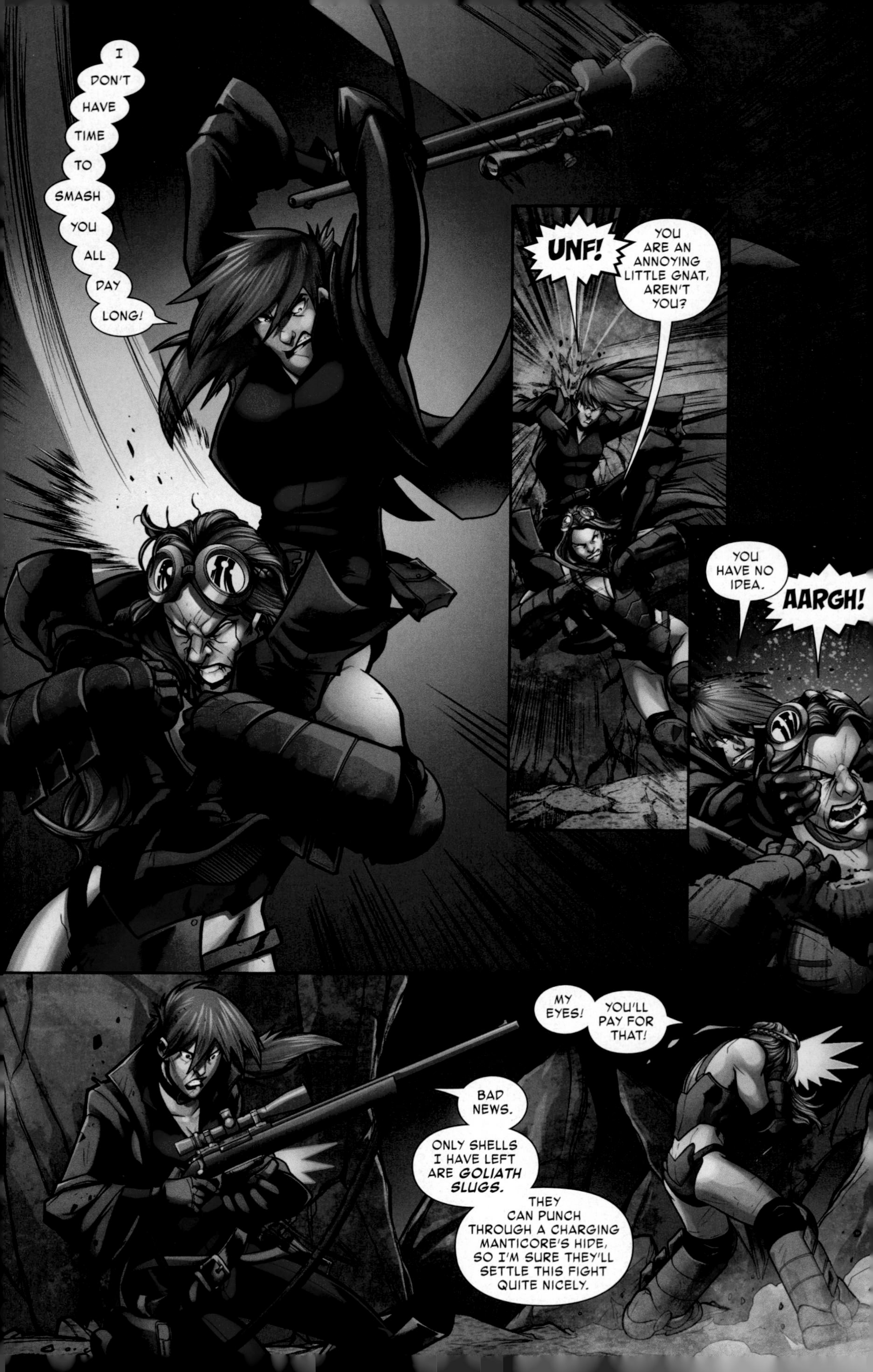
I DON'T HAVE TIME TO SMASH YOU ALL DAY LONG!
UNF!
YOU ARE AN ANNOYING LITTLE GNAT, AREN'T YOU?
YOU HAVE NO IDEA.
AARGH!
MY EYES!
YOU'LL PAY FOR THAT!
BAD NEWS.
ONLY SHELLS I HAVE LEFT ARE GOLIATH SLUGS.
THEY CAN PUNCH THROUGH A CHARGING MANTICORE'S HIDE, SO I'M SURE THEY'LL SETTLE THIS FIGHT QUITE NICELY.

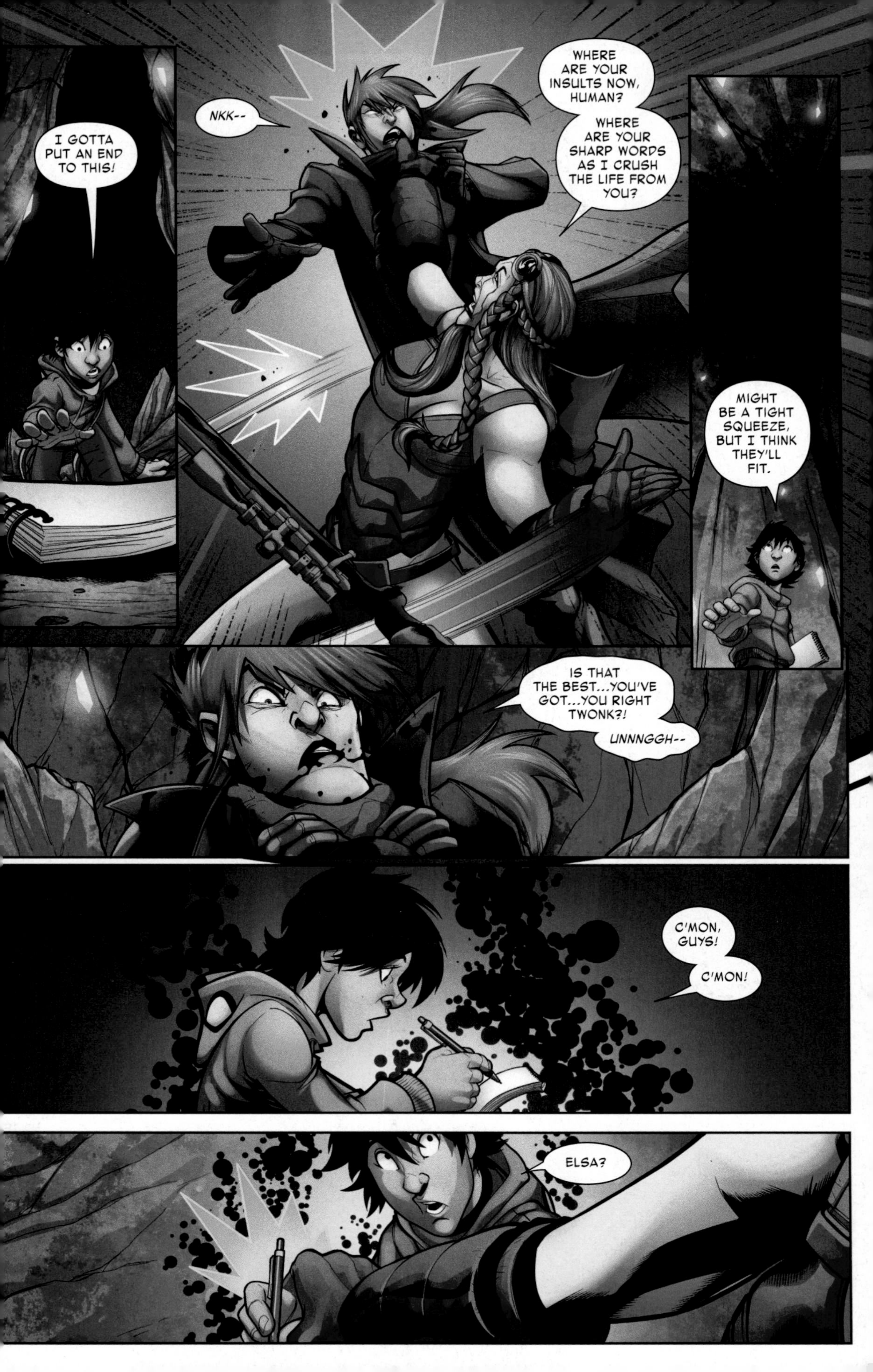
I GOTTA PUT AN END TO THIS!
NKK--
WHERE ARE YOUR INSULTS NOW, HUMAN?
WHERE ARE YOUR SHARP WORDS AS I CRUSH THE LIFE FROM YOU?
MIGHT BE A TIGHT SQUEEZE, BUT I THINK THEY'LL FIT.
IS THAT THE BEST...YOU'VE GOT...YOU RIGHT TWONK?!
UNNNGGH--
C'MON, GUYS!
C'MON!
ELSA?

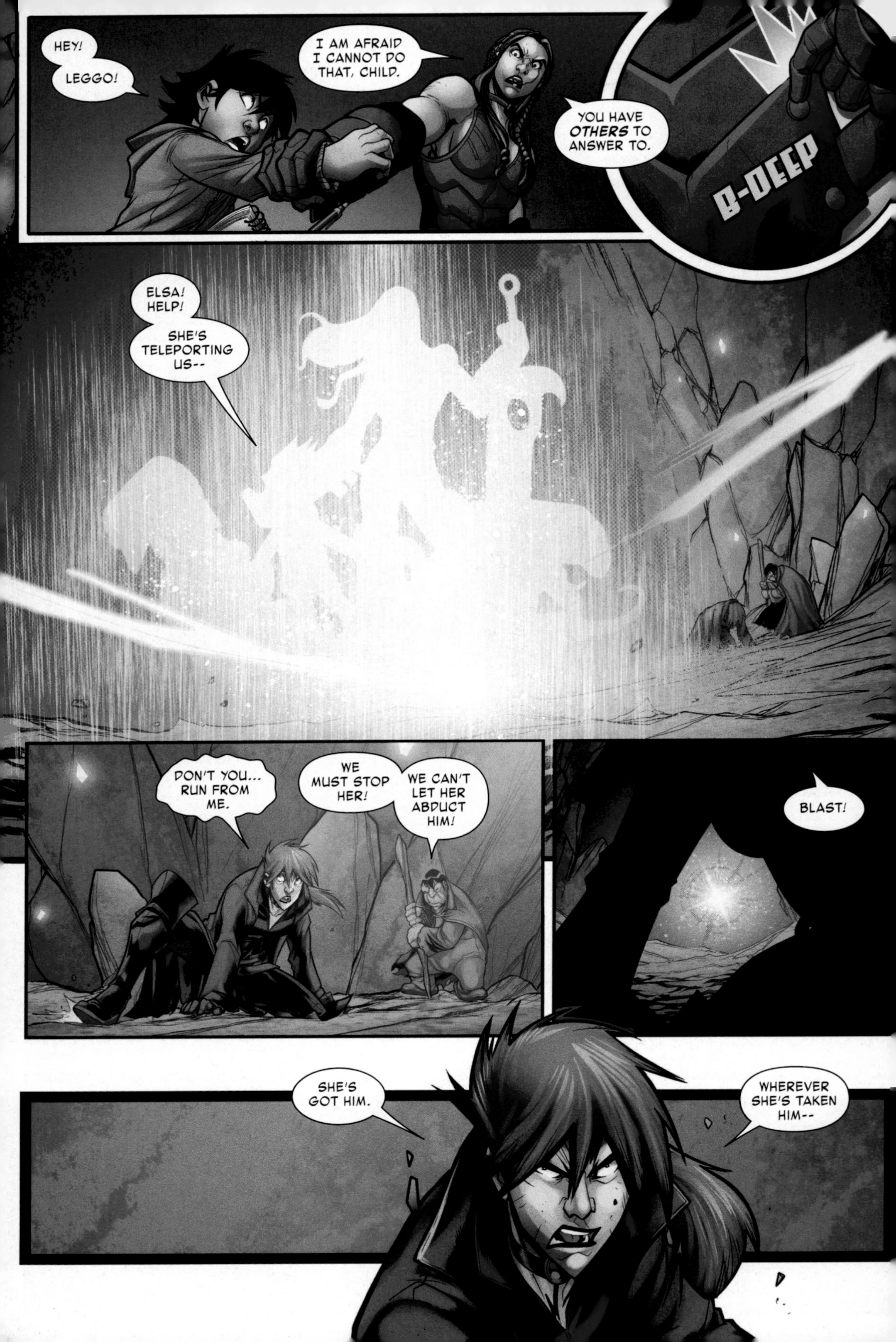
HEY!
LEGGO!
I AM AFRAID I CANNOT DO THAT, CHILD.
YOU HAVE OTHERS TO ANSWER TO.
B-DEEP
ELSA! HELP!
SHE'S TELEPORTING US--
DON'T YOU... RUN FROM ME.
WE MUST STOP HER!
WE CAN'T LET HER ABDUCT HIM!
BLAST!
SHE'S GOT HIM.
WHEREVER SHE'S TAKEN HIM--

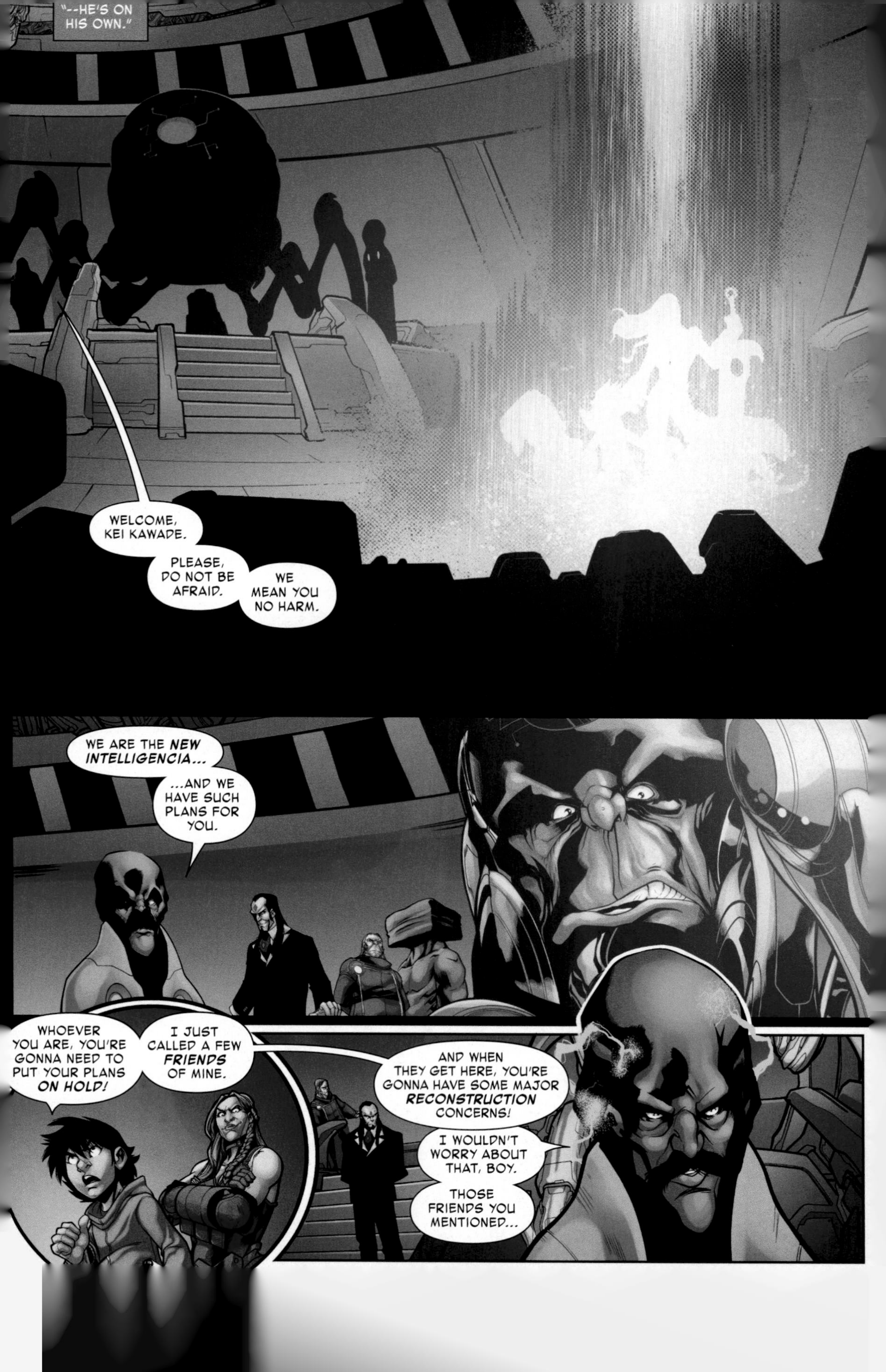
"--HE'S ON HIS OWN."
WELCOME, KEI KAWADE.
PLEASE, DO NOT BE AFRAID.
WE MEAN YOU NO HARM.
WE ARE THE NEW INTELLIGENCIA...
...AND WE HAVE SUCH PLANS FOR YOU.
WHOEVER YOU ARE, YOU'RE GONNA NEED TO PUT YOUR PLANS ON HOLD!
I JUST CALLED A FEW FRIENDS OF MINE.
AND WHEN THEY GET HERE, YOU'RE GONNA HAVE SOME MAJOR RECONSTRUCTION CONCERNS!
I WOULDN'T WORRY ABOUT THAT, BOY.
THOSE FRIENDS YOU MENTIONED...

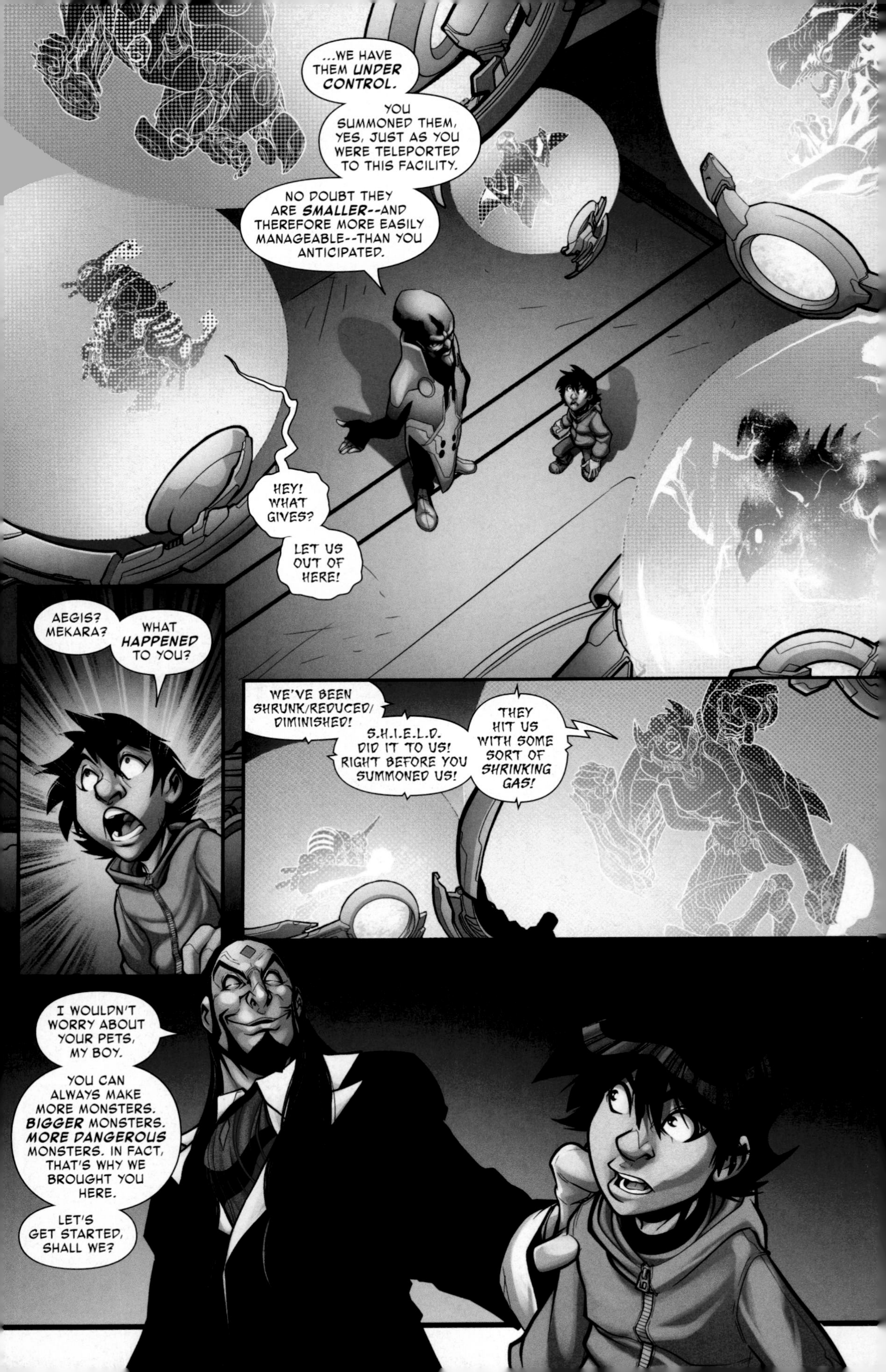
...WE HAVE THEM UNDER CONTROL.
YOU SUMMONED THEM, YES, JUST AS YOU WERE TELEPORTED TO THIS FACILITY.
NO DOUBT THEY ARE SMALLER--AND THEREFORE MORE EASILY MANAGEABLE--THAN YOU ANTICIPATED.
HEY! WHAT GIVES?
LET US OUT OF HERE!
AEGIS? MEKARA?
WHAT HAPPENED TO YOU?
WE'VE BEEN SHRUNK/REDUCED/DIMINISHED!
S.H.I.E.L.D. DID IT TO US! RIGHT BEFORE YOU SUMMONED US!
THEY HIT US WITH SOME SORT OF SHRINKING GAS!
I WOULDN'T WORRY ABOUT YOUR PETS, MY BOY.
YOU CAN ALWAYS MAKE MORE MONSTERS. BIGGER MONSTERS. MORE DANGEROUS MONSTERS. IN FACT, THAT'S WHY WE BROUGHT YOU HERE.
LET'S GET STARTED, SHALL WE?

#1 ACTION FIGURE VARIANT BY
JOHN TYLER CHRISTOPHER

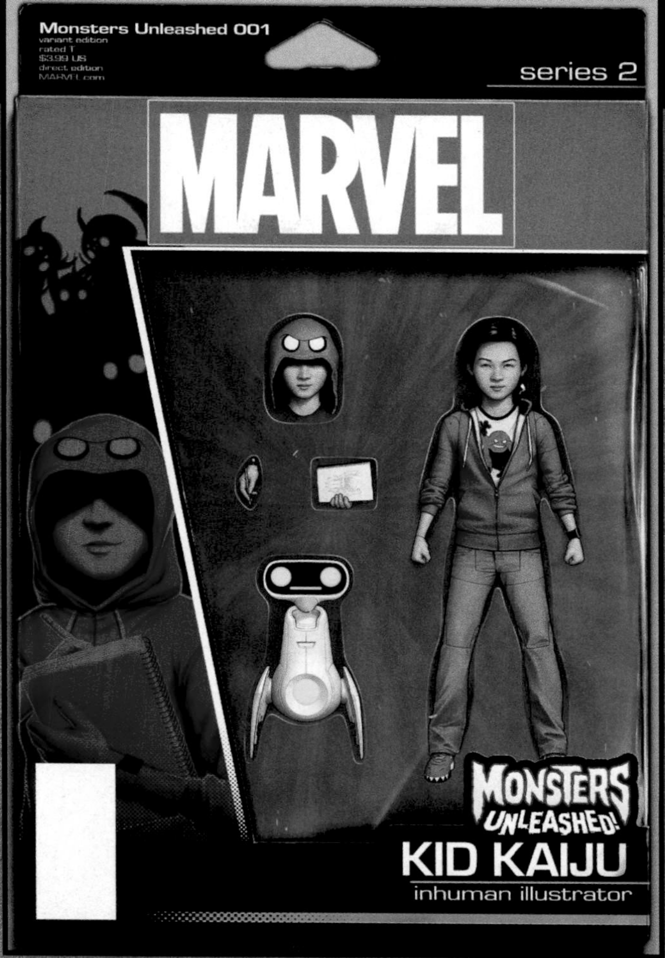
Monsters Unleashed 001
variant edition
rated T
$3.99 US
direct edition
MARVEL.com
series 2
MARVEL
MONSTERS UNLEASHED!
KID KAIJU
inhuman illustrator

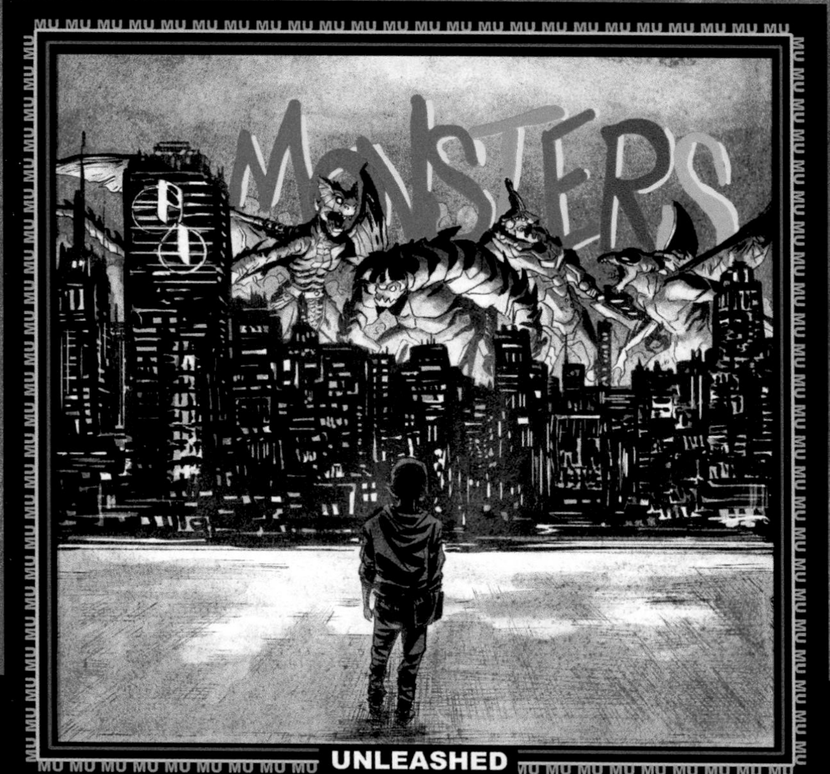
MONSTERS
UNLEASHED

#1 HIP-HOP VARIANT BY
SANFORD GREENE

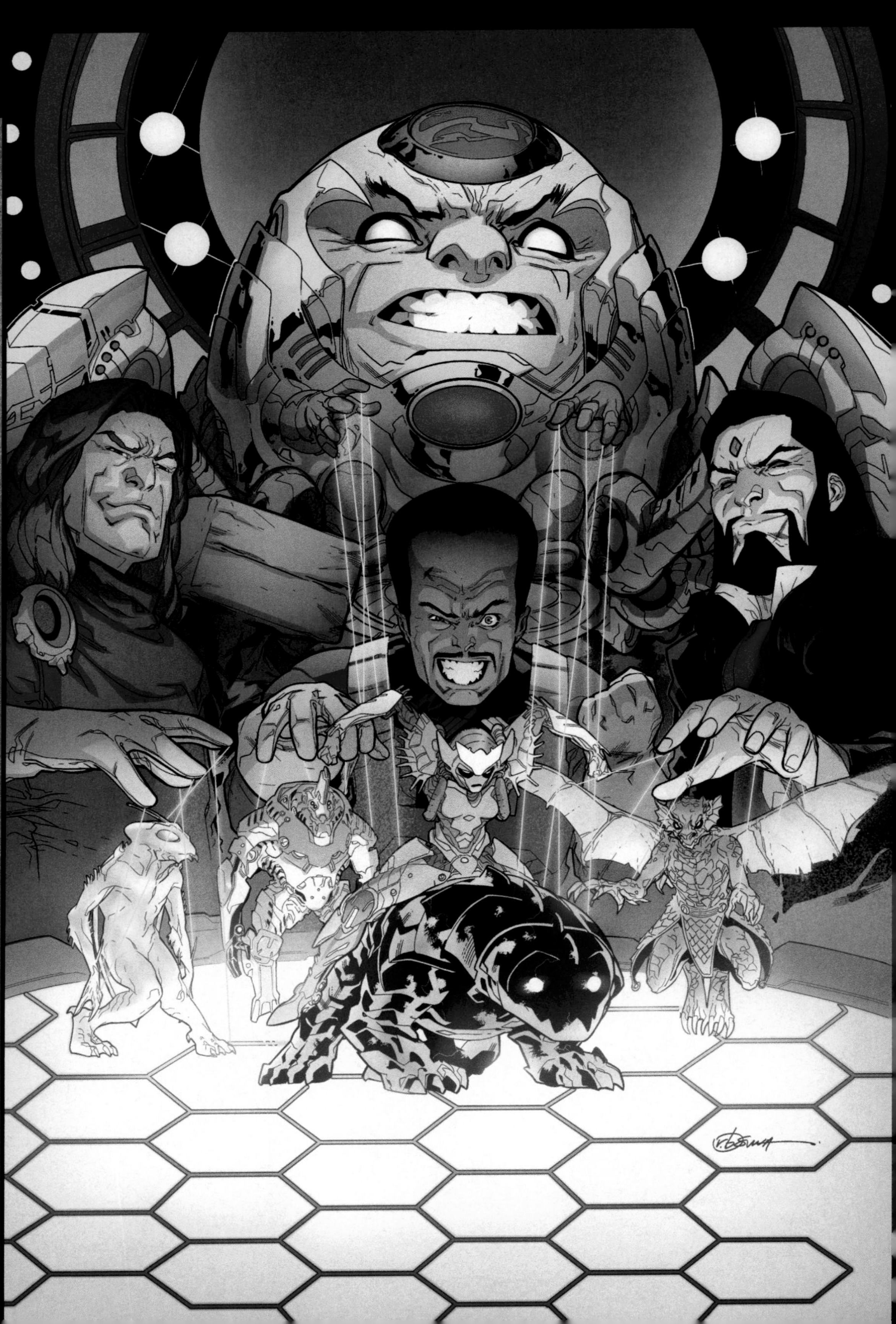

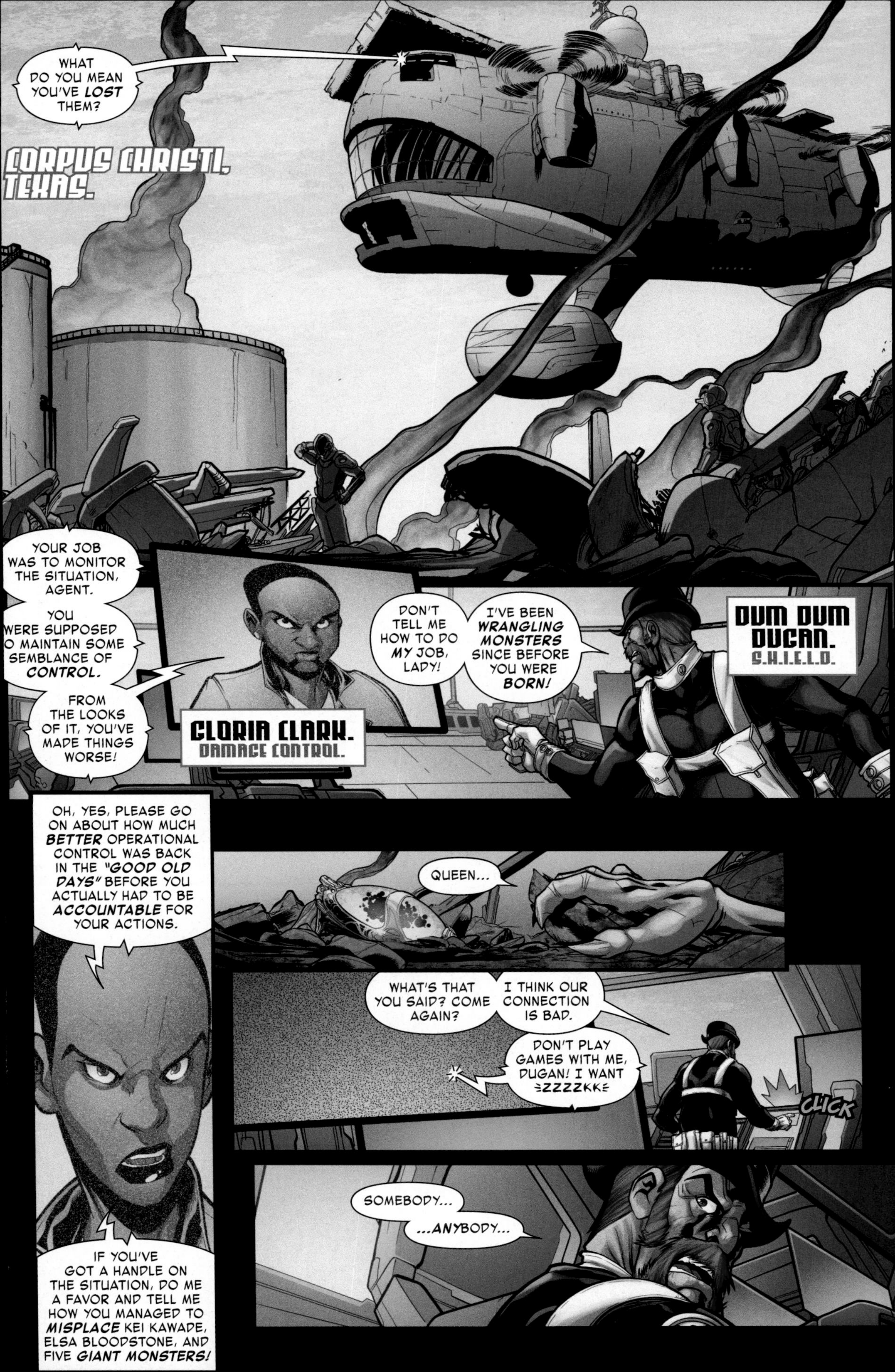
WHAT DO YOU MEAN YOU'VE LOST THEM?
CORPUS CHRISTI, TEXAS.
YOUR JOB WAS TO MONITOR THE SITUATION, AGENT.
YOU WERE SUPPOSED TO MAINTAIN SOME SEMBLANCE OF CONTROL.
FROM THE LOOKS OF IT, YOU'VE MADE THINGS WORSE!
GLORIA CLARK. DAMAGE CONTROL.
DON'T TELL ME HOW TO DO MY JOB, LADY!
I'VE BEEN WRANGLING MONSTERS SINCE BEFORE YOU WERE BORN!
DUM DUM DUGAN. S.H.I.E.L.D.
OH, YES, PLEASE GO ON ABOUT HOW MUCH BETTER OPERATIONAL CONTROL WAS BACK IN THE "GOOD OLD DAYS" BEFORE YOU ACTUALLY HAD TO BE ACCOUNTABLE FOR YOUR ACTIONS.
IF YOU'VE GOT A HANDLE ON THE SITUATION, DO ME A FAVOR AND TELL ME HOW YOU MANAGED TO MISPLACE KEI KAWADE, ELSA BLOODSTONE, AND FIVE GIANT MONSTERS!
QUEEN...
WHAT'S THAT YOU SAID? COME AGAIN?
I THINK OUR CONNECTION IS BAD.
DON'T PLAY GAMES WITH ME, DUGAN! I WANT ZZZZKK
CLICK
SOMEBODY...
...ANYBODY...

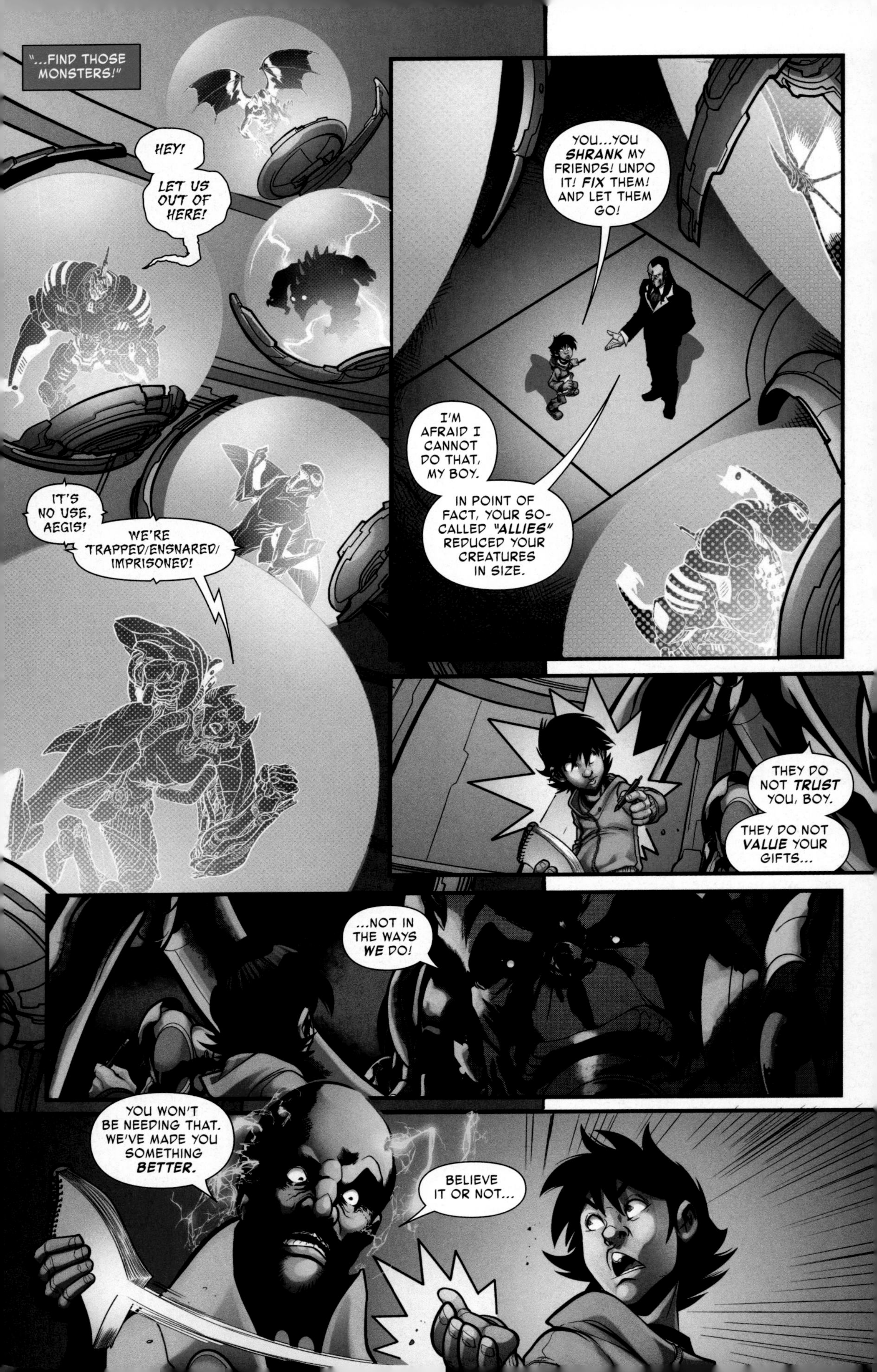
"...FIND THOSE MONSTERS!"
HEY!
LET US OUT OF HERE!
IT'S NO USE, AEGIS!
WE'RE TRAPPED/ENSNARED/IMPRISONED!
YOU...YOU SHRANK MY FRIENDS! UNDO IT! FIX THEM! AND LET THEM GO!
I'M AFRAID I CANNOT DO THAT, MY BOY.
IN POINT OF FACT, YOUR SO-CALLED "ALLIES" REDUCED YOUR CREATURES IN SIZE.
THEY DO NOT TRUST YOU, BOY.
THEY DO NOT VALUE YOUR GIFTS...
...NOT IN THE WAYS WE DO!
YOU WON'T BE NEEDING THAT. WE'VE MADE YOU SOMETHING BETTER.
BELIEVE IT OR NOT...

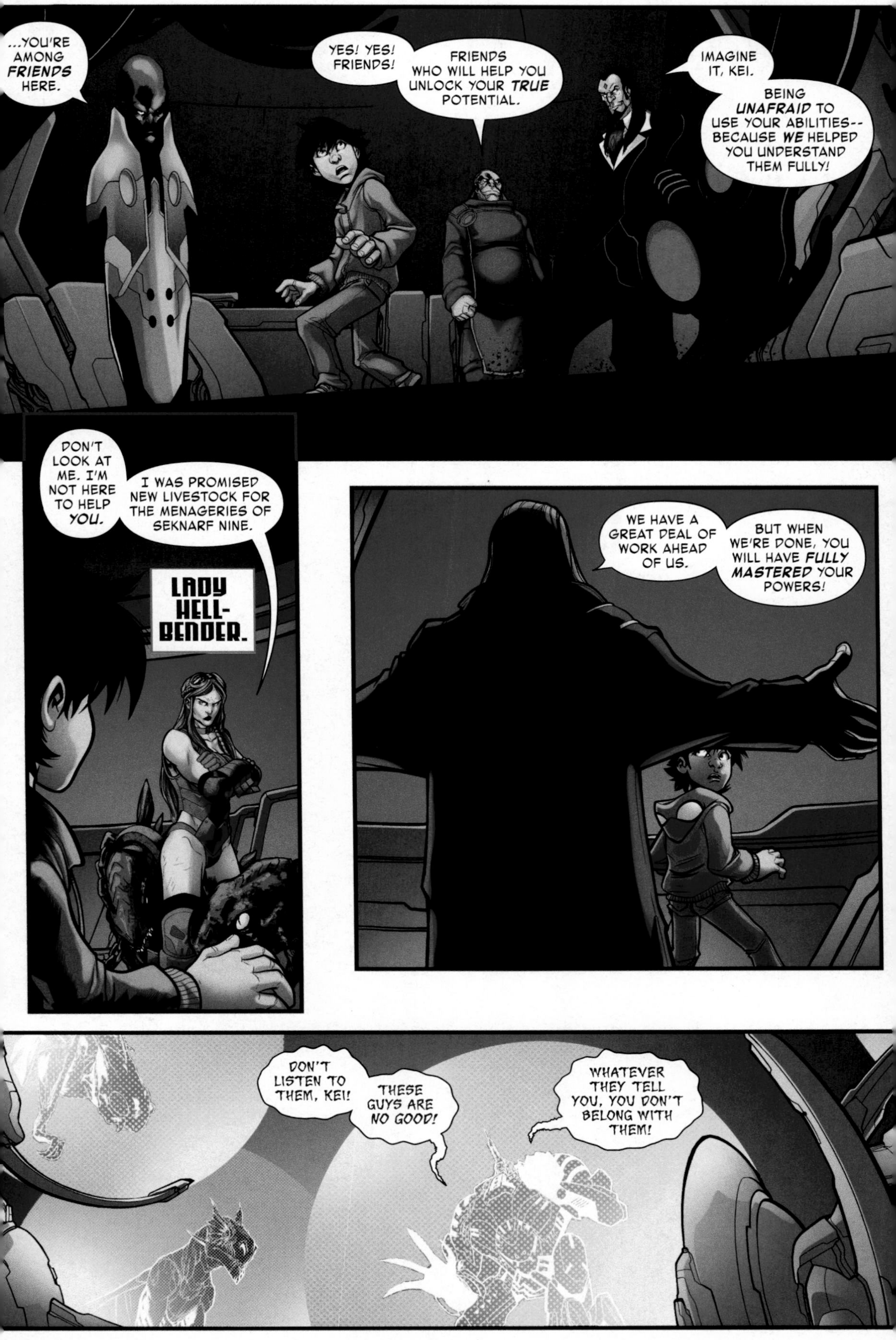
...YOU'RE AMONG FRIENDS HERE.
YES! YES! FRIENDS!
FRIENDS WHO WILL HELP YOU UNLOCK YOUR TRUE POTENTIAL.
IMAGINE IT, KEI.
BEING UNAFRAID TO USE YOUR ABILITIES--BECAUSE WE HELPED YOU UNDERSTAND THEM FULLY!
DON'T LOOK AT ME. I'M NOT HERE TO HELP YOU.
I WAS PROMISED NEW LIVESTOCK FOR THE MENAGERIES OF SEKNARF NINE.
LADY HELL-BENDER.
WE HAVE A GREAT DEAL OF WORK AHEAD OF US.
BUT WHEN WE'RE DONE, YOU WILL HAVE FULLY MASTERED YOUR POWERS!
DON'T LISTEN TO THEM, KEI!
THESE GUYS ARE NO GOOD!
WHATEVER THEY TELL YOU, YOU DON'T BELONG WITH THEM!

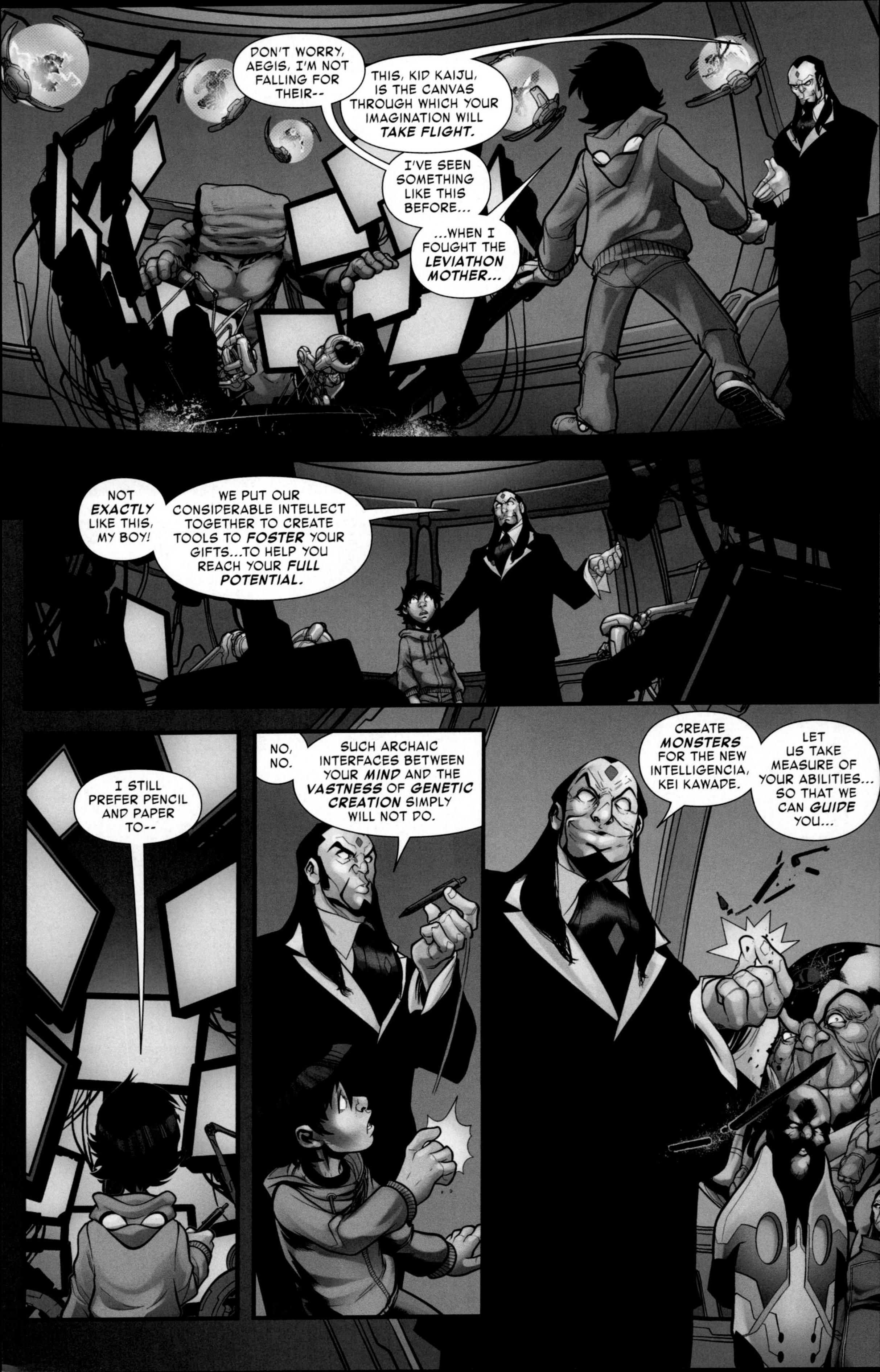
DON'T WORRY, AEGIS, I'M NOT FALLING FOR THEIR--
THIS, KID KAIJU, IS THE CANVAS THROUGH WHICH YOUR IMAGINATION WILL TAKE FLIGHT.
I'VE SEEN SOMETHING LIKE THIS BEFORE...
...WHEN I FOUGHT THE LEVIATHON MOTHER...
NOT EXACTLY LIKE THIS, MY BOY!
WE PUT OUR CONSIDERABLE INTELLECT TOGETHER TO CREATE TOOLS TO FOSTER YOUR GIFTS...TO HELP YOU REACH YOUR FULL POTENTIAL.
I STILL PREFER PENCIL AND PAPER TO--
NO, NO.
SUCH ARCHAIC INTERFACES BETWEEN YOUR MIND AND THE VASTNESS OF GENETIC CREATION SIMPLY WILL NOT DO.
CREATE MONSTERS FOR THE NEW INTELLIGENCIA, KEI KAWADE.
LET US TAKE MEASURE OF YOUR ABILITIES... SO THAT WE CAN GUIDE YOU...

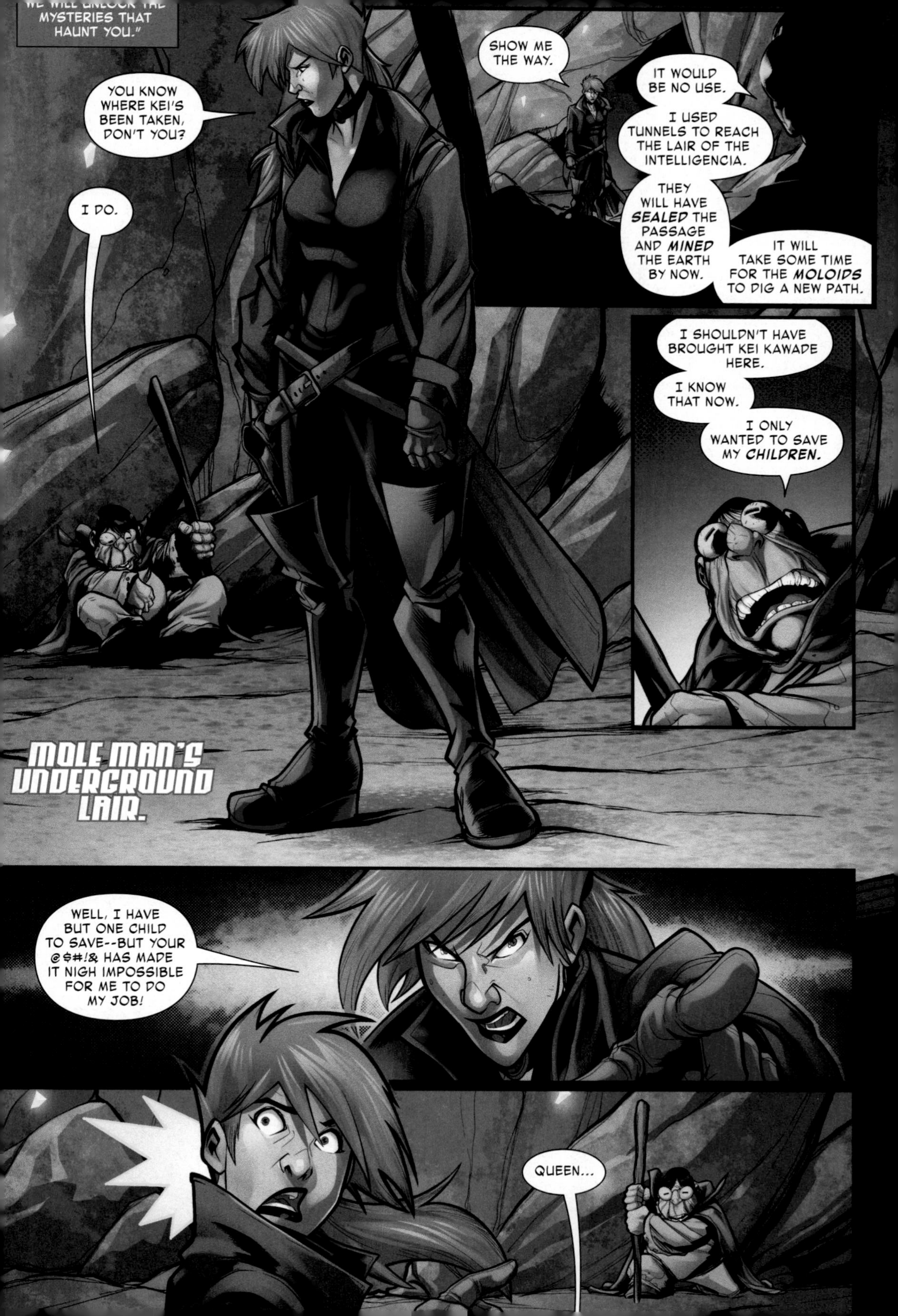
MYSTERIES THAT HAUNT YOU."
YOU KNOW WHERE KEI'S BEEN TAKEN, DON'T YOU?
I DO.
SHOW ME THE WAY.
IT WOULD BE NO USE.
I USED TUNNELS TO REACH THE LAIR OF THE INTELLIGENCIA.
THEY WILL HAVE SEALED THE PASSAGE AND MINED THE EARTH BY NOW.
IT WILL TAKE SOME TIME FOR THE MOLOIDS TO DIG A NEW PATH.
I SHOULDN'T HAVE BROUGHT KEI KAWADE HERE.
I KNOW THAT NOW.
I ONLY WANTED TO SAVE MY CHILDREN.
MOLE MAN'S UNDERGROUND LAIR.
WELL, I HAVE BUT ONE CHILD TO SAVE--BUT YOUR @$#!& HAS MADE IT NIGH IMPOSSIBLE FOR ME TO DO MY JOB!
QUEEN...

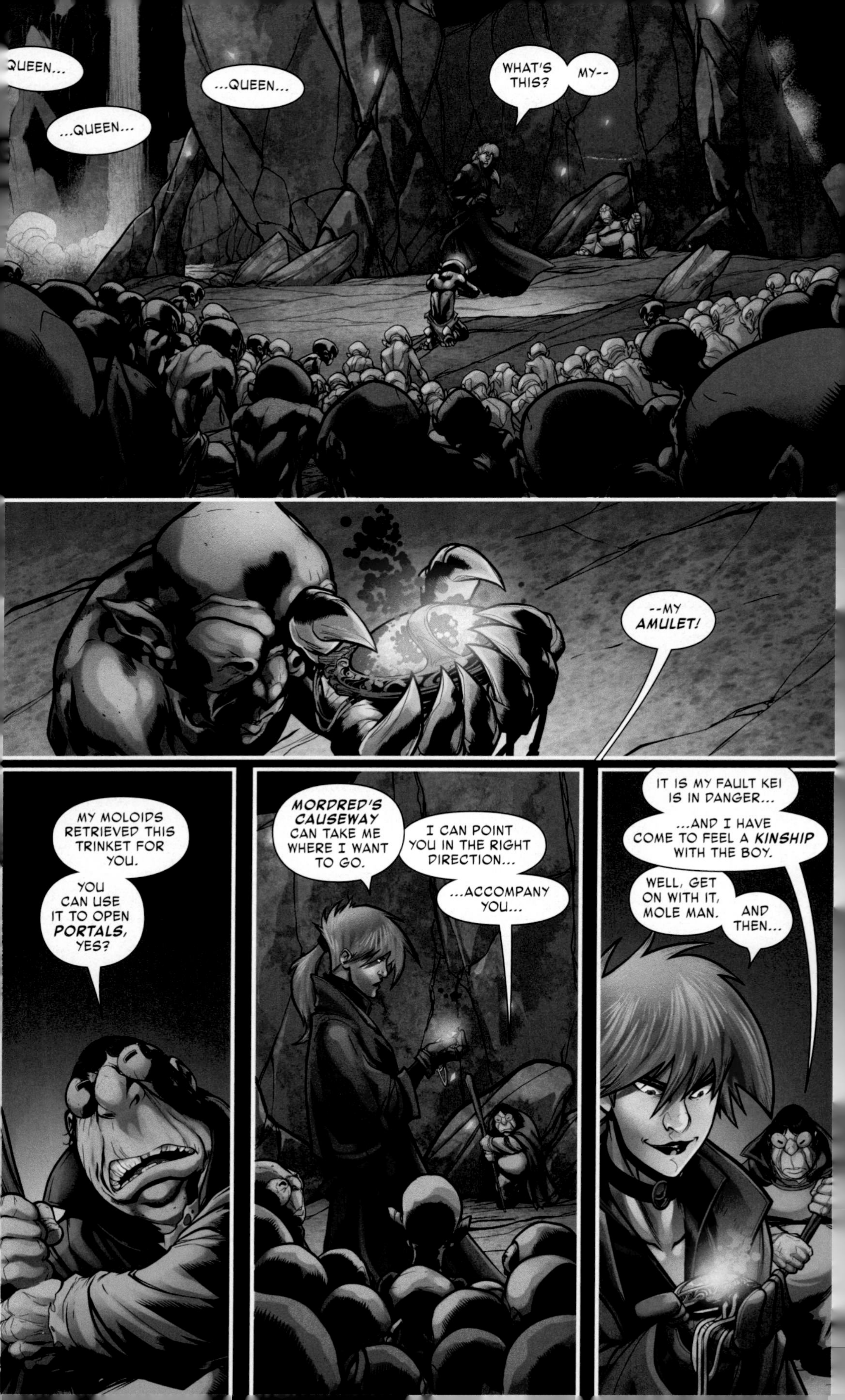
QUEEN...
...QUEEN...
...QUEEN...
WHAT'S THIS?
MY--
--MY AMULET!
MY MOLOIDS RETRIEVED THIS TRINKET FOR YOU.
YOU CAN USE IT TO OPEN PORTALS, YES?
MORDRED'S CAUSEWAY CAN TAKE ME WHERE I WANT TO GO.
I CAN POINT YOU IN THE RIGHT DIRECTION...
...ACCOMPANY YOU...
IT IS MY FAULT KEI IS IN DANGER...
...AND I HAVE COME TO FEEL A KINSHIP WITH THE BOY.
WELL, GET ON WITH IT, MOLE MAN.
AND THEN...

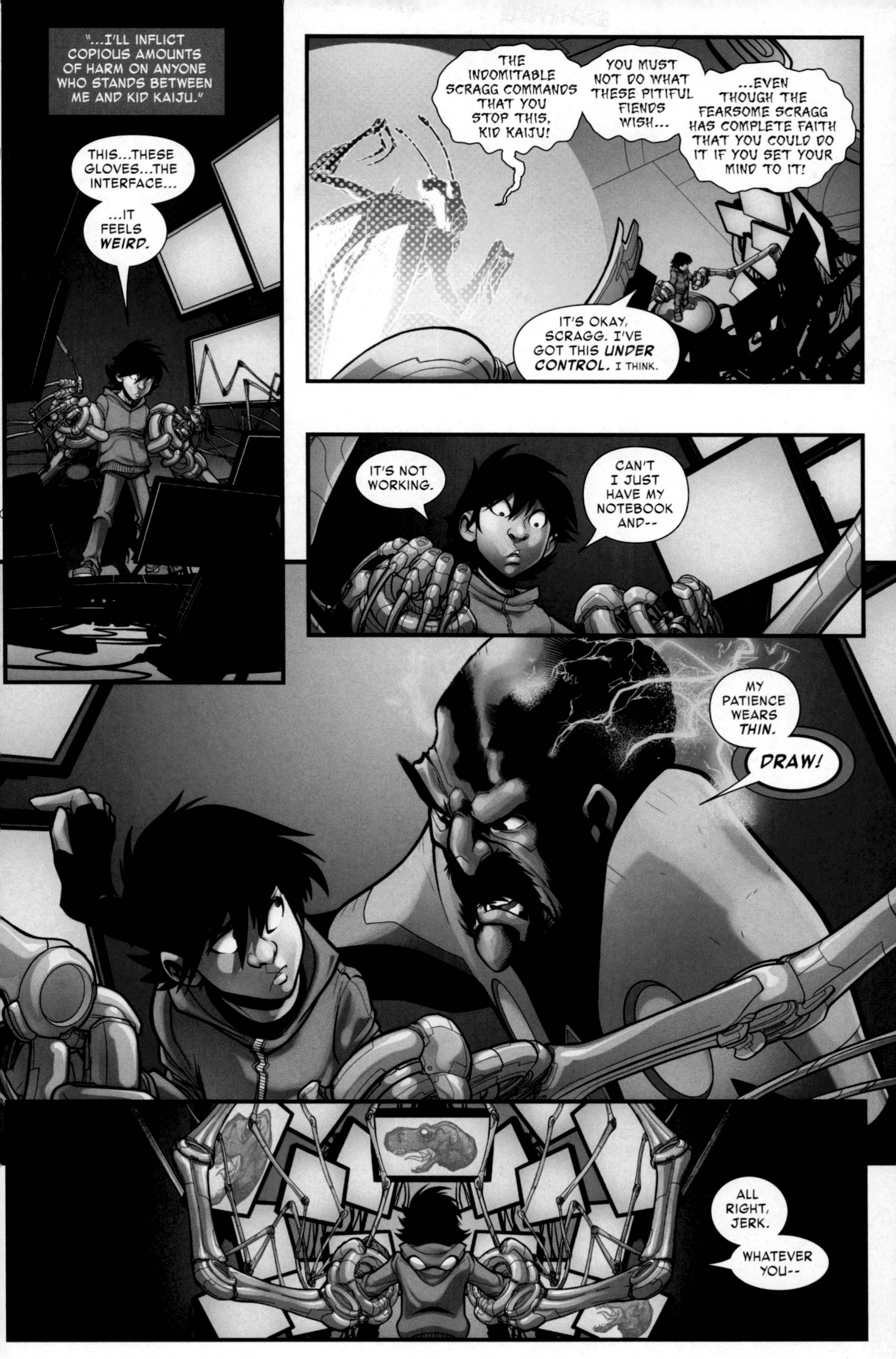
"...I'LL INFLICT COPIOUS AMOUNTS OF HARM ON ANYONE WHO STANDS BETWEEN ME AND KID KAIJU."
THIS...THESE GLOVES...THE INTERFACE...
...IT FEELS WEIRD.
THE INDOMITABLE SCRAGG COMMANDS THAT YOU STOP THIS, KID KAIJU!
YOU MUST NOT DO WHAT THESE PITIFUL FIENDS WISH...
...EVEN THOUGH THE FEARSOME SCRAGG HAS COMPLETE FAITH THAT YOU COULD DO IT IF YOU SET YOUR MIND TO IT!
IT'S OKAY, SCRAGG. I'VE GOT THIS UNDER CONTROL. I THINK.
IT'S NOT WORKING.
CAN'T I JUST HAVE MY NOTEBOOK AND--
MY PATIENCE WEARS THIN.
DRAW!
ALL RIGHT, JERK.
WHATEVER YOU--

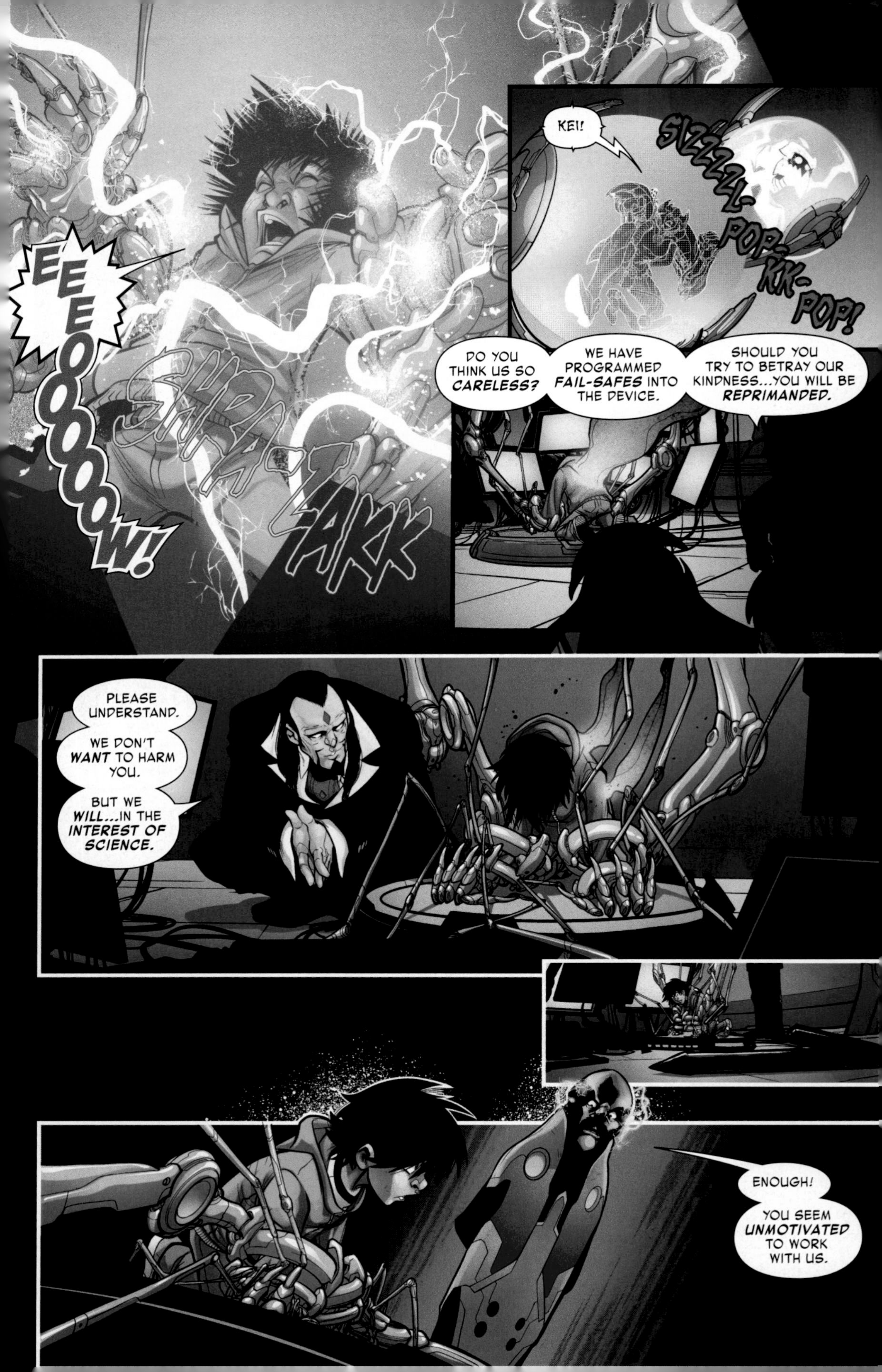

EEEOOOOOOOW!
SHRA-ZAKK
KEI!
SIZZZZL-POP-KK-POP!
DO YOU THINK US SO CARELESS?
WE HAVE PROGRAMMED FAIL-SAFES INTO THE DEVICE.
SHOULD YOU TRY TO BETRAY OUR KINDNESS...YOU WILL BE REPRIMANDED.
PLEASE UNDERSTAND.
WE DON'T WANT TO HARM YOU.
BUT WE WILL...IN THE INTEREST OF SCIENCE.
ENOUGH!
YOU SEEM UNMOTIVATED TO WORK WITH US.

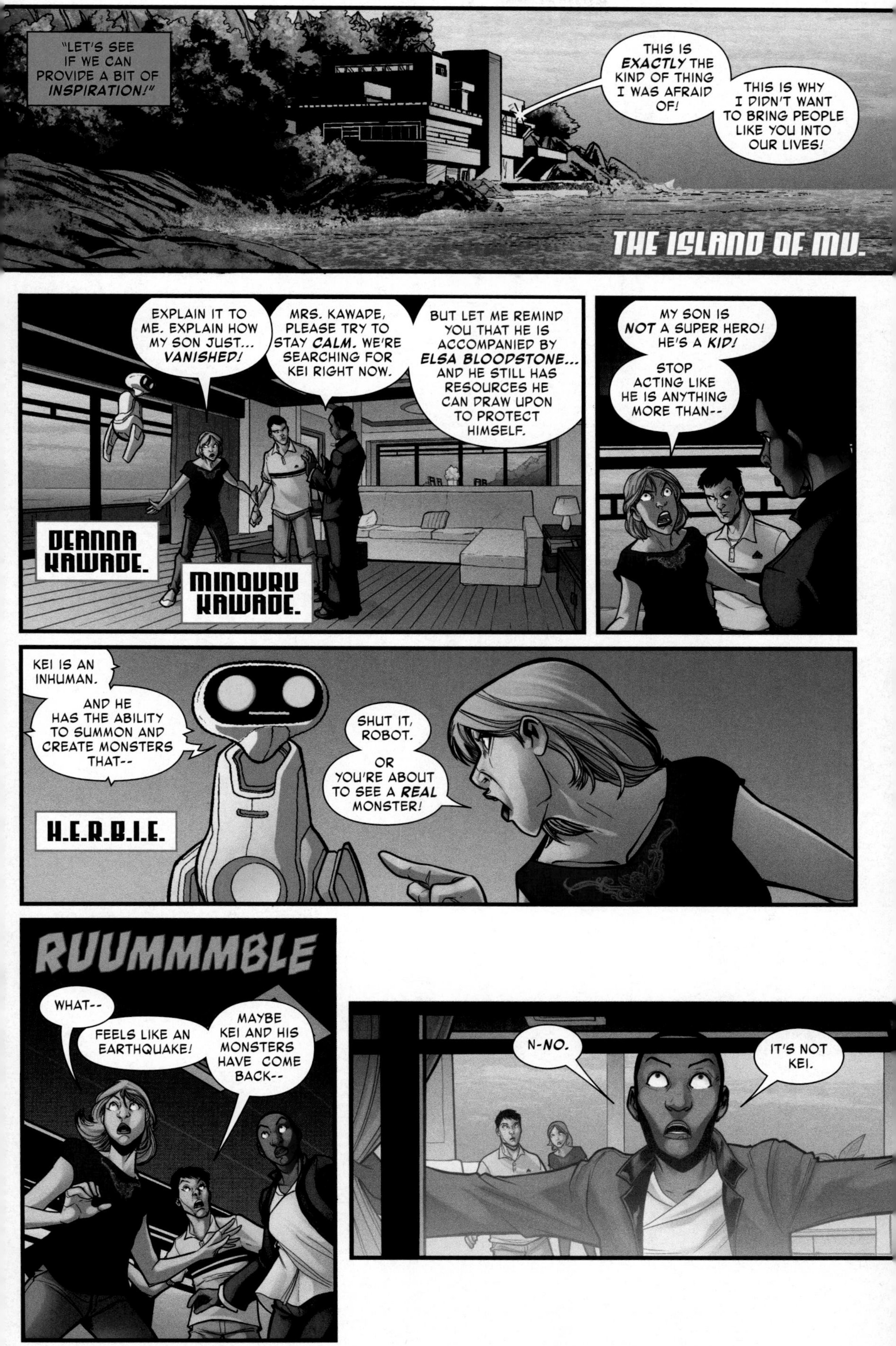
"LET'S SEE IF WE CAN PROVIDE A BIT OF *INSPIRATION!*"
THIS IS *EXACTLY* THE KIND OF THING I WAS AFRAID OF!
THIS IS WHY I DIDN'T WANT TO BRING PEOPLE LIKE YOU INTO OUR LIVES!
THE ISLAND OF MU.
EXPLAIN IT TO ME. EXPLAIN HOW MY SON JUST... *VANISHED!*
MRS. KAWADE, PLEASE TRY TO STAY *CALM.* WE'RE SEARCHING FOR KEI RIGHT NOW.
BUT LET ME REMIND YOU THAT HE IS ACCOMPANIED BY *ELSA BLOODSTONE...* AND HE STILL HAS RESOURCES HE CAN DRAW UPON TO PROTECT HIMSELF.
DEANNA KAWADE.
MINORU KAWADE.
MY SON IS *NOT* A SUPER HERO! HE'S A *KID!*
STOP ACTING LIKE HE IS ANYTHING MORE THAN--
KEI IS AN INHUMAN.
AND HE HAS THE ABILITY TO SUMMON AND CREATE MONSTERS THAT--
H.E.R.B.I.E.
SHUT IT, ROBOT.
OR YOU'RE ABOUT TO SEE A *REAL* MONSTER!
RUUMMMBLE
WHAT--
FEELS LIKE AN EARTHQUAKE!
MAYBE KEI AND HIS MONSTERS HAVE COME BACK--
N-*NO.*
IT'S NOT KEI.

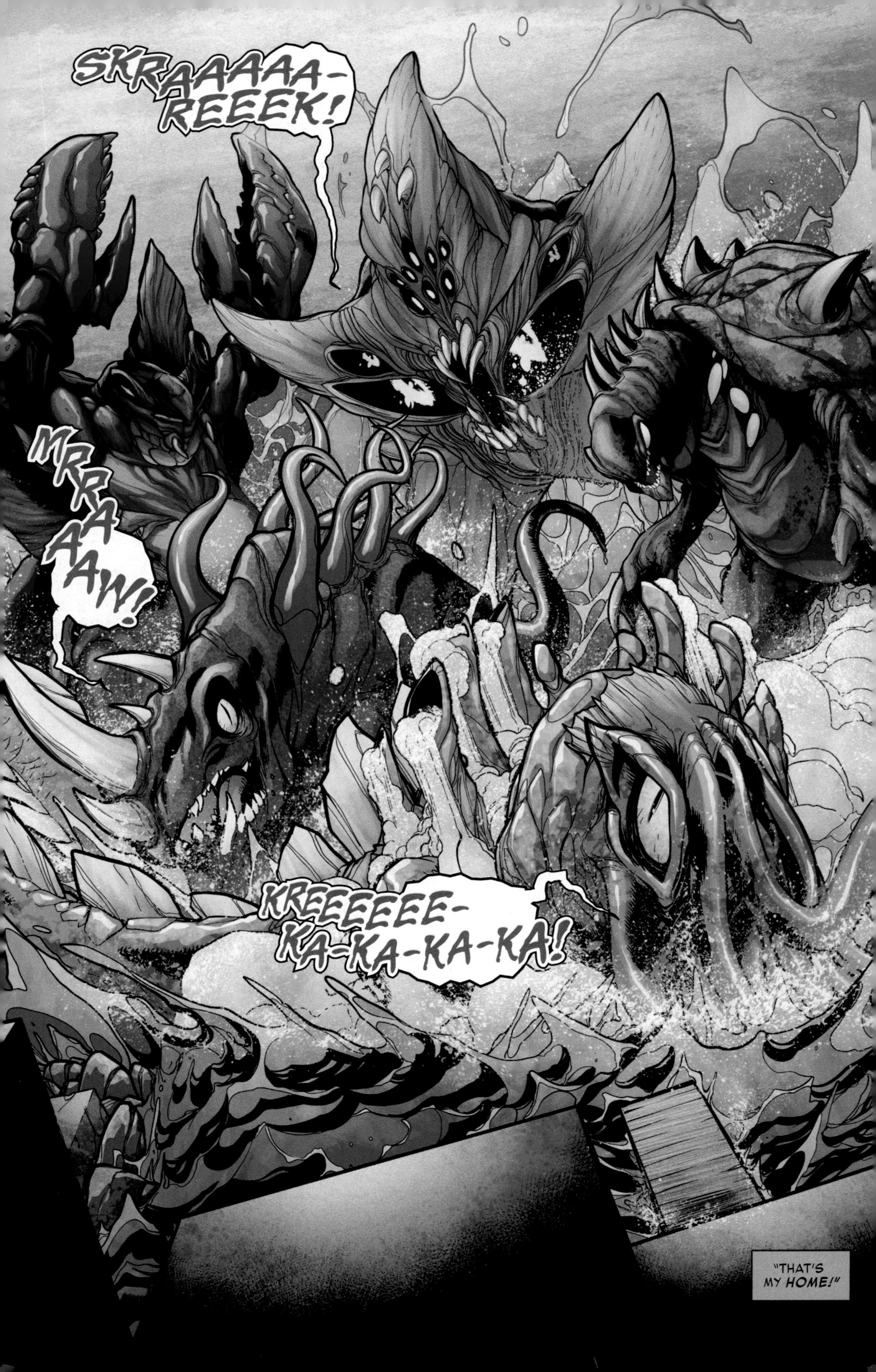
SKRAAAAA-REEEK!
MRRAAAW!
KREEEEEE-KA-KA-KA-KA!
"THAT'S MY *HOME!*"

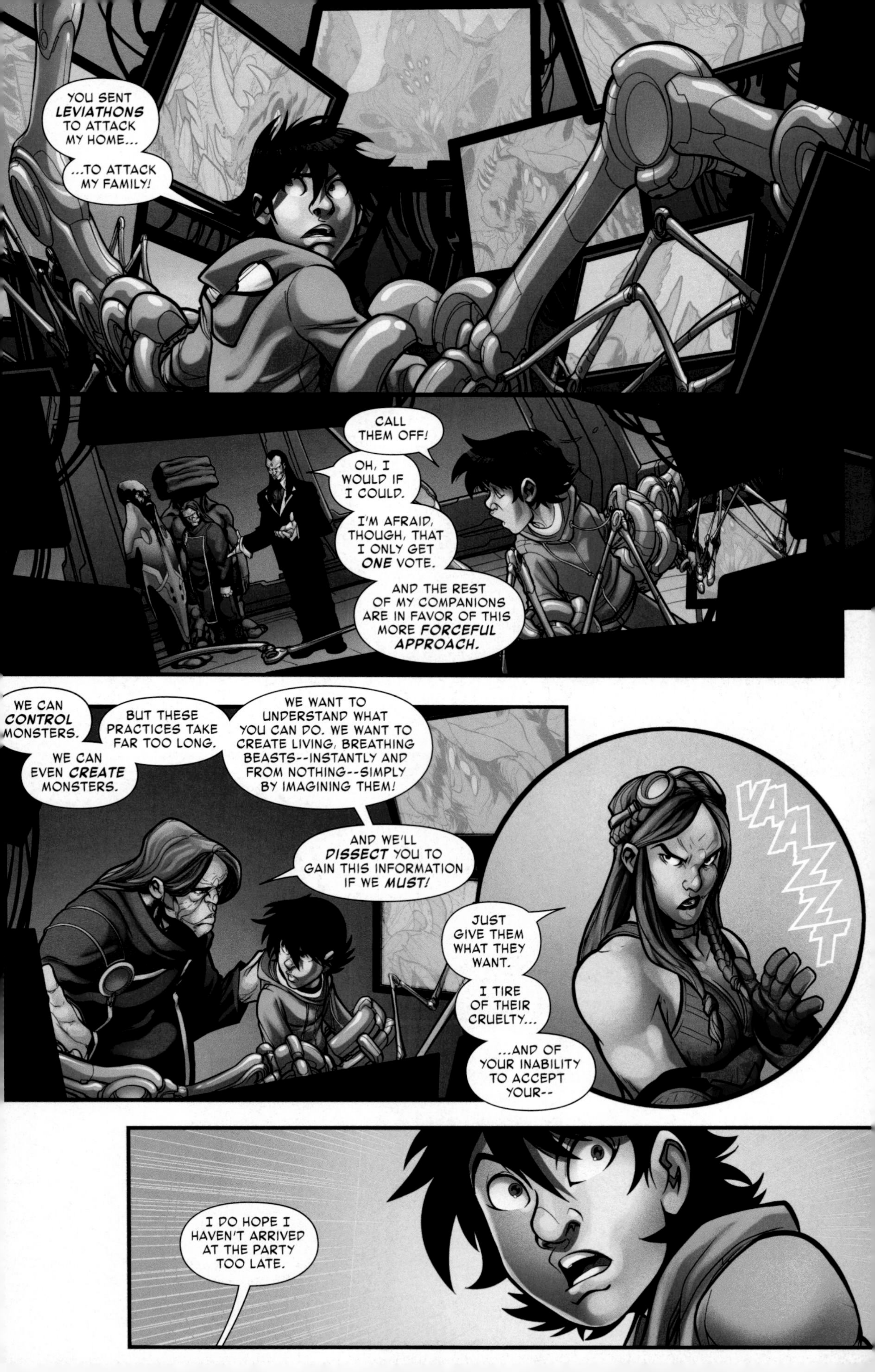
YOU SENT LEVIATHONS TO ATTACK MY HOME...
...TO ATTACK MY FAMILY!
CALL THEM OFF!
OH, I WOULD IF I COULD.
I'M AFRAID, THOUGH, THAT I ONLY GET ONE VOTE.
AND THE REST OF MY COMPANIONS ARE IN FAVOR OF THIS MORE FORCEFUL APPROACH.
WE CAN CONTROL MONSTERS.
WE CAN EVEN CREATE MONSTERS.
BUT THESE PRACTICES TAKE FAR TOO LONG.
WE WANT TO UNDERSTAND WHAT YOU CAN DO. WE WANT TO CREATE LIVING, BREATHING BEASTS--INSTANTLY AND FROM NOTHING--SIMPLY BY IMAGINING THEM!
AND WE'LL DISSECT YOU TO GAIN THIS INFORMATION IF WE MUST!
VAZZZT
JUST GIVE THEM WHAT THEY WANT.
I TIRE OF THEIR CRUELTY...
...AND OF YOUR INABILITY TO ACCEPT YOUR--
I DO HOPE I HAVEN'T ARRIVED AT THE PARTY TOO LATE.

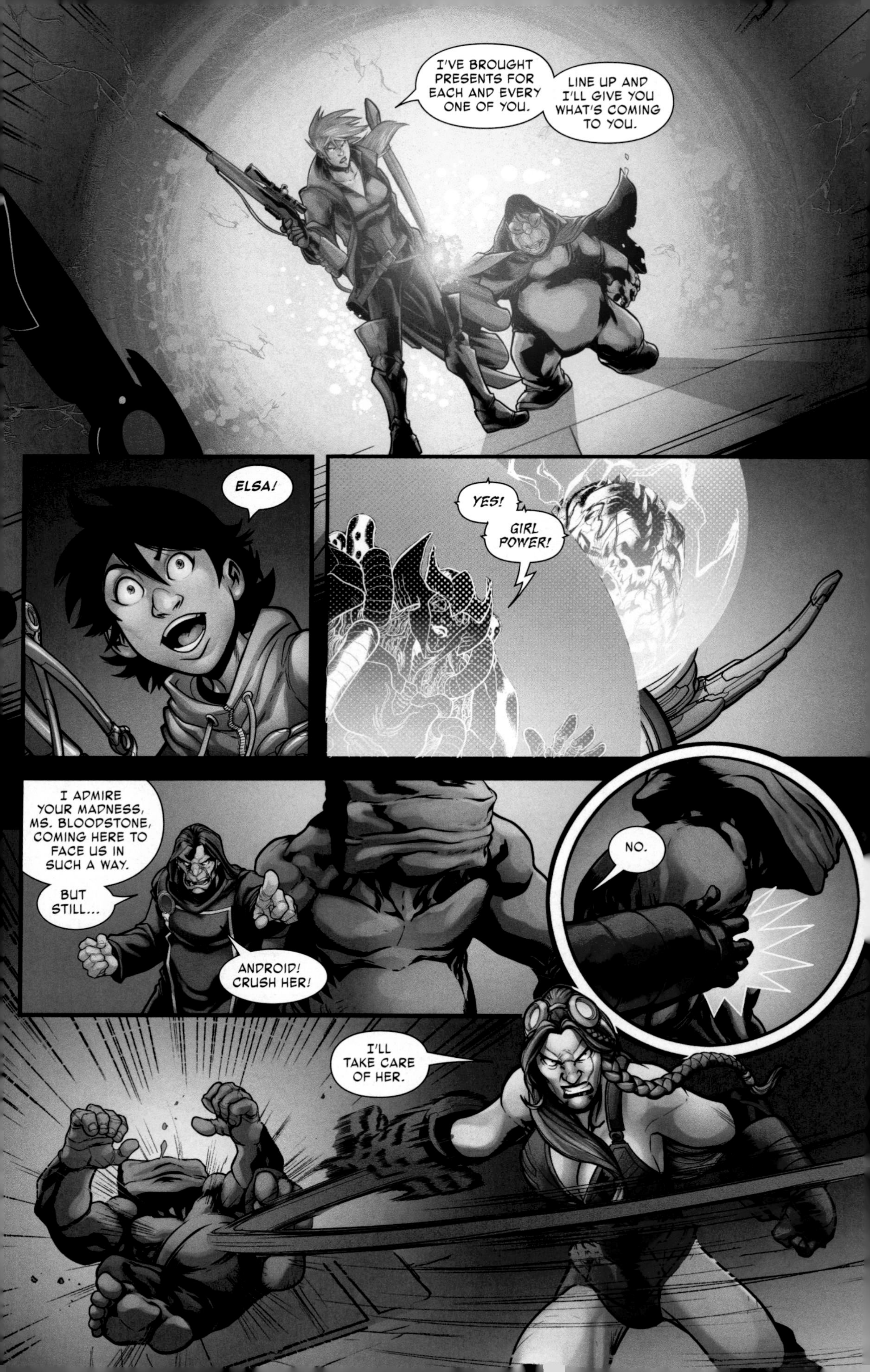
I'VE BROUGHT PRESENTS FOR EACH AND EVERY ONE OF YOU.
LINE UP AND I'LL GIVE YOU WHAT'S COMING TO YOU.
ELSA!
YES!
GIRL POWER!
I ADMIRE YOUR MADNESS, MS. BLOODSTONE, COMING HERE TO FACE US IN SUCH A WAY.
BUT STILL...
ANDROID! CRUSH HER!
NO.
I'LL TAKE CARE OF HER.

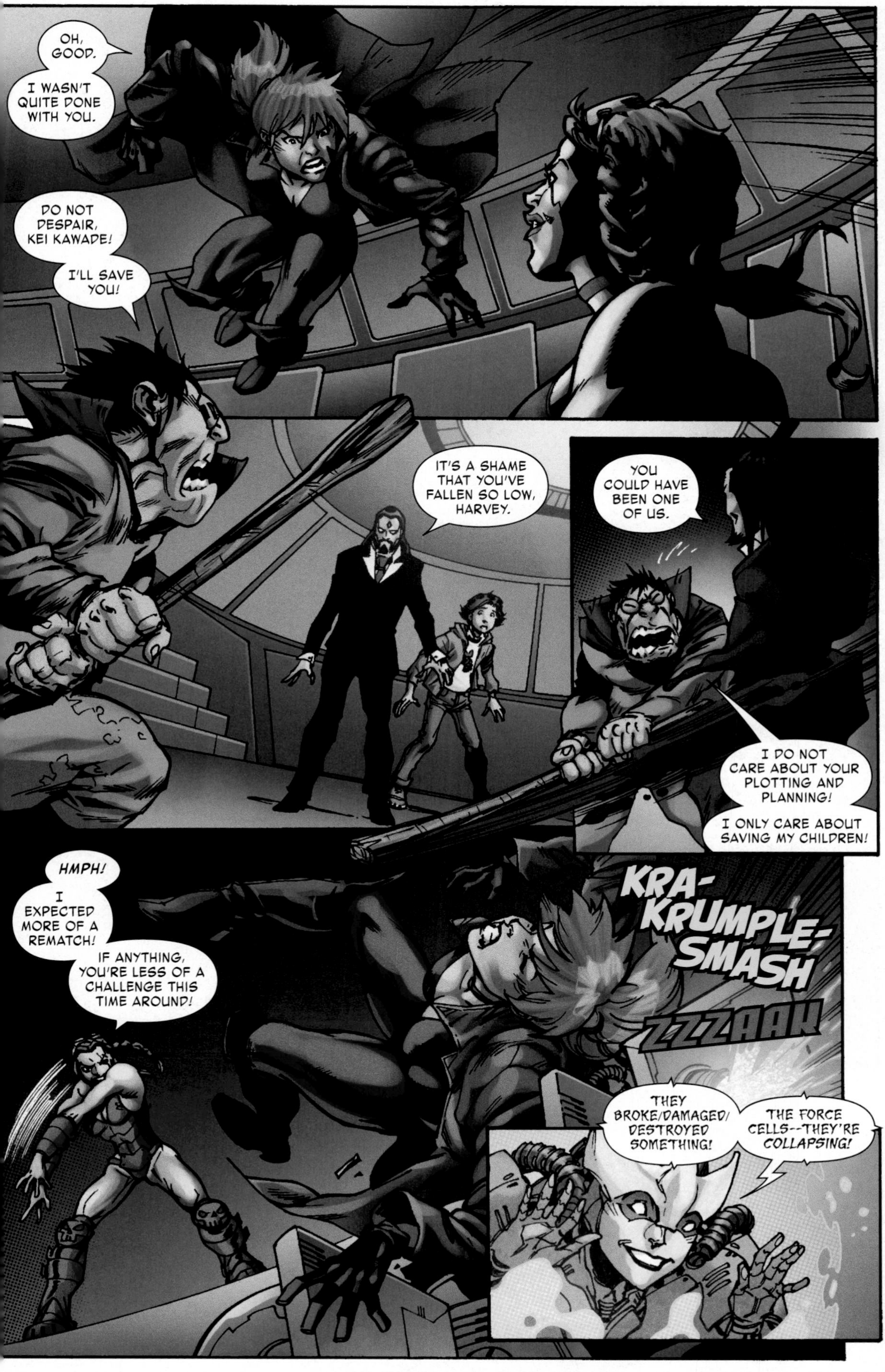
OH, GOOD.
I WASN'T QUITE DONE WITH YOU.
DO NOT DESPAIR, KEI KAWADE!
I'LL SAVE YOU!
IT'S A SHAME THAT YOU'VE FALLEN SO LOW, HARVEY.
YOU COULD HAVE BEEN ONE OF US.
I DO NOT CARE ABOUT YOUR PLOTTING AND PLANNING!
I ONLY CARE ABOUT SAVING MY CHILDREN!
HMPH!
I EXPECTED MORE OF A REMATCH!
IF ANYTHING, YOU'RE LESS OF A CHALLENGE THIS TIME AROUND!
KRA-KRUMPLE-SMASH
ZZZAAK
THEY BROKE/DAMAGED/ DESTROYED SOMETHING!
THE FORCE CELLS--THEY'RE COLLAPSING!

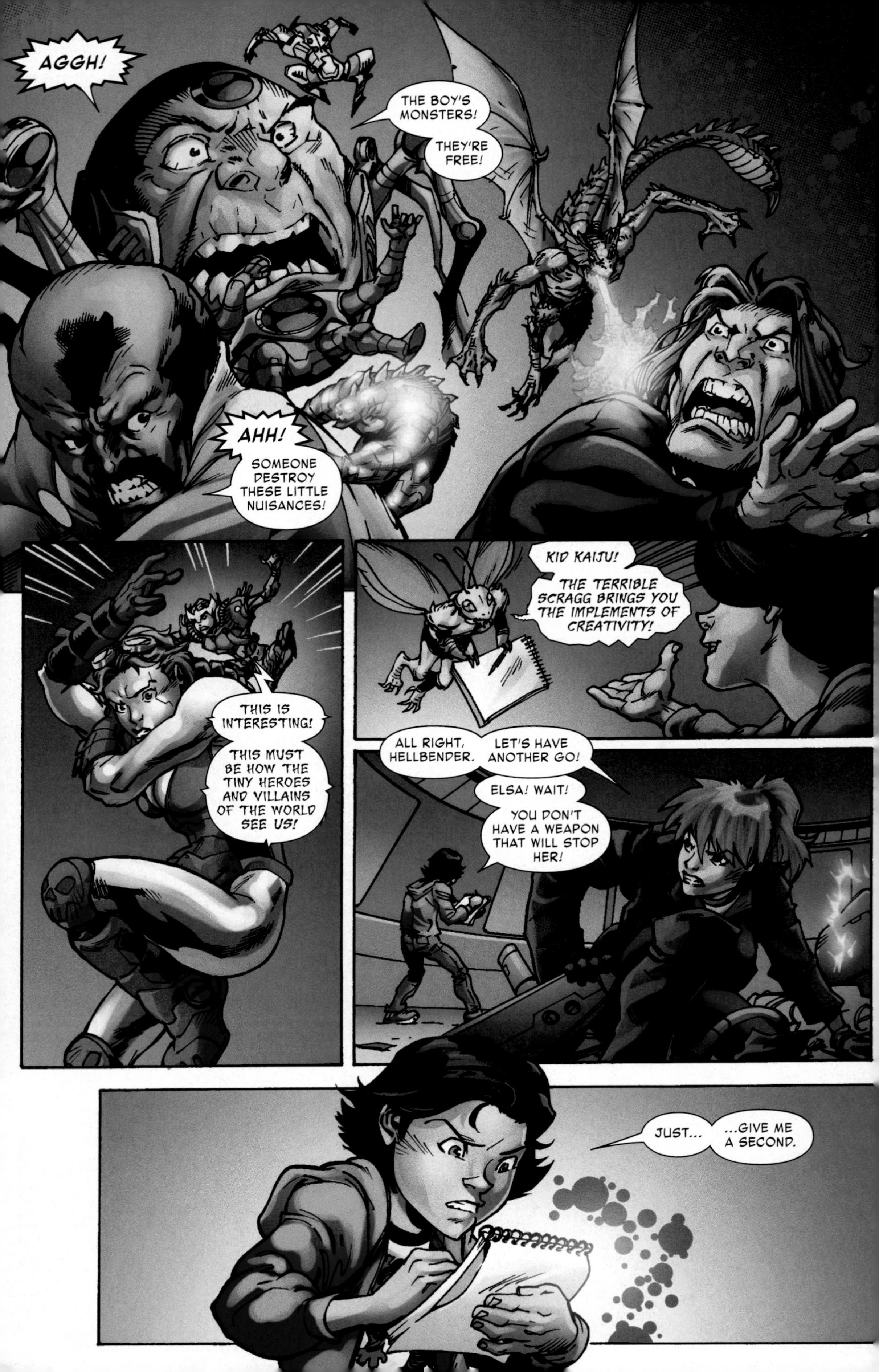
AGGH!
THE BOY'S MONSTERS!
THEY'RE FREE!
AHH!
SOMEONE DESTROY THESE LITTLE NUISANCES!
THIS IS INTERESTING!
THIS MUST BE HOW THE TINY HEROES AND VILLAINS OF THE WORLD SEE US!
KID KAIJU!
THE TERRIBLE SCRAGG BRINGS YOU THE IMPLEMENTS OF CREATIVITY!
ALL RIGHT, HELLBENDER.
LET'S HAVE ANOTHER GO!
ELSA! WAIT!
YOU DON'T HAVE A WEAPON THAT WILL STOP HER!
JUST...
...GIVE ME A SECOND.

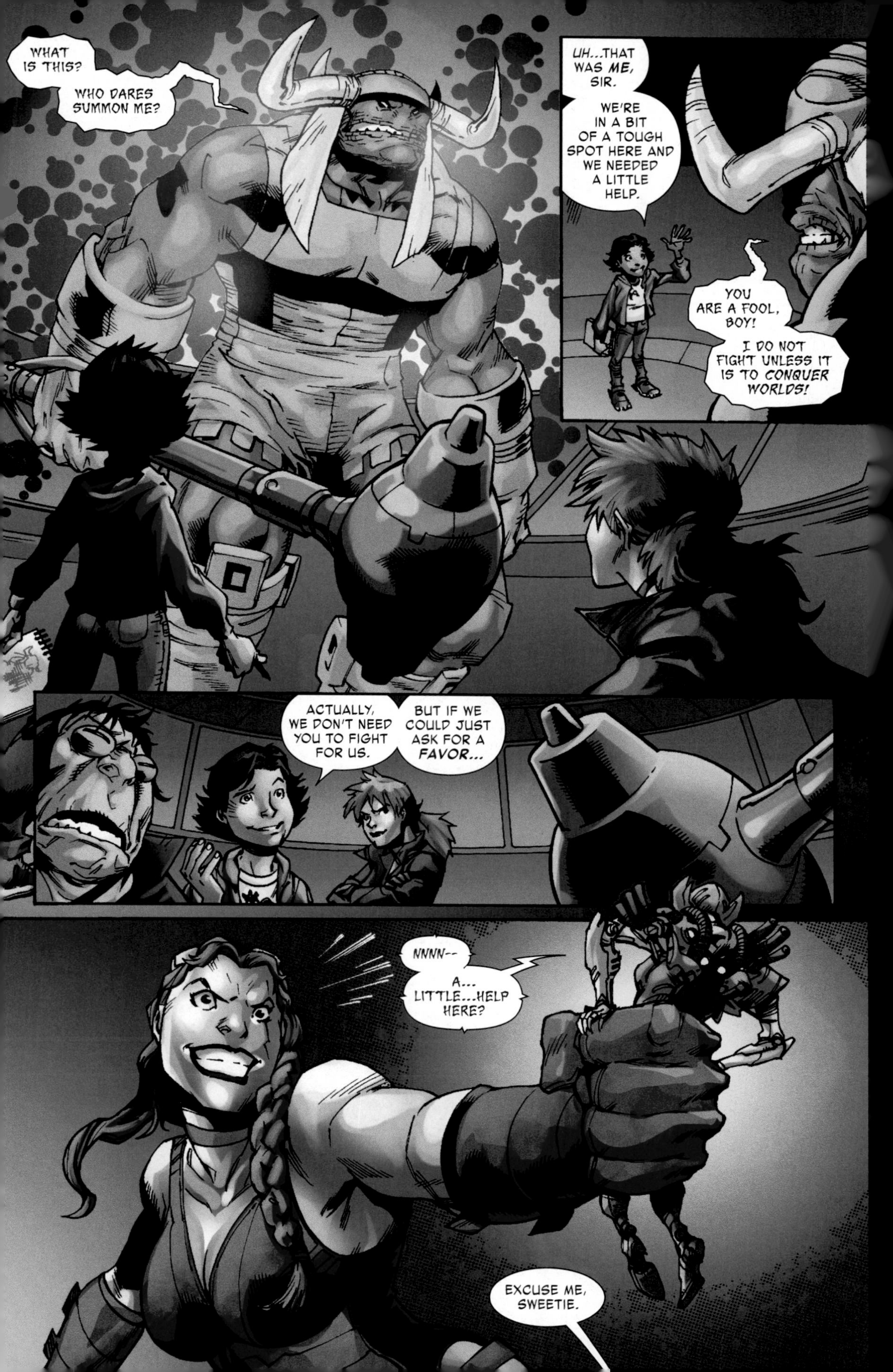
WHAT IS THIS?
WHO DARES SUMMON ME?
UH...THAT WAS ME, SIR.
WE'RE IN A BIT OF A TOUGH SPOT HERE AND WE NEEDED A LITTLE HELP.
YOU ARE A FOOL, BOY!
I DO NOT FIGHT UNLESS IT IS TO CONQUER WORLDS!
ACTUALLY, WE DON'T NEED YOU TO FIGHT FOR US.
BUT IF WE COULD JUST ASK FOR A FAVOR...
NNNN--
A... LITTLE...HELP HERE?
EXCUSE ME, SWEETIE.

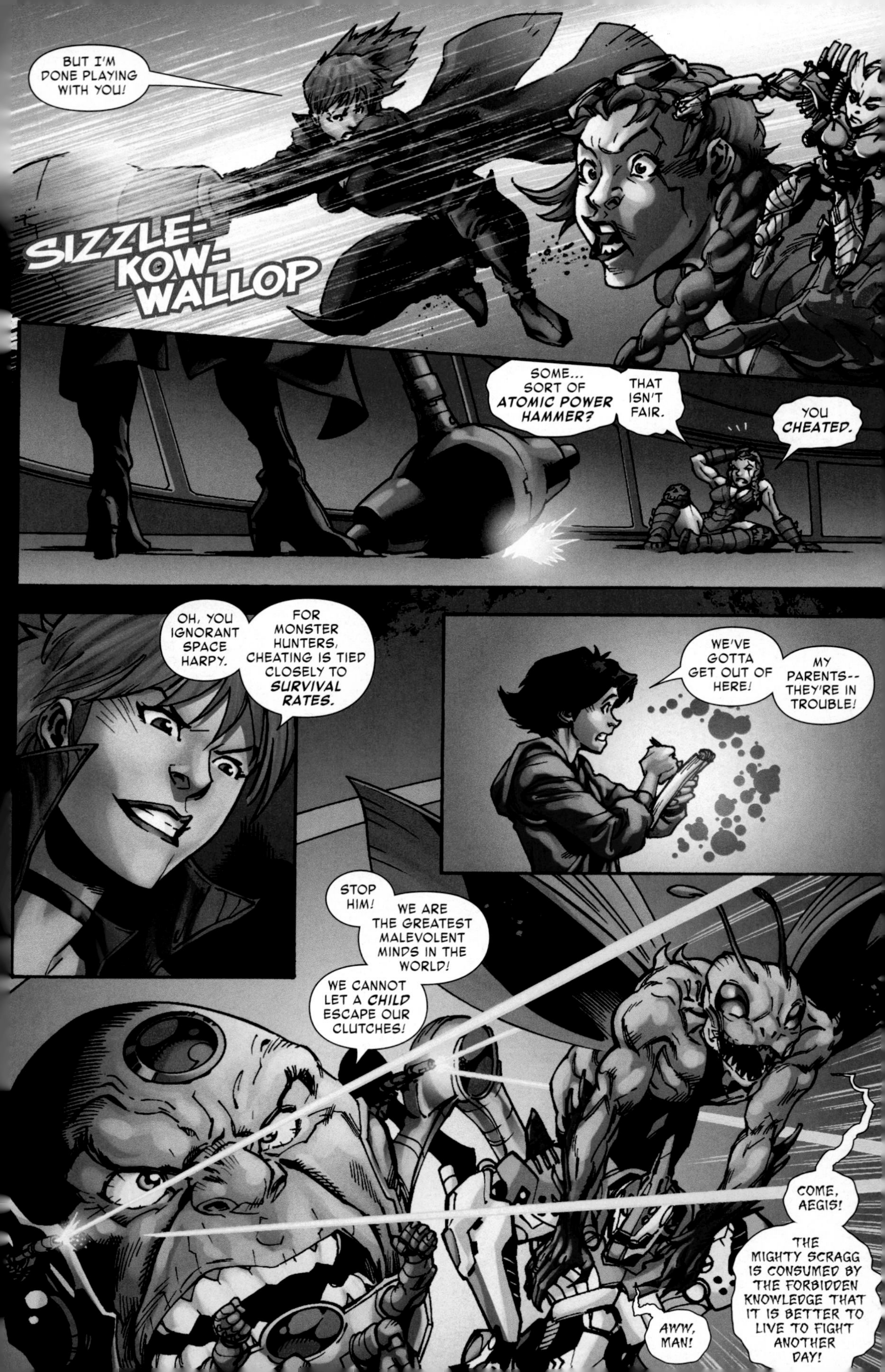
BUT I'M DONE PLAYING WITH YOU!
SIZZLE-KOW-WALLOP
SOME... SORT OF ATOMIC POWER HAMMER?
THAT ISN'T FAIR.
YOU CHEATED.
OH, YOU IGNORANT SPACE HARPY.
FOR MONSTER HUNTERS, CHEATING IS TIED CLOSELY TO SURVIVAL RATES.
WE'VE GOTTA GET OUT OF HERE!
MY PARENTS-- THEY'RE IN TROUBLE!
STOP HIM!
WE ARE THE GREATEST MALEVOLENT MINDS IN THE WORLD!
WE CANNOT LET A CHILD ESCAPE OUR CLUTCHES!
COME, AEGIS!
THE MIGHTY SCRAGG IS CONSUMED BY THE FORBIDDEN KNOWLEDGE THAT IT IS BETTER TO LIVE TO FIGHT ANOTHER DAY!
AWW, MAN!

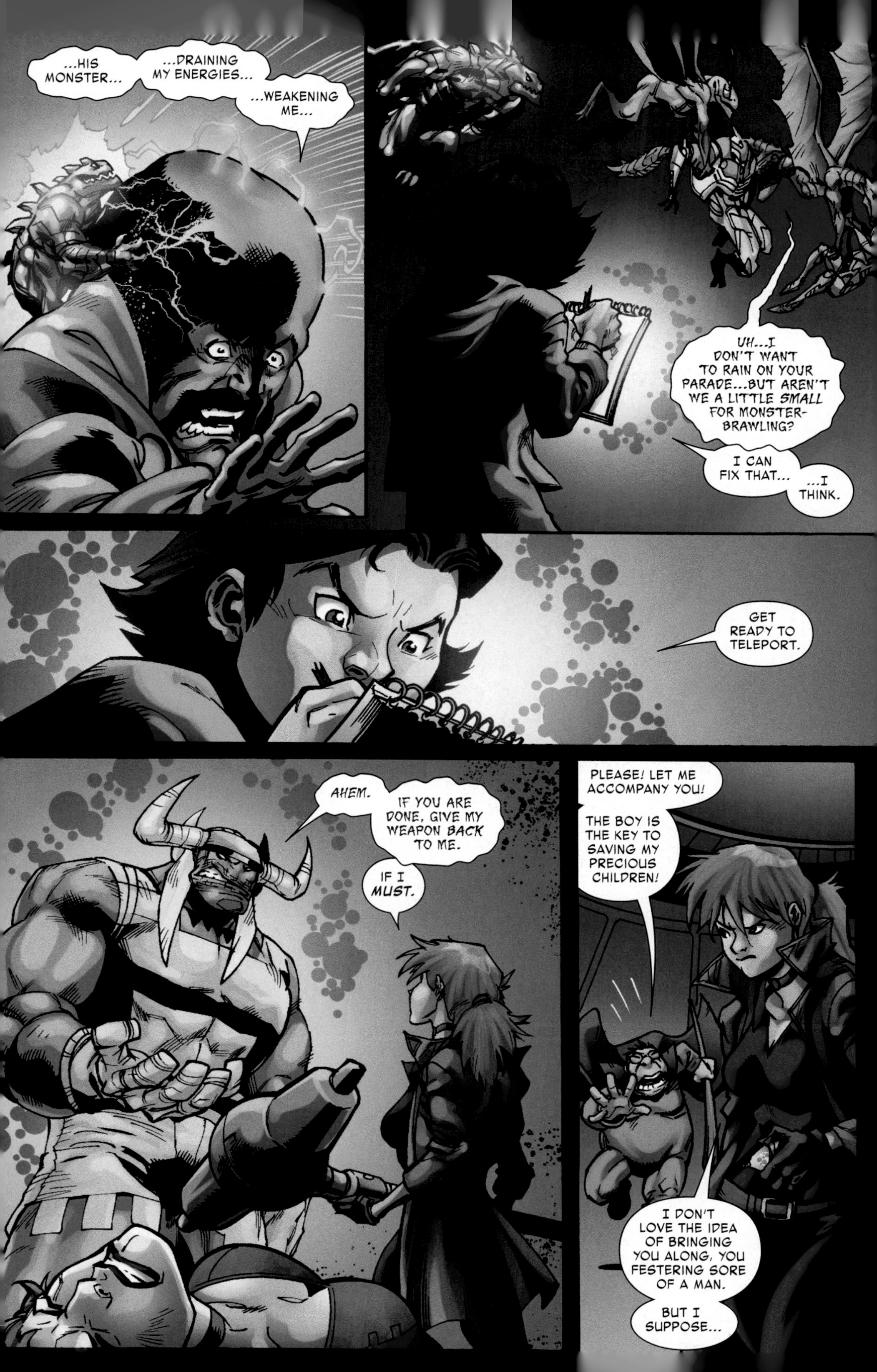
...HIS MONSTER...
...DRAINING MY ENERGIES...
...WEAKENING ME...
UH...I DON'T WANT TO RAIN ON YOUR PARADE...BUT AREN'T WE A LITTLE SMALL FOR MONSTER-BRAWLING?
I CAN FIX THAT...
...I THINK.
GET READY TO TELEPORT.
AHEM.
IF YOU ARE DONE, GIVE MY WEAPON BACK TO ME.
IF I MUST.
PLEASE! LET ME ACCOMPANY YOU!
THE BOY IS THE KEY TO SAVING MY PRECIOUS CHILDREN!
I DON'T LOVE THE IDEA OF BRINGING YOU ALONG, YOU FESTERING SORE OF A MAN.
BUT I SUPPOSE...

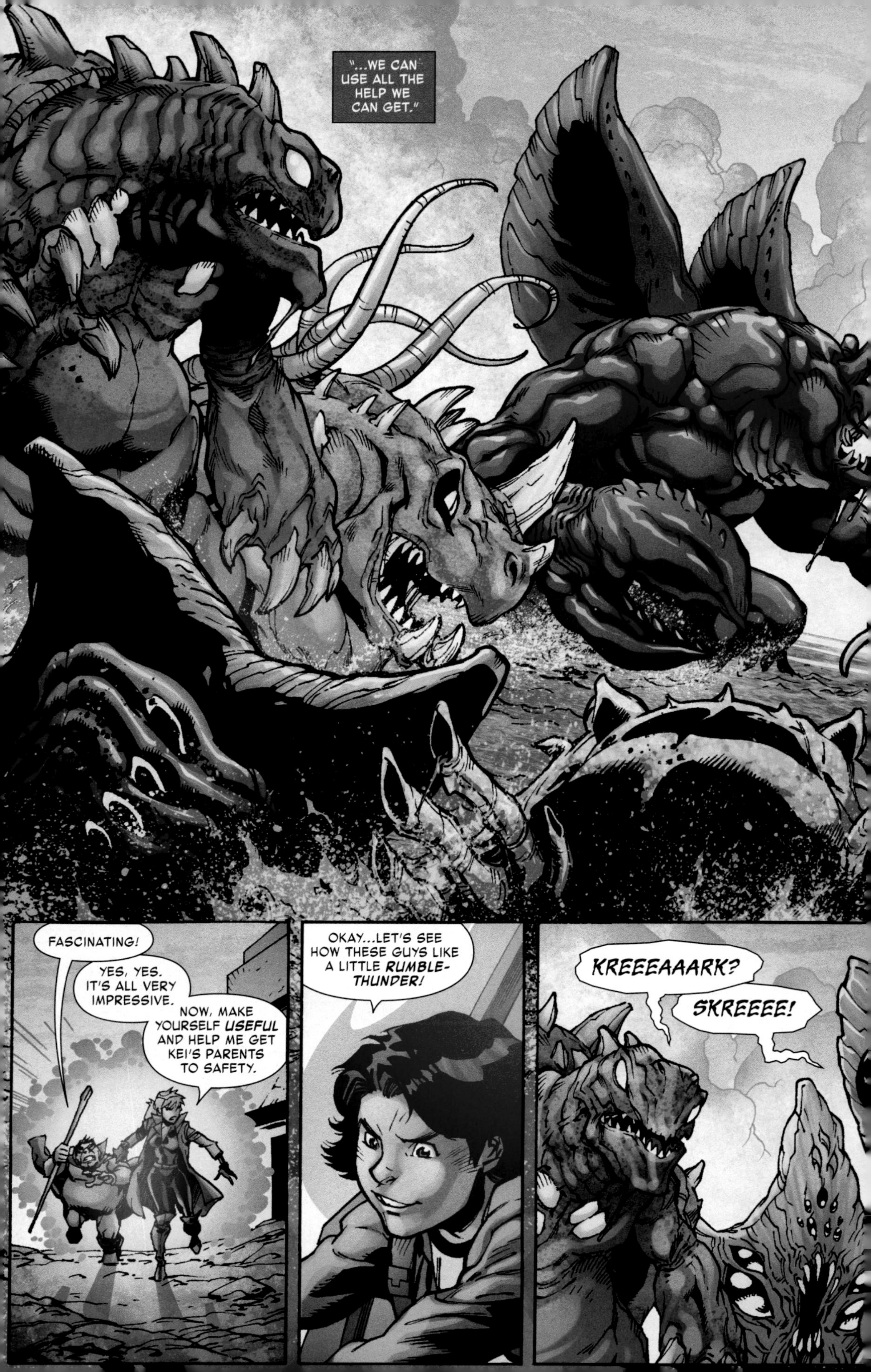
"...WE CAN USE ALL THE HELP WE CAN GET."
FASCINATING!
YES, YES. IT'S ALL VERY IMPRESSIVE.
NOW, MAKE YOURSELF USEFUL AND HELP ME GET KEI'S PARENTS TO SAFETY.
OKAY...LET'S SEE HOW THESE GUYS LIKE A LITTLE RUMBLE-THUNDER!
KREEEAAARK?
SKREEEE!

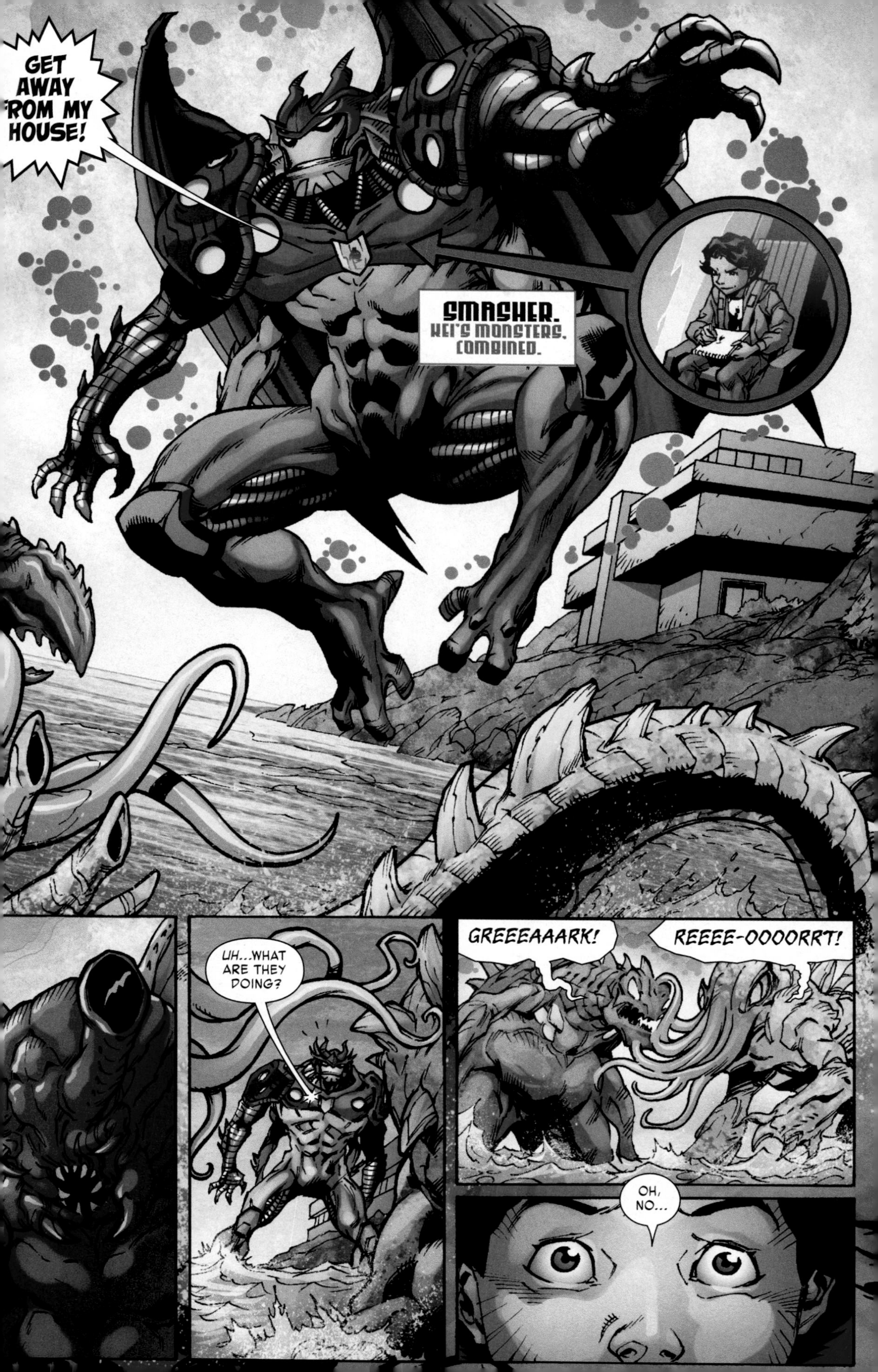

GET AWAY 'ROM MY HOUSE!
SMASHER. KEI'S MONSTERS, COMBINED.
UH...WHAT ARE THEY DOING?
GREEEAAARK!
REEEE-OOOORRT!
OH, NO...

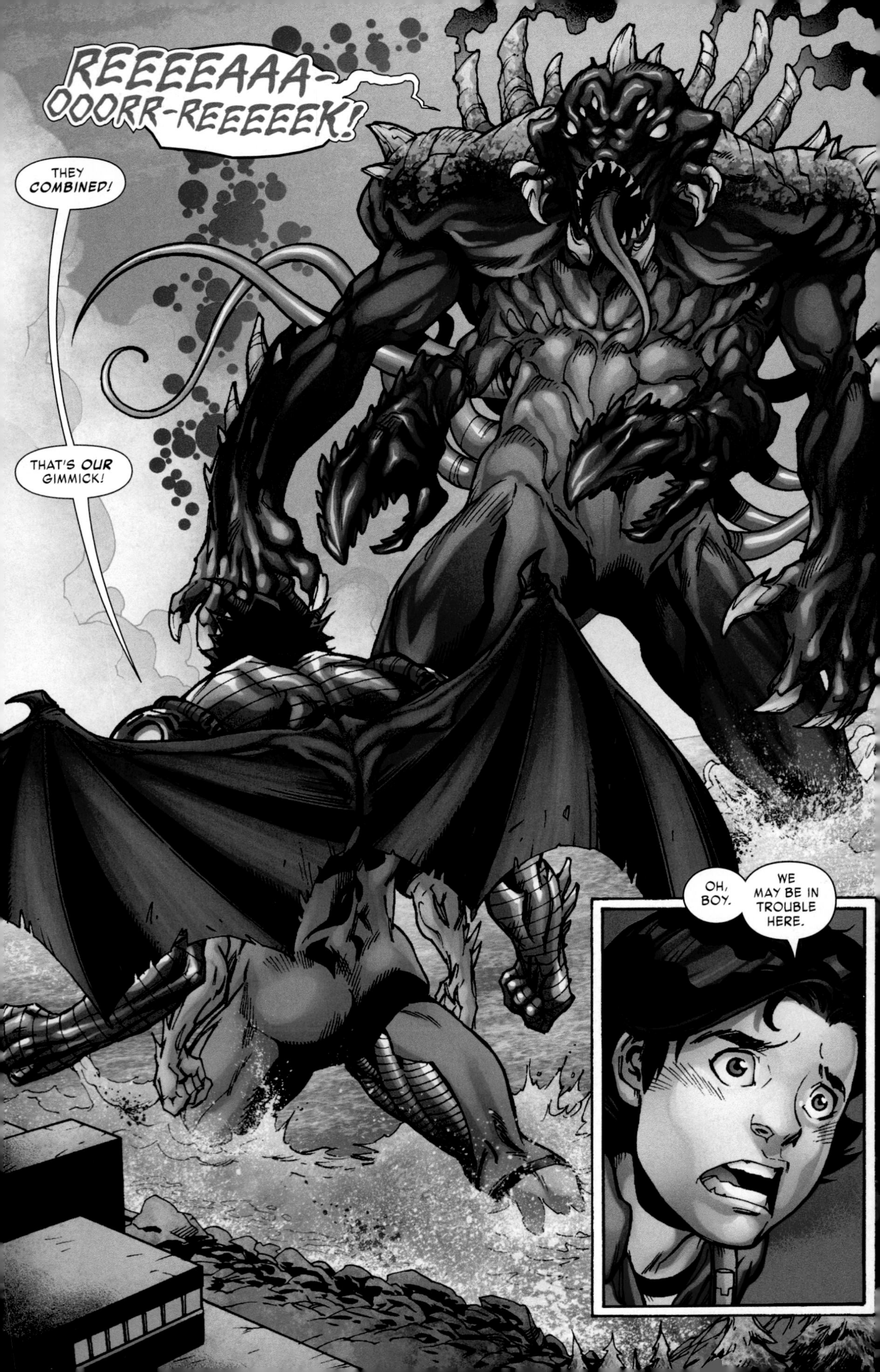
REEEEAAA-OOORR-REEEEEK!
THEY *COMBINED!*
THAT'S *OUR* GIMMICK!
OH, BOY.
WE MAY BE IN TROUBLE HERE.

#2 VARIANT BY
DAVID NAKAYAMA

#3 VARIANT BY
DAVID BALDEÓN &
ROMULO FAJARDO JR.

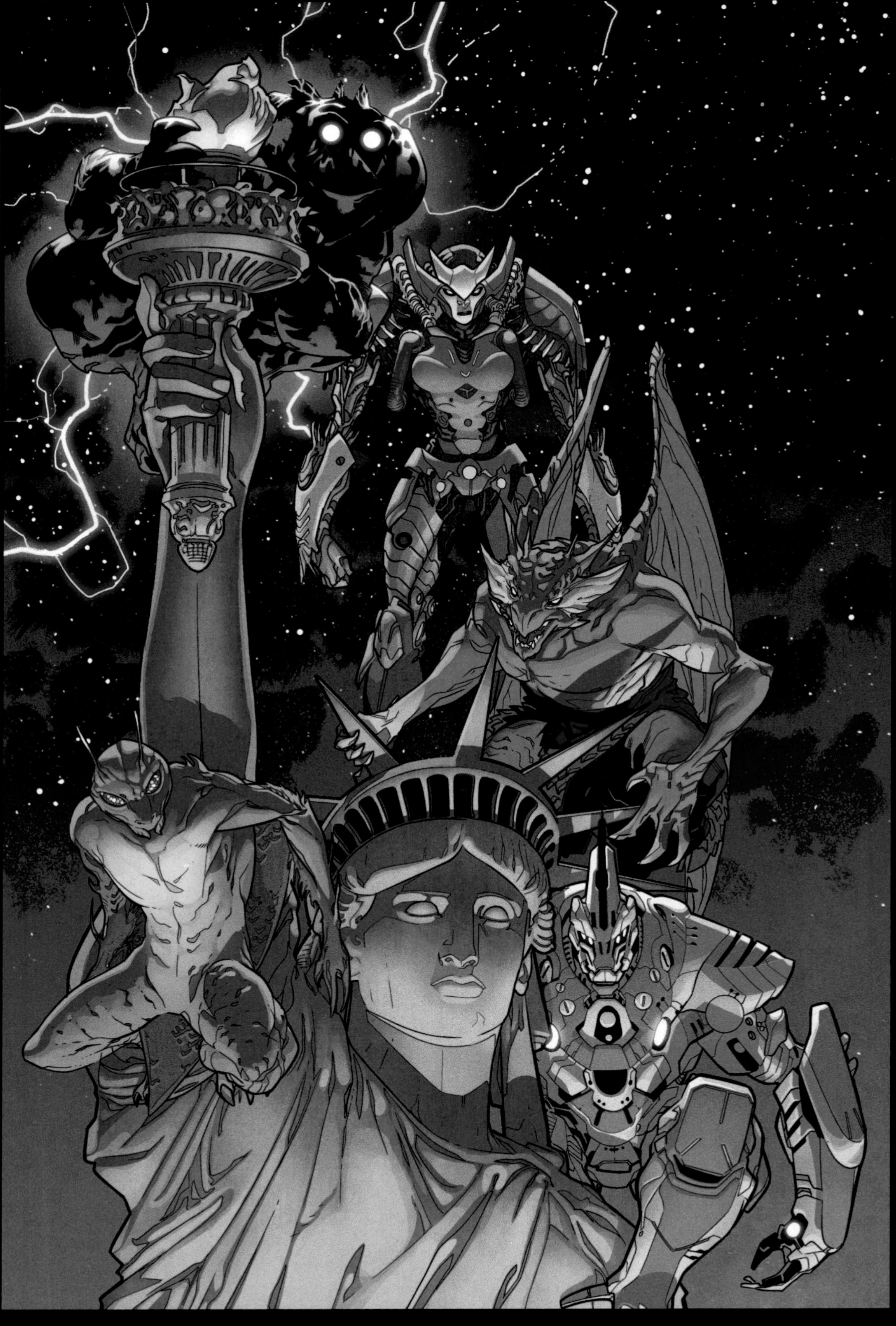

#5

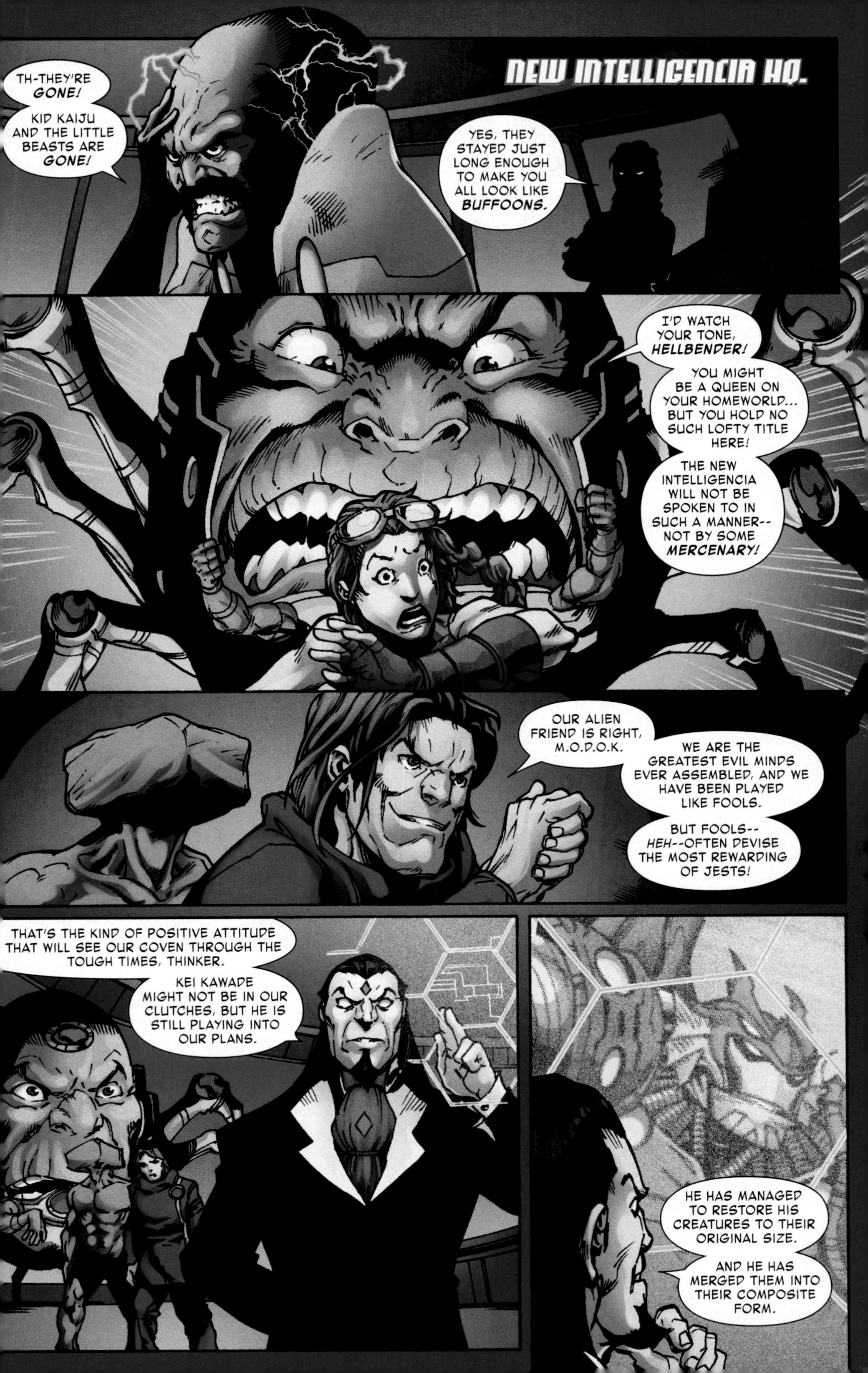
NEW INTELLIGENCIA HQ.
TH-THEY'RE GONE!
KID KAIJU AND THE LITTLE BEASTS ARE GONE!
YES, THEY STAYED JUST LONG ENOUGH TO MAKE YOU ALL LOOK LIKE BUFFOONS.
I'D WATCH YOUR TONE, HELLBENDER!
YOU MIGHT BE A QUEEN ON YOUR HOMEWORLD... BUT YOU HOLD NO SUCH LOFTY TITLE HERE!
THE NEW INTELLIGENCIA WILL NOT BE SPOKEN TO IN SUCH A MANNER-- NOT BY SOME MERCENARY!
OUR ALIEN FRIEND IS RIGHT, M.O.D.O.K.
WE ARE THE GREATEST EVIL MINDS EVER ASSEMBLED, AND WE HAVE BEEN PLAYED LIKE FOOLS.
BUT FOOLS-- HEH--OFTEN DEVISE THE MOST REWARDING OF JESTS!
THAT'S THE KIND OF POSITIVE ATTITUDE THAT WILL SEE OUR COVEN THROUGH THE TOUGH TIMES, THINKER.
KEI KAWADE MIGHT NOT BE IN OUR CLUTCHES, BUT HE IS STILL PLAYING INTO OUR PLANS.
HE HAS MANAGED TO RESTORE HIS CREATURES TO THEIR ORIGINAL SIZE.
AND HE HAS MERGED THEM INTO THEIR COMPOSITE FORM.

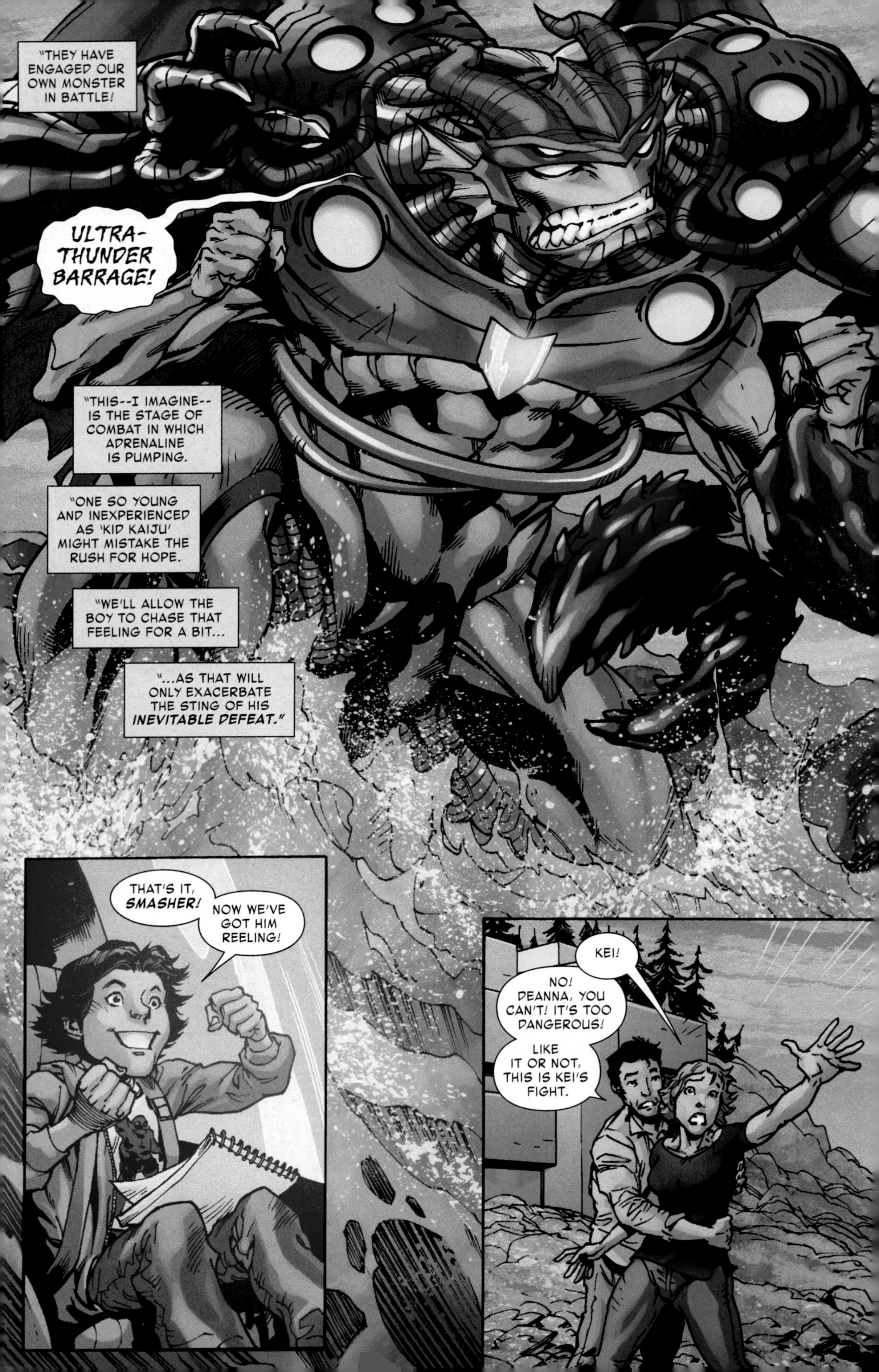
"THEY HAVE ENGAGED OUR OWN MONSTER IN BATTLE!
ULTRA-THUNDER BARRAGE!
"THIS--I IMAGINE--IS THE STAGE OF COMBAT IN WHICH ADRENALINE IS PUMPING.
"ONE SO YOUNG AND INEXPERIENCED AS 'KID KAIJU' MIGHT MISTAKE THE RUSH FOR HOPE.
"WE'LL ALLOW THE BOY TO CHASE THAT FEELING FOR A BIT...
"...AS THAT WILL ONLY EXACERBATE THE STING OF HIS INEVITABLE DEFEAT."
THAT'S IT, SMASHER!
NOW WE'VE GOT HIM REELING!
KEI!
NO! DEANNA, YOU CAN'T! IT'S TOO DANGEROUS!
LIKE IT OR NOT, THIS IS KEI'S FIGHT.

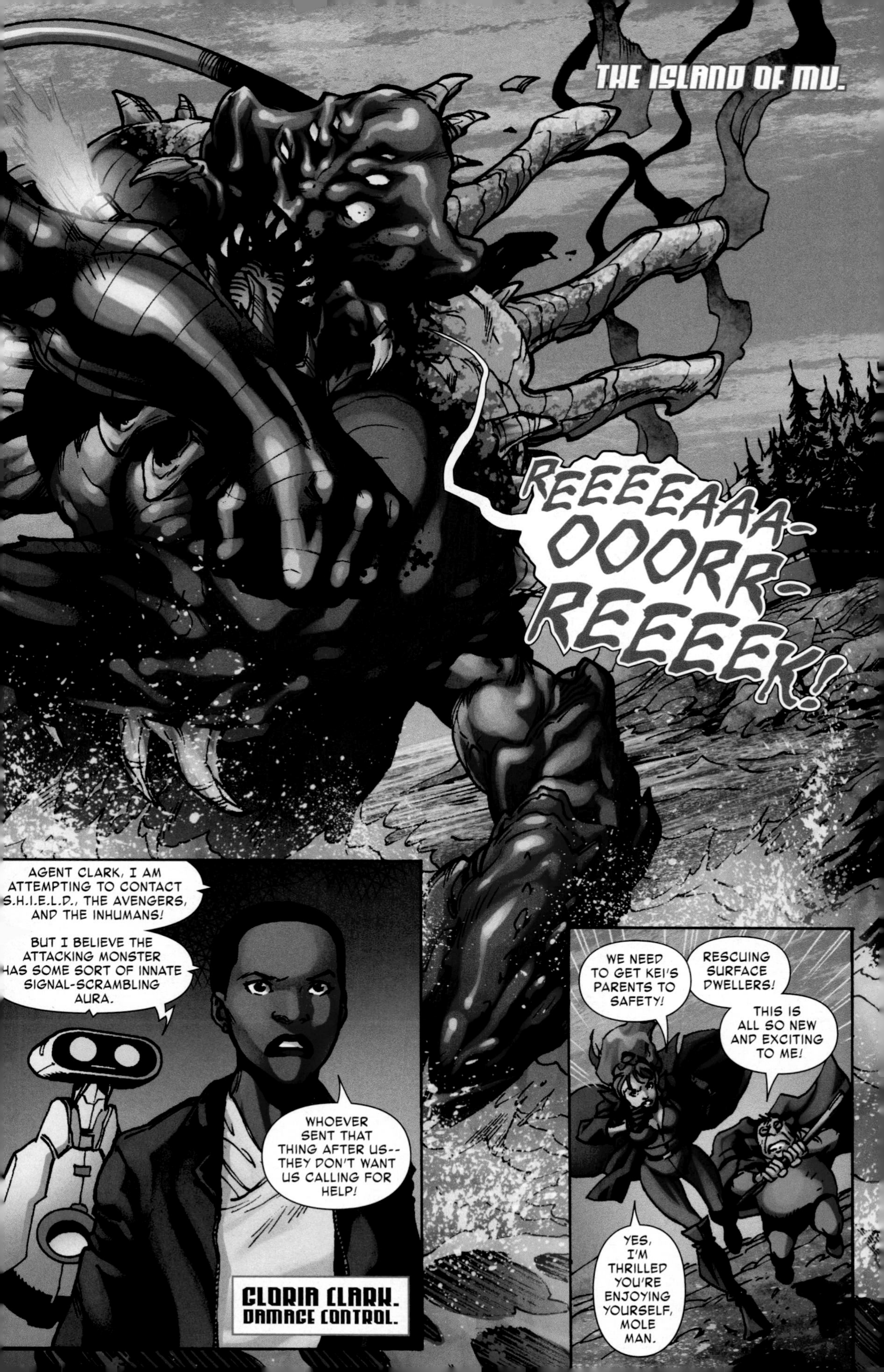
THE ISLAND OF MU.
REEEEAAA-OOORR-REEEEK!
AGENT CLARK, I AM ATTEMPTING TO CONTACT S.H.I.E.L.D., THE AVENGERS, AND THE INHUMANS!
BUT I BELIEVE THE ATTACKING MONSTER HAS SOME SORT OF INNATE SIGNAL-SCRAMBLING AURA.
WHOEVER SENT THAT THING AFTER US--THEY DON'T WANT US CALLING FOR HELP!
GLORIA CLARK. DAMAGE CONTROL.
WE NEED TO GET KEI'S PARENTS TO SAFETY!
RESCUING SURFACE DWELLERS!
THIS IS ALL SO NEW AND EXCITING TO ME!
YES, I'M THRILLED YOU'RE ENJOYING YOURSELF, MOLE MAN.

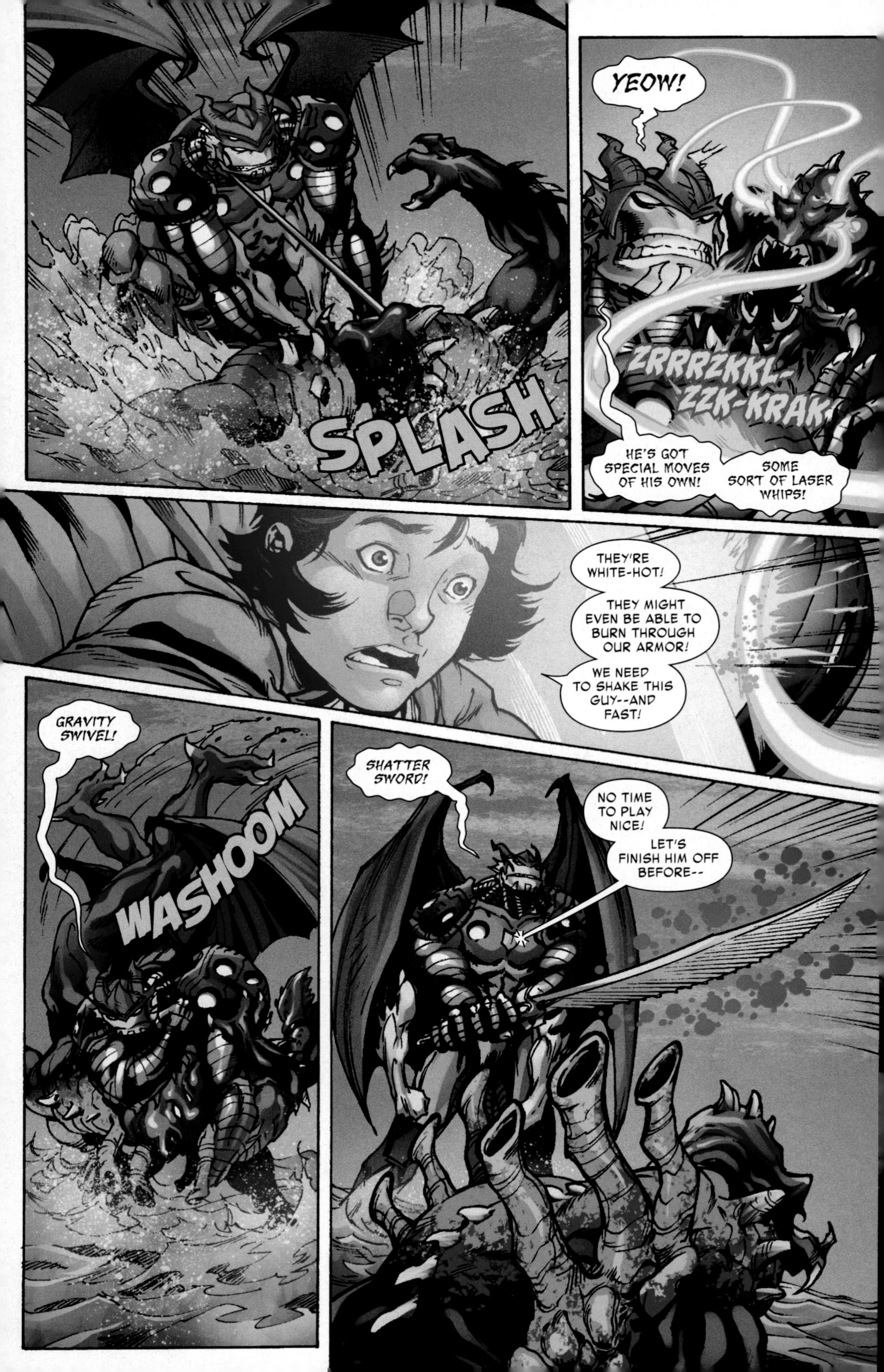
SPLASH
YEOW!
ZRRRZKKL-ZZK-KRAK
HE'S GOT SPECIAL MOVES OF HIS OWN!
SOME SORT OF LASER WHIPS!
THEY'RE WHITE-HOT!
THEY MIGHT EVEN BE ABLE TO BURN THROUGH OUR ARMOR!
WE NEED TO SHAKE THIS GUY--AND FAST!
GRAVITY SWIVEL!
WASHOOM
SHATTER SWORD!
NO TIME TO PLAY NICE!
LET'S FINISH HIM OFF BEFORE--

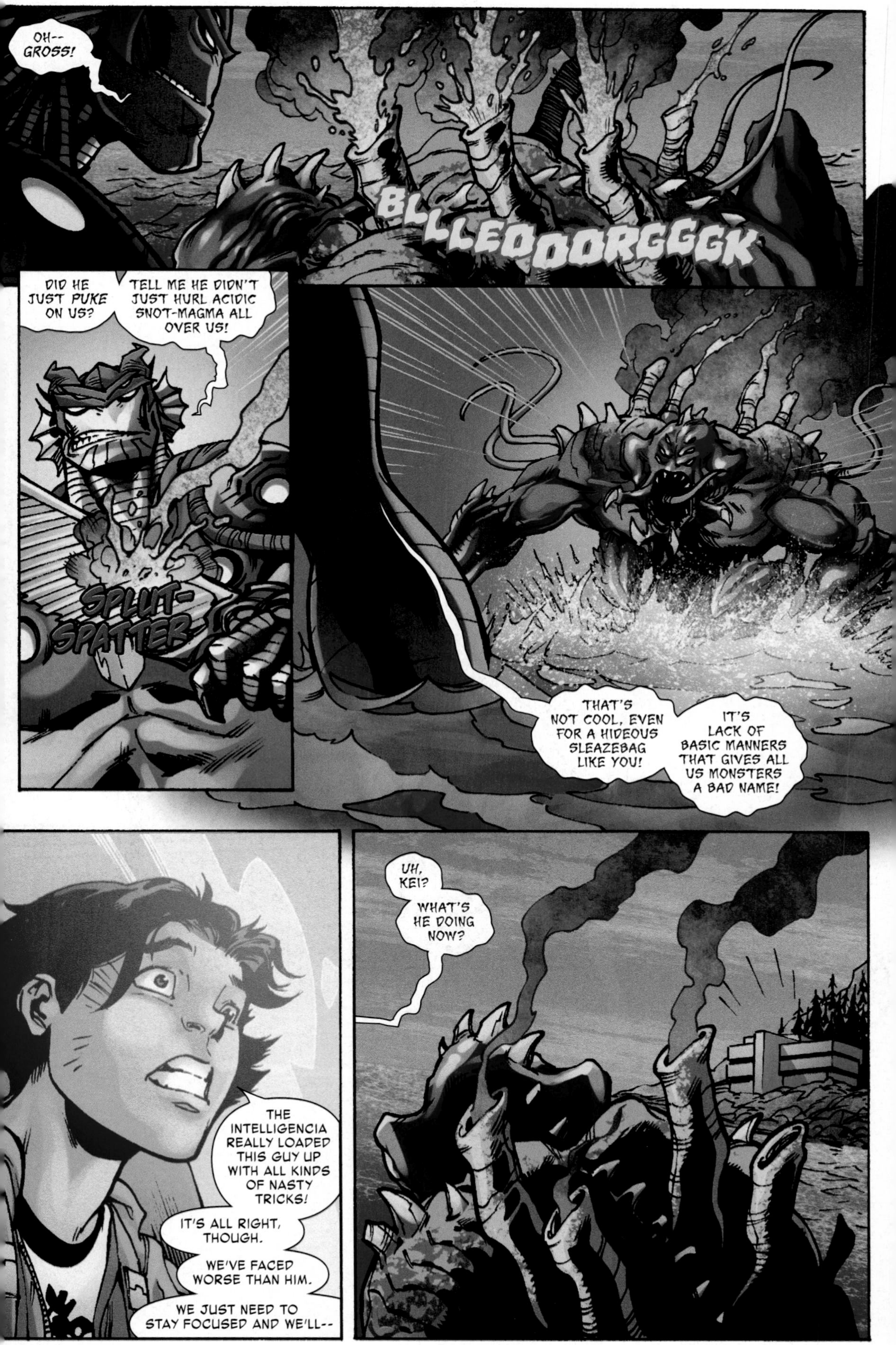
OH-- GROSS!
BLLLEDOORGGGK
DID HE JUST PUKE ON US?
TELL ME HE DIDN'T JUST HURL ACIDIC SNOT-MAGMA ALL OVER US!
SPLUT-SPATTER
THAT'S NOT COOL, EVEN FOR A HIDEOUS SLEAZEBAG LIKE YOU!
IT'S LACK OF BASIC MANNERS THAT GIVES ALL US MONSTERS A BAD NAME!
THE INTELLIGENCIA REALLY LOADED THIS GUY UP WITH ALL KINDS OF NASTY TRICKS!
IT'S ALL RIGHT, THOUGH.
WE'VE FACED WORSE THAN HIM.
WE JUST NEED TO STAY FOCUSED AND WE'LL--
UH, KEI?
WHAT'S HE DOING NOW?

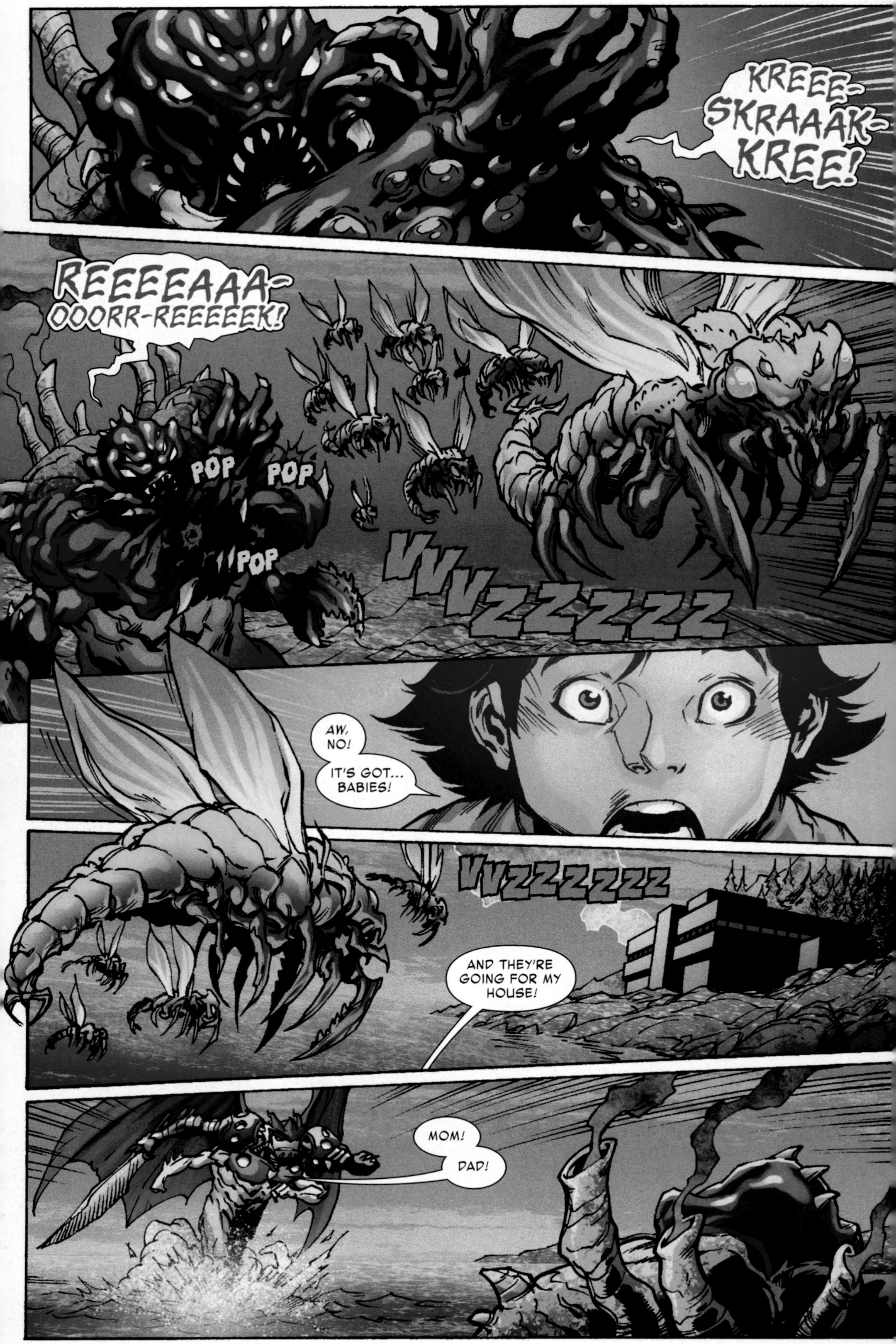
KREEE-SKRAAAK-KREE!
REEEEAAA-OOORR-REEEEEK!
POP
POP
POP
VVVZZZZZZ
AW, NO!
IT'S GOT... BABIES!
VVZZZZZZ
AND THEY'RE GOING FOR MY HOUSE!
MOM!
DAD!

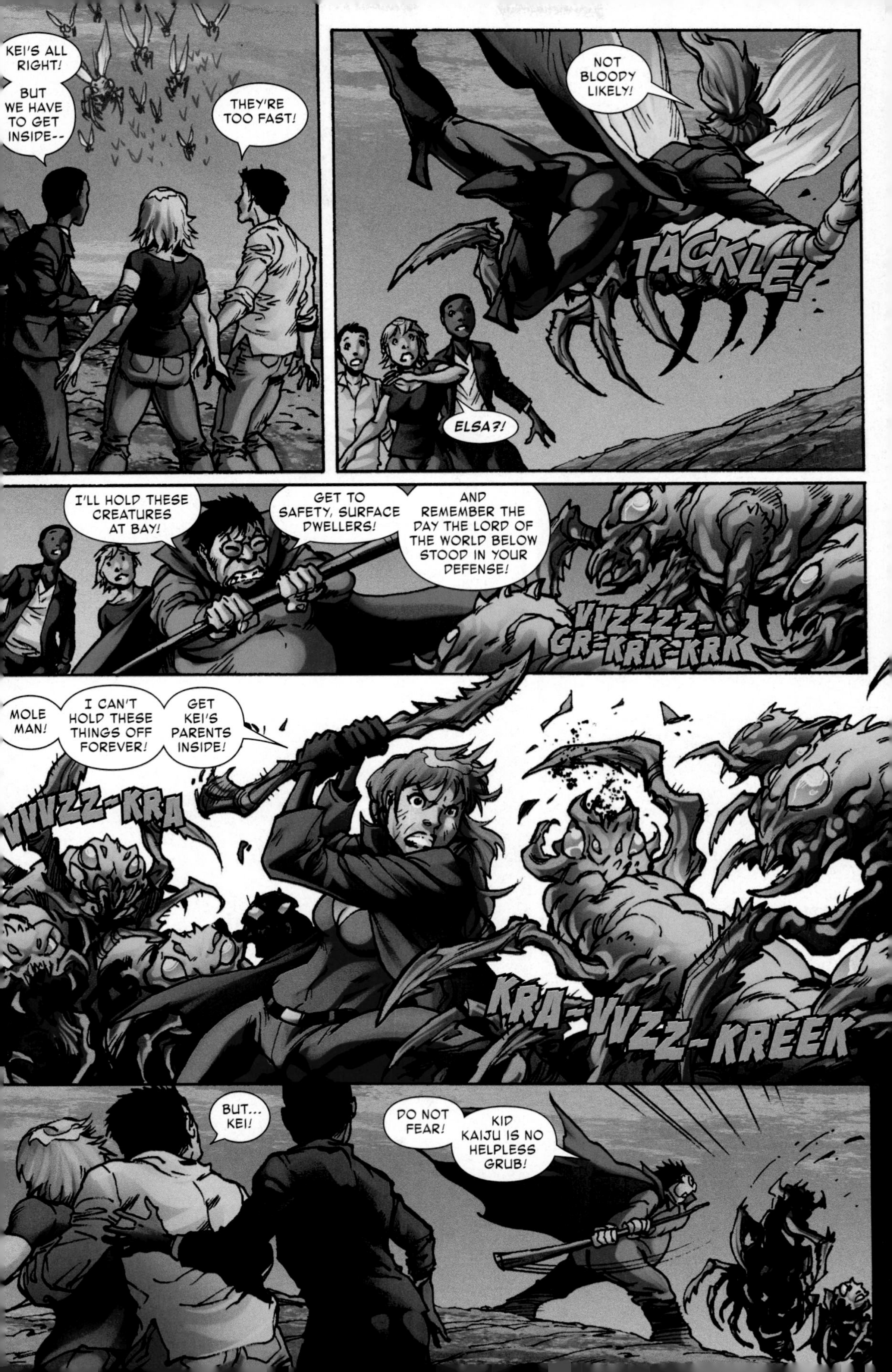
KEI'S ALL RIGHT!
BUT WE HAVE TO GET INSIDE--
THEY'RE TOO FAST!
NOT BLOODY LIKELY!
TACKLE!
ELSA?!
I'LL HOLD THESE CREATURES AT BAY!
GET TO SAFETY, SURFACE DWELLERS!
AND REMEMBER THE DAY THE LORD OF THE WORLD BELOW STOOD IN YOUR DEFENSE!
VVZZZZ-GR-KRK-KRK
MOLE MAN!
I CAN'T HOLD THESE THINGS OFF FOREVER!
GET KEI'S PARENTS INSIDE!
VVVZZ-KRA
KRA-VVZZ-KREEK
BUT... KEI!
DO NOT FEAR!
KID KAIJU IS NO HELPLESS GRUB!

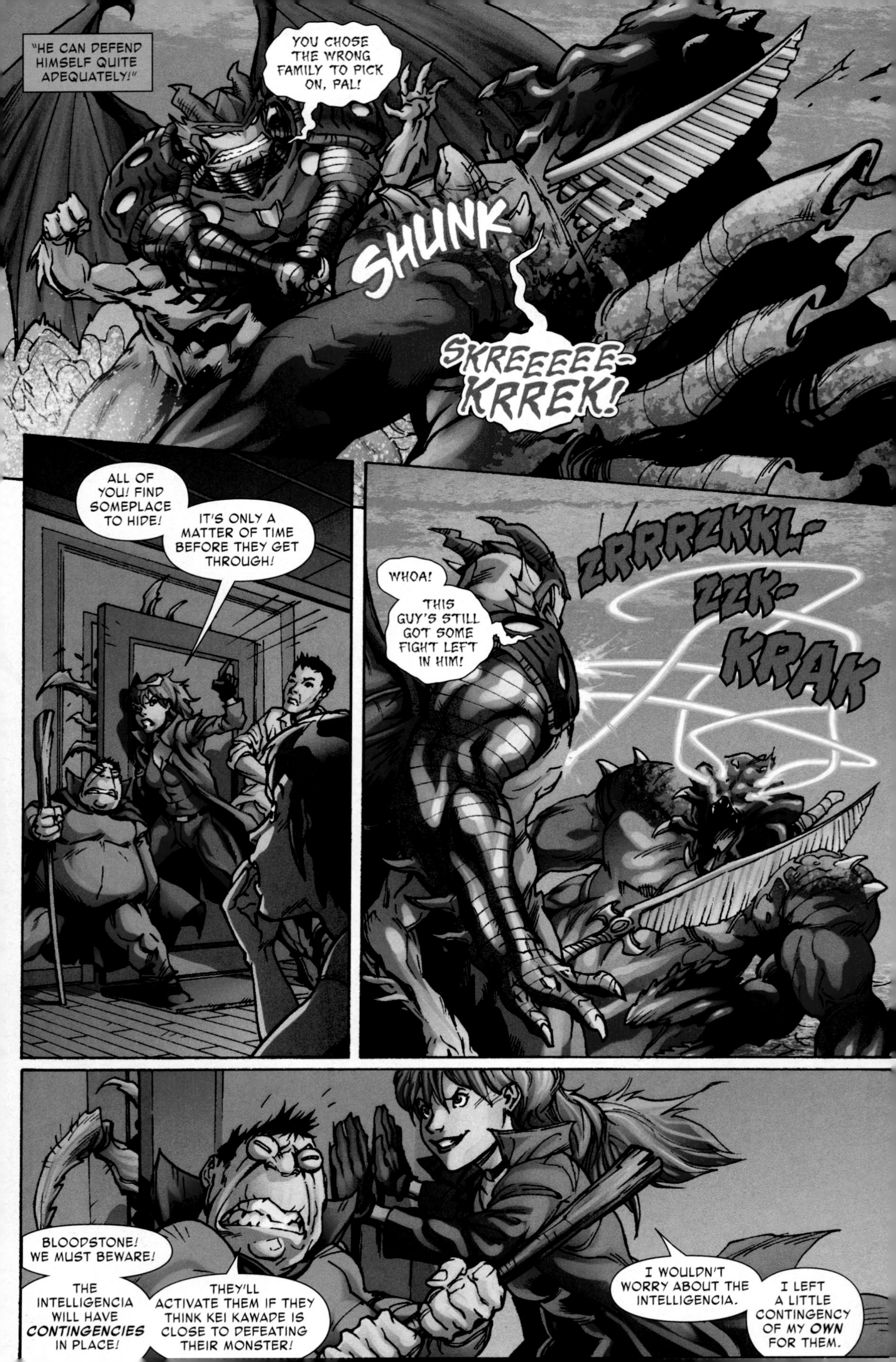
"HE CAN DEFEND HIMSELF QUITE ADEQUATELY!"
YOU CHOSE THE WRONG FAMILY TO PICK ON, PAL!
SHUNK
SKREEEEEE-KRREK!
ALL OF YOU! FIND SOMEPLACE TO HIDE!
IT'S ONLY A MATTER OF TIME BEFORE THEY GET THROUGH!
ZRRRZKKL-ZZK-KRAK
WHOA!
THIS GUY'S STILL GOT SOME FIGHT LEFT IN HIM!
BLOODSTONE! WE MUST BEWARE!
THE INTELLIGENCIA WILL HAVE *CONTINGENCIES* IN PLACE!
THEY'LL ACTIVATE THEM IF THEY THINK KEI KAWADE IS CLOSE TO DEFEATING THEIR MONSTER!
I WOULDN'T WORRY ABOUT THE INTELLIGENCIA.
I LEFT A LITTLE CONTINGENCY OF MY *OWN* FOR THEM.

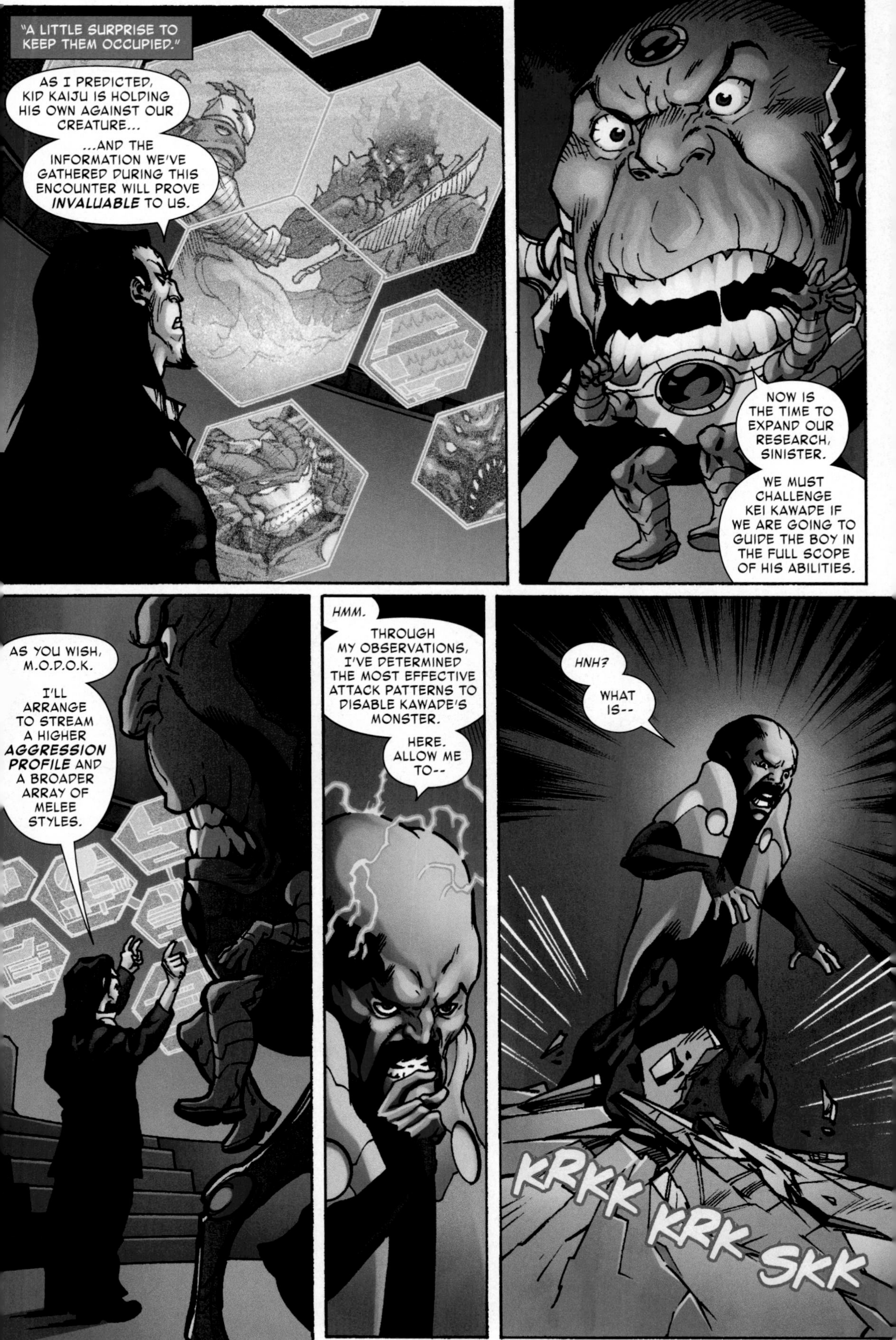

"A LITTLE SURPRISE TO KEEP THEM OCCUPIED."
AS I PREDICTED, KID KAIJU IS HOLDING HIS OWN AGAINST OUR CREATURE...
...AND THE INFORMATION WE'VE GATHERED DURING THIS ENCOUNTER WILL PROVE *INVALUABLE* TO US.
NOW IS THE TIME TO EXPAND OUR RESEARCH, SINISTER.
WE MUST CHALLENGE KEI KAWADE IF WE ARE GOING TO GUIDE THE BOY IN THE FULL SCOPE OF HIS ABILITIES.
AS YOU WISH, M.O.D.O.K.
I'LL ARRANGE TO STREAM A HIGHER *AGGRESSION PROFILE* AND A BROADER ARRAY OF MELEE STYLES.
HMM.
THROUGH MY OBSERVATIONS, I'VE DETERMINED THE MOST EFFECTIVE ATTACK PATTERNS TO DISABLE KAWADE'S MONSTER.
HERE. ALLOW ME TO--
HNH?
WHAT IS--
KRKK KRK SKK

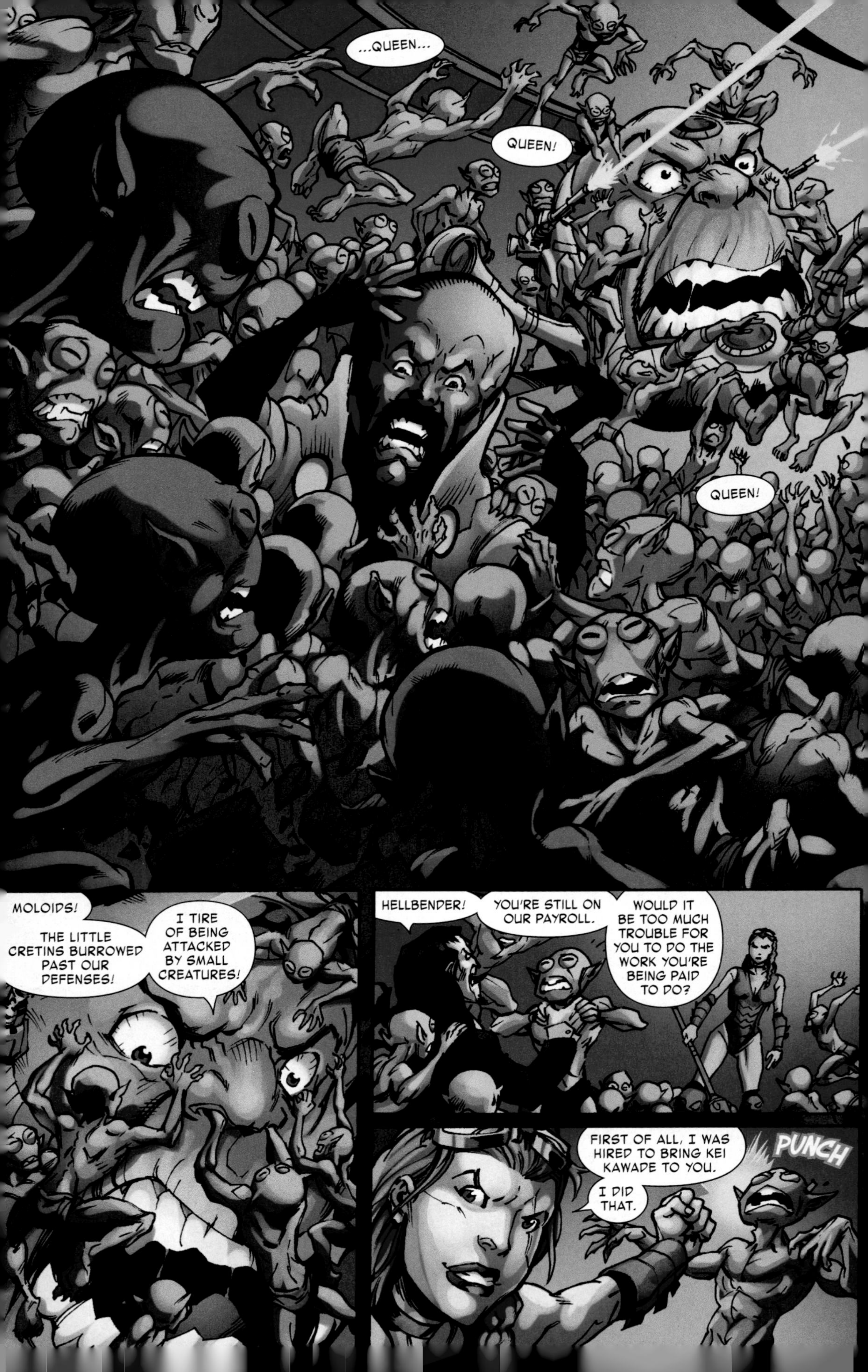
...QUEEN...
QUEEN!
QUEEN!
MOLOIDS!
THE LITTLE CRETINS BURROWED PAST OUR DEFENSES!
I TIRE OF BEING ATTACKED BY SMALL CREATURES!
HELLBENDER!
YOU'RE STILL ON OUR PAYROLL.
WOULD IT BE TOO MUCH TROUBLE FOR YOU TO DO THE WORK YOU'RE BEING PAID TO DO?
FIRST OF ALL, I WAS HIRED TO BRING KEI KAWADE TO YOU.
I DID THAT.
PUNCH

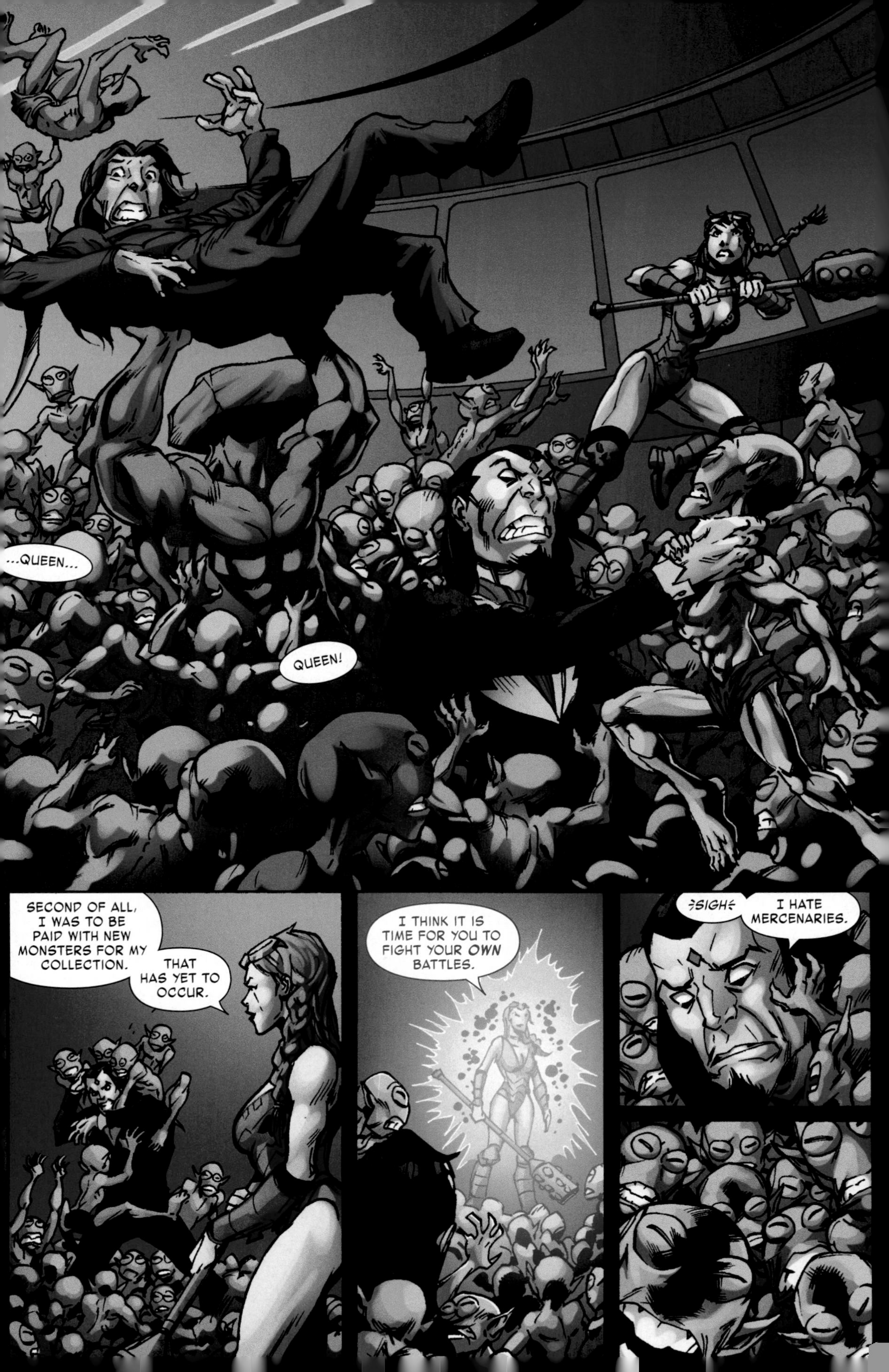
...QUEEN...
QUEEN!
SECOND OF ALL, I WAS TO BE PAID WITH NEW MONSTERS FOR MY COLLECTION.
THAT HAS YET TO OCCUR.
I THINK IT IS TIME FOR YOU TO FIGHT YOUR *OWN* BATTLES.
SIGH
I HATE MERCENARIES.

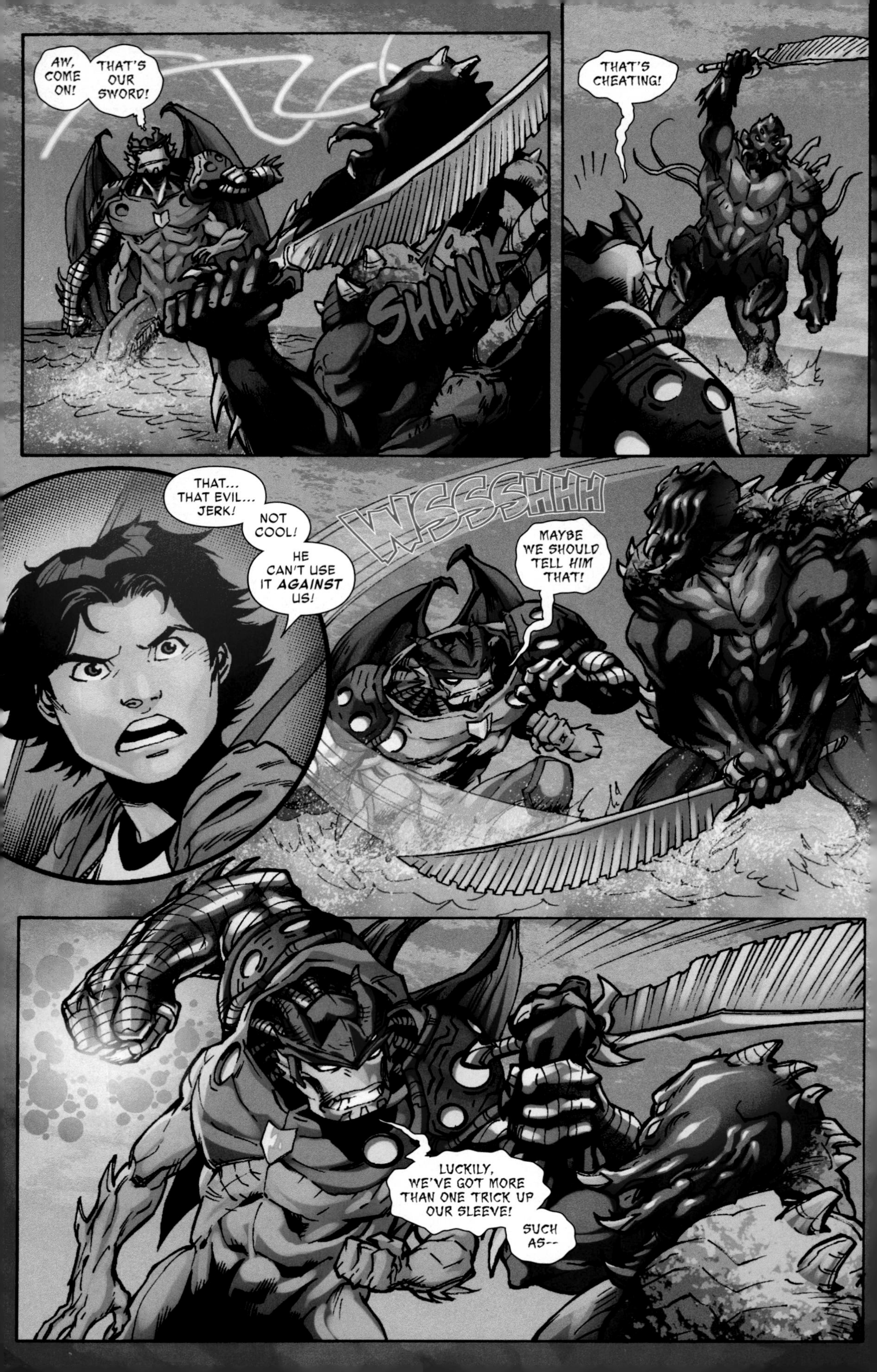
AW, COME ON!
THAT'S OUR SWORD!
SHUNK
THAT'S CHEATING!
THAT... THAT EVIL... JERK!
NOT COOL!
HE CAN'T USE IT AGAINST US!
WSSSHHH
MAYBE WE SHOULD TELL HIM THAT!
LUCKILY, WE'VE GOT MORE THAN ONE TRICK UP OUR SLEEVE!
SUCH AS--

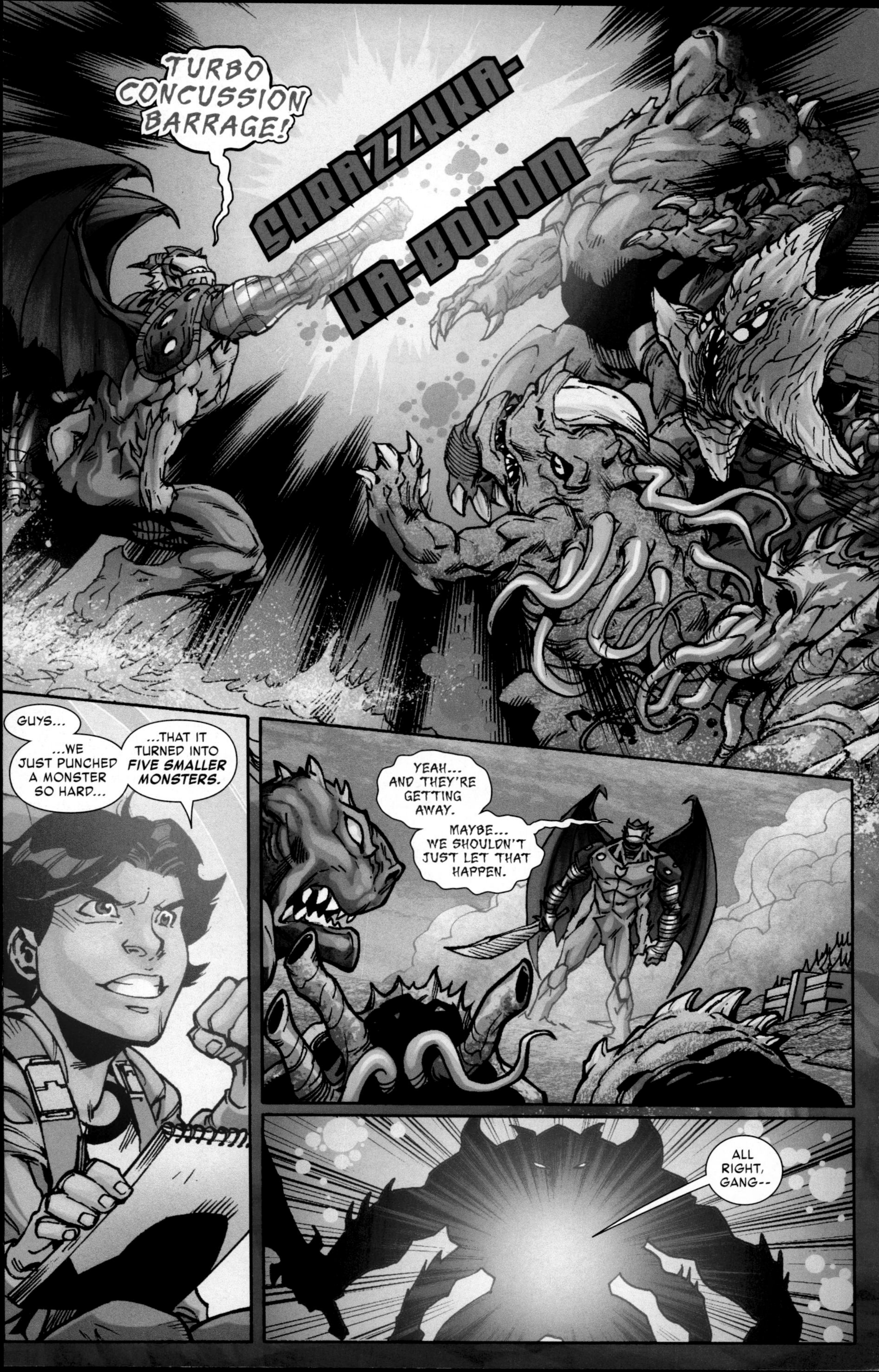
TURBO CONCUSSION BARRAGE!
SHRAZZZKKA-KA-BOOOM
GUYS...
...WE JUST PUNCHED A MONSTER SO HARD...
...THAT IT TURNED INTO FIVE SMALLER MONSTERS.
YEAH... AND THEY'RE GETTING AWAY.
MAYBE... WE SHOULDN'T JUST LET THAT HAPPEN.
ALL RIGHT, GANG--

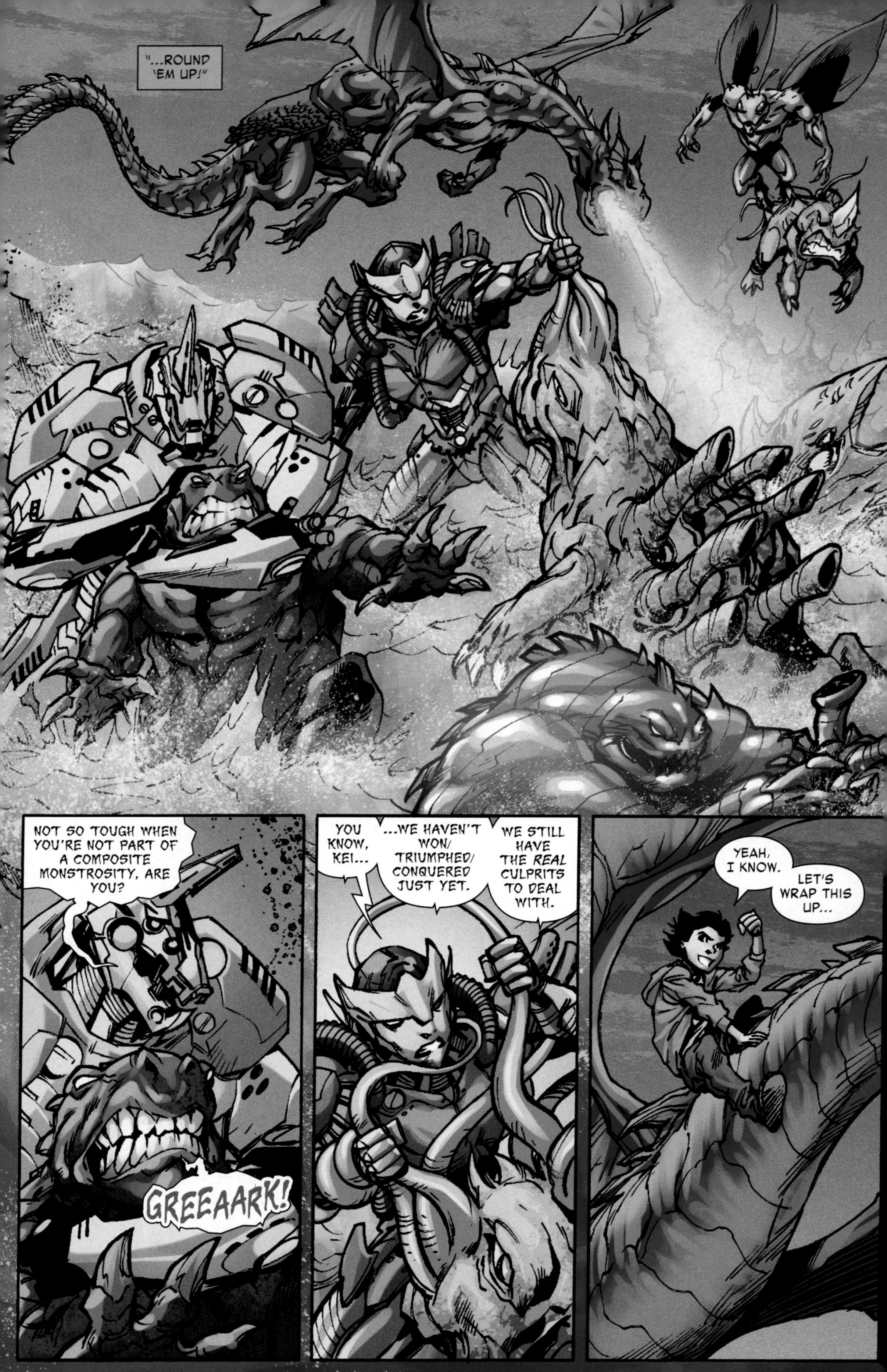
"...ROUND 'EM UP!"
NOT SO TOUGH WHEN YOU'RE NOT PART OF A COMPOSITE MONSTROSITY, ARE YOU?
GREEAARK!
YOU KNOW, KEI...
...WE HAVEN'T WON/ TRIUMPHED/ CONQUERED JUST YET.
WE STILL HAVE THE *REAL* CULPRITS TO DEAL WITH.
YEAH, I KNOW.
LET'S WRAP THIS UP...

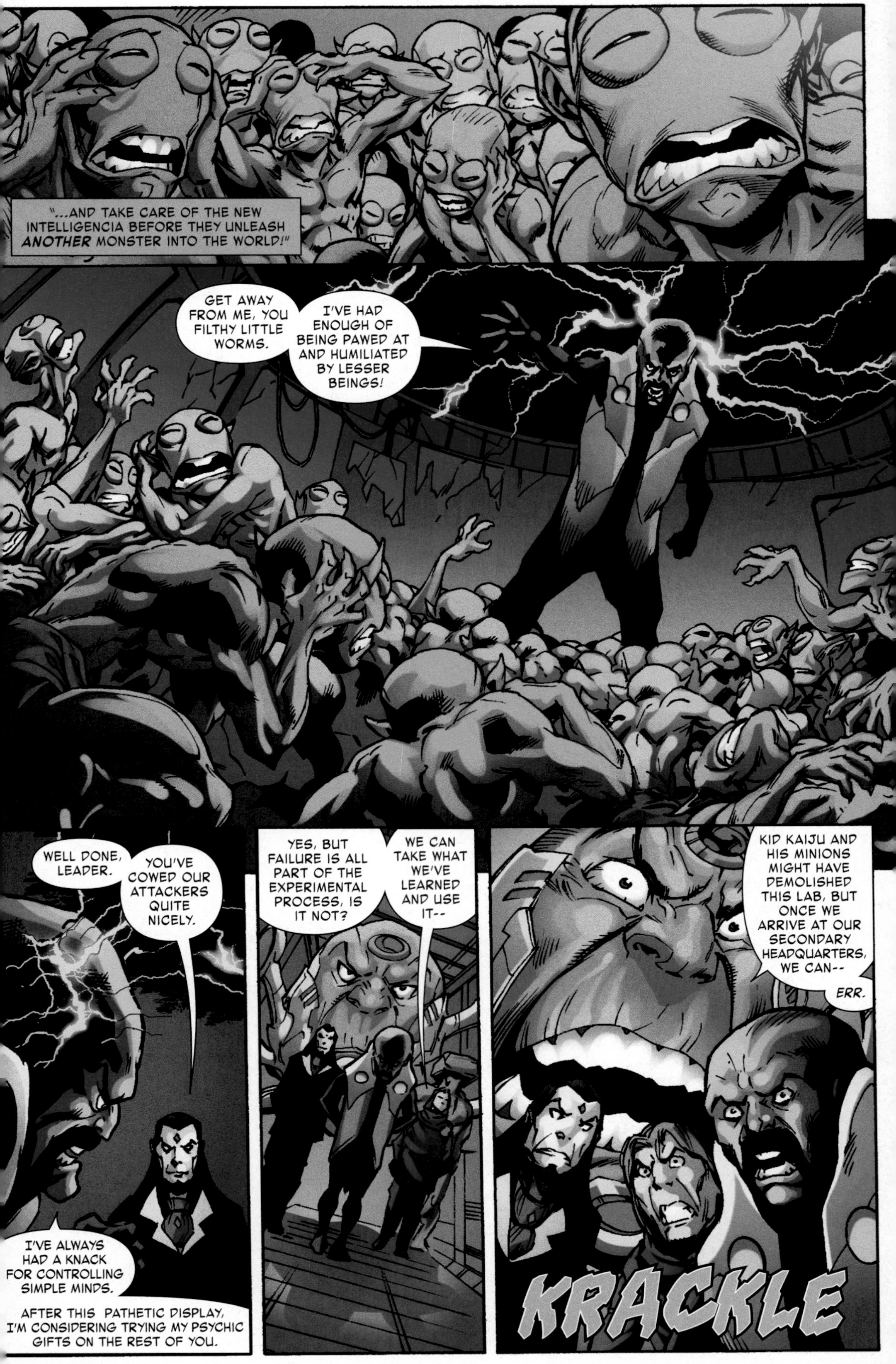
"...AND TAKE CARE OF THE NEW INTELLIGENCIA BEFORE THEY UNLEASH ANOTHER MONSTER INTO THE WORLD!"
GET AWAY FROM ME, YOU FILTHY LITTLE WORMS.
I'VE HAD ENOUGH OF BEING PAWED AT AND HUMILIATED BY LESSER BEINGS!
WELL DONE, LEADER.
YOU'VE COWED OUR ATTACKERS QUITE NICELY.
I'VE ALWAYS HAD A KNACK FOR CONTROLLING SIMPLE MINDS.
AFTER THIS PATHETIC DISPLAY, I'M CONSIDERING TRYING MY PSYCHIC GIFTS ON THE REST OF YOU.
YES, BUT FAILURE IS ALL PART OF THE EXPERIMENTAL PROCESS, IS IT NOT?
WE CAN TAKE WHAT WE'VE LEARNED AND USE IT--
KID KAIJU AND HIS MINIONS MIGHT HAVE DEMOLISHED THIS LAB, BUT ONCE WE ARRIVE AT OUR SECONDARY HEADQUARTERS, WE CAN--
ERR.
KRACKLE

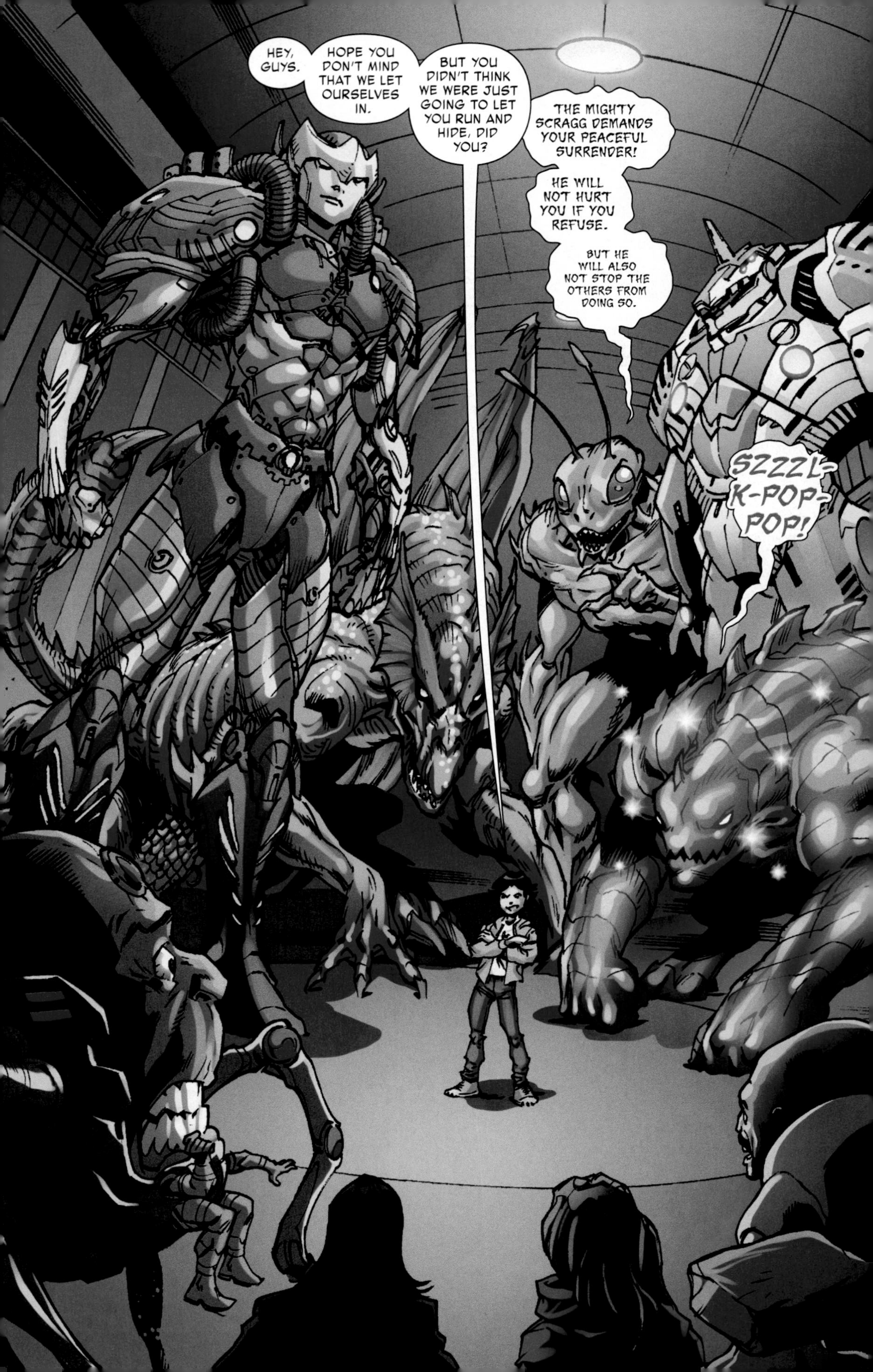
HEY, GUYS.
HOPE YOU DON'T MIND THAT WE LET OURSELVES IN.
BUT YOU DIDN'T THINK WE WERE JUST GOING TO LET YOU RUN AND HIDE, DID YOU?
THE MIGHTY SCRAGG DEMANDS YOUR PEACEFUL SURRENDER!
HE WILL NOT HURT YOU IF YOU REFUSE.
BUT HE WILL ALSO NOT STOP THE OTHERS FROM DOING SO.
SZZZL-K-POP-POP!

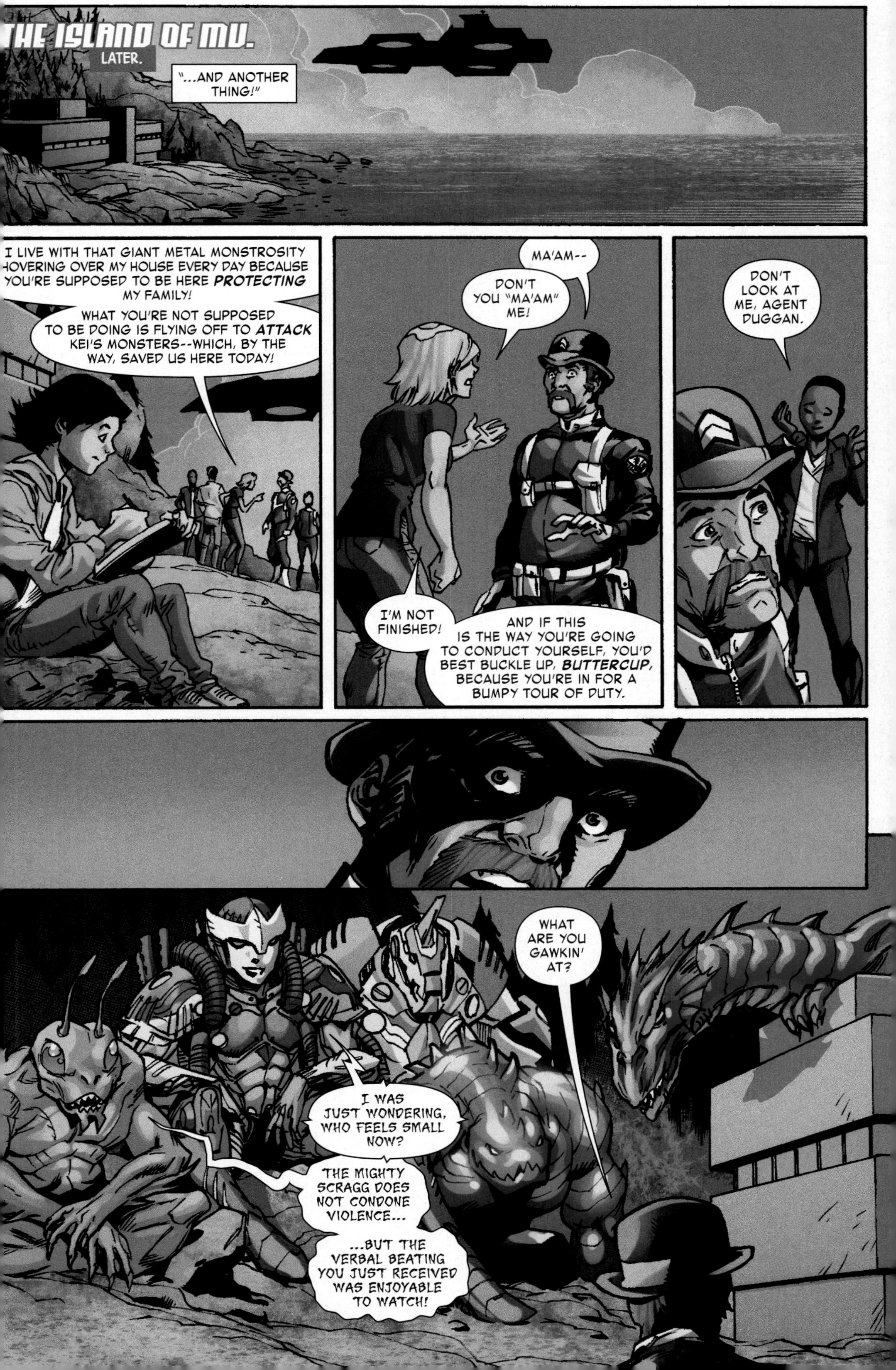
THE ISLAND OF MU.
LATER.
"...AND ANOTHER THING!"
I LIVE WITH THAT GIANT METAL MONSTROSITY HOVERING OVER MY HOUSE EVERY DAY BECAUSE YOU'RE SUPPOSED TO BE HERE PROTECTING MY FAMILY!
WHAT YOU'RE NOT SUPPOSED TO BE DOING IS FLYING OFF TO ATTACK KEI'S MONSTERS--WHICH, BY THE WAY, SAVED US HERE TODAY!
MA'AM--
DON'T YOU "MA'AM" ME!
I'M NOT FINISHED!
AND IF THIS IS THE WAY YOU'RE GOING TO CONDUCT YOURSELF, YOU'D BEST BUCKLE UP, BUTTERCUP, BECAUSE YOU'RE IN FOR A BUMPY TOUR OF DUTY.
DON'T LOOK AT ME, AGENT DUGGAN.
WHAT ARE YOU GAWKIN' AT?
I WAS JUST WONDERING, WHO FEELS SMALL NOW?
THE MIGHTY SCRAGG DOES NOT CONDONE VIOLENCE...
...BUT THE VERBAL BEATING YOU JUST RECEIVED WAS ENJOYABLE TO WATCH!

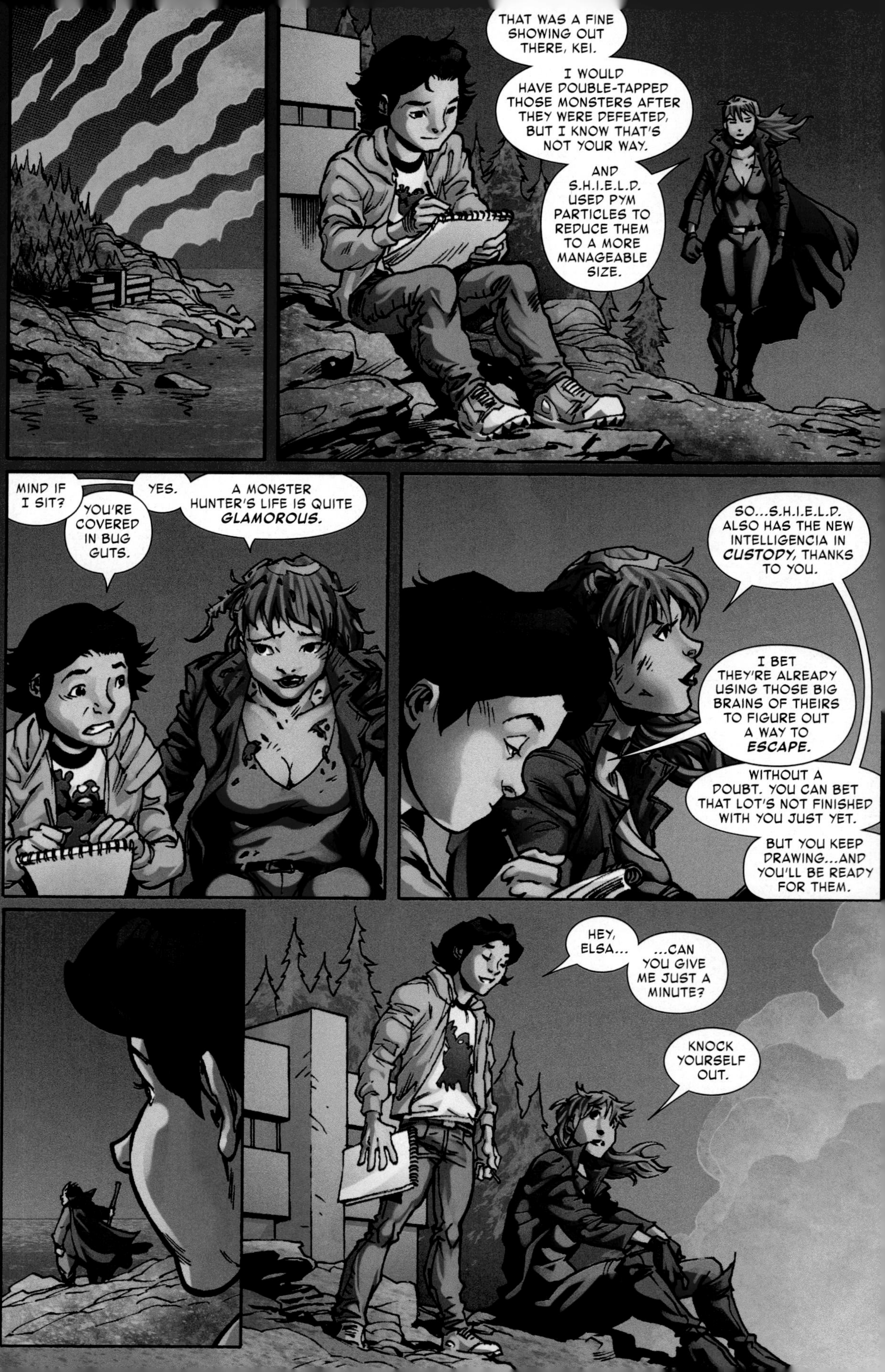
THAT WAS A FINE SHOWING OUT THERE, KEI.
I WOULD HAVE DOUBLE-TAPPED THOSE MONSTERS AFTER THEY WERE DEFEATED, BUT I KNOW THAT'S NOT YOUR WAY.
AND S.H.I.E.L.D. USED PYM PARTICLES TO REDUCE THEM TO A MORE MANAGEABLE SIZE.
MIND IF I SIT?
YES.
YOU'RE COVERED IN BUG GUTS.
A MONSTER HUNTER'S LIFE IS QUITE GLAMOROUS.
SO...S.H.I.E.L.D. ALSO HAS THE NEW INTELLIGENCIA IN CUSTODY, THANKS TO YOU.
I BET THEY'RE ALREADY USING THOSE BIG BRAINS OF THEIRS TO FIGURE OUT A WAY TO ESCAPE.
WITHOUT A DOUBT. YOU CAN BET THAT LOT'S NOT FINISHED WITH YOU JUST YET.
BUT YOU KEEP DRAWING...AND YOU'LL BE READY FOR THEM.
HEY, ELSA...
...CAN YOU GIVE ME JUST A MINUTE?
KNOCK YOURSELF OUT.

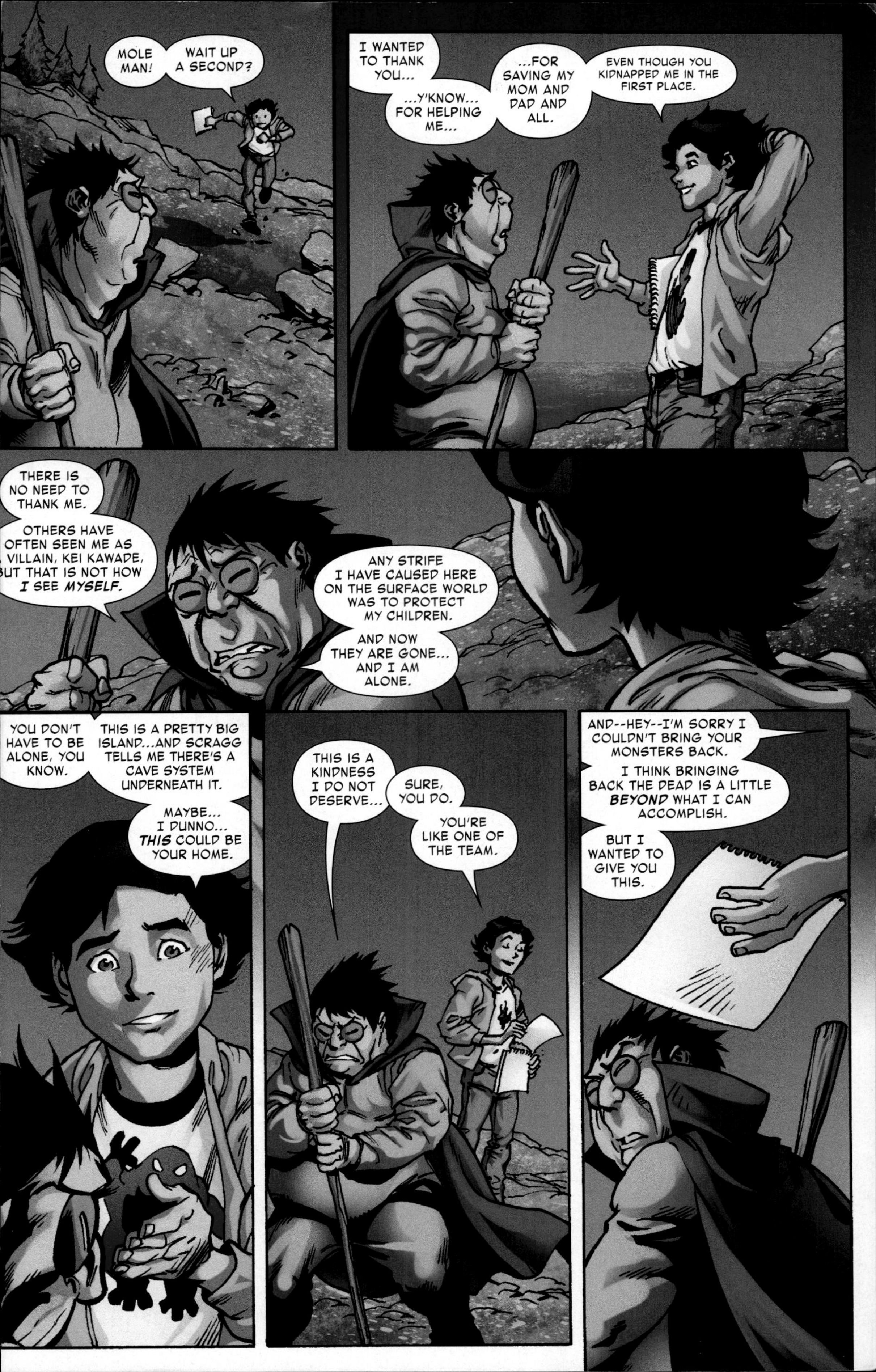
MOLE MAN!
WAIT UP A SECOND?
I WANTED TO THANK YOU...
...Y'KNOW... FOR HELPING ME...
...FOR SAVING MY MOM AND DAD AND ALL.
EVEN THOUGH YOU KIDNAPPED ME IN THE FIRST PLACE.
THERE IS NO NEED TO THANK ME.
OTHERS HAVE OFTEN SEEN ME AS VILLAIN, KEI KAWADE, BUT THAT IS NOT HOW I SEE MYSELF.
ANY STRIFE I HAVE CAUSED HERE ON THE SURFACE WORLD WAS TO PROTECT MY CHILDREN.
AND NOW THEY ARE GONE... AND I AM ALONE.
YOU DON'T HAVE TO BE ALONE, YOU KNOW.
THIS IS A PRETTY BIG ISLAND...AND SCRAGG TELLS ME THERE'S A CAVE SYSTEM UNDERNEATH IT.
MAYBE... I DUNNO... THIS COULD BE YOUR HOME.
THIS IS A KINDNESS I DO NOT DESERVE...
SURE, YOU DO.
YOU'RE LIKE ONE OF THE TEAM.
AND--HEY--I'M SORRY I COULDN'T BRING YOUR MONSTERS BACK.
I THINK BRINGING BACK THE DEAD IS A LITTLE BEYOND WHAT I CAN ACCOMPLISH.
BUT I WANTED TO GIVE YOU THIS.

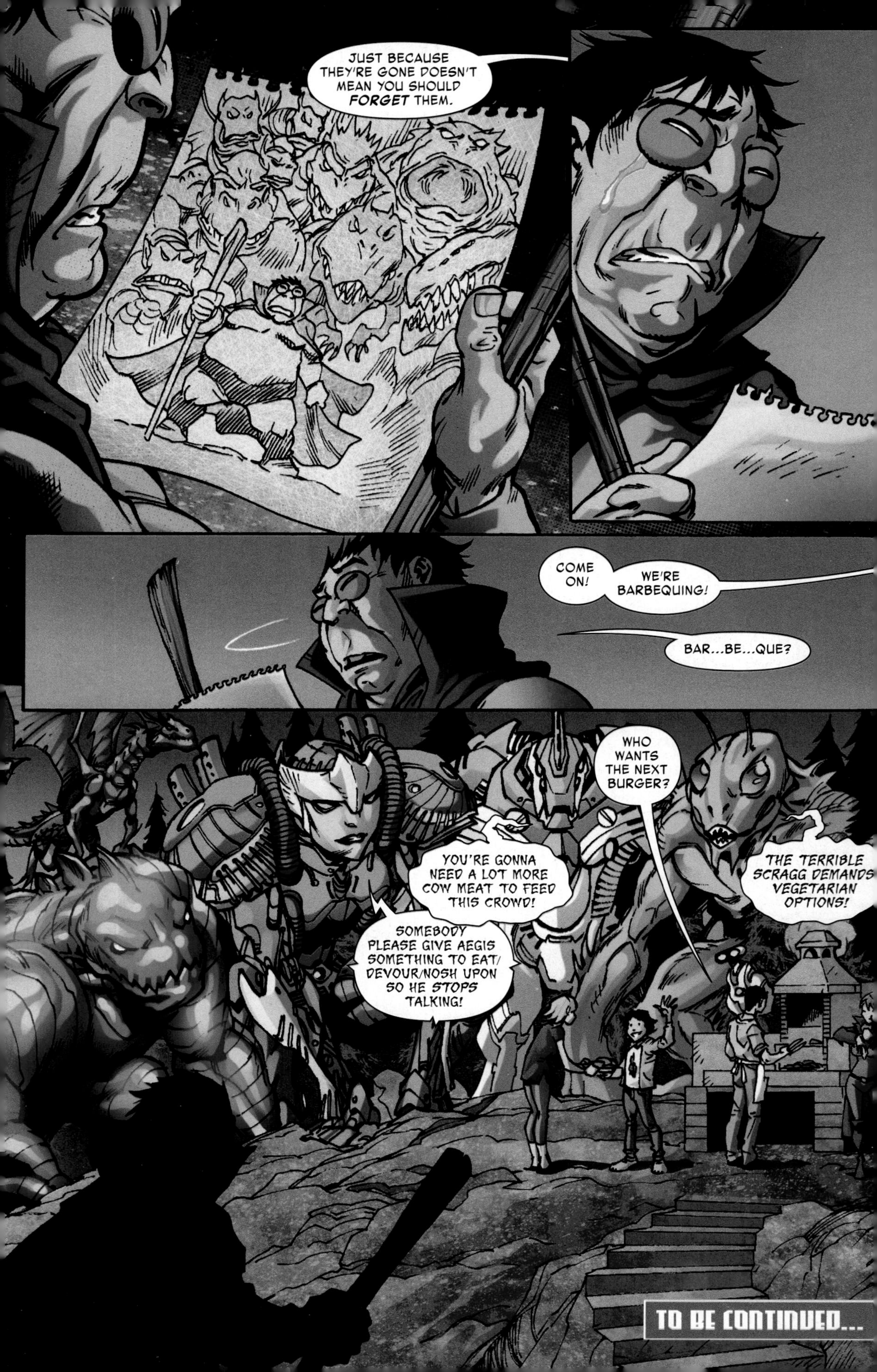
JUST BECAUSE THEY'RE GONE DOESN'T MEAN YOU SHOULD FORGET THEM.
COME ON!
WE'RE BARBEQUING!
BAR...BE...QUE?
WHO WANTS THE NEXT BURGER?
YOU'RE GONNA NEED A LOT MORE COW MEAT TO FEED THIS CROWD!
THE TERRIBLE SCRAGG DEMANDS VEGETARIAN OPTIONS!
SOMEBODY PLEASE GIVE AEGIS SOMETHING TO EAT/ DEVOUR/NOSH UPON SO HE STOPS TALKING!
TO BE CONTINUED...